KT-229-793

ENGLISH SILVER COINAGE
from 1649

ENGLISH
SILVER COINAGE
from 1649

BY

P. ALAN RAYNER

LONDON

English Silver Coinage 1649–1949 by H. A. Seaby
First Edition 1949
English Silver Coinage from 1649 by P. A. Rayner
Second Edition 1957
Third (Revised) Edition 1968
Fourth (Revised) Edition 1974
English Silver Coinage from 1649
Fifth (Revised) Edition by P. A. Rayner 1992

Typeset by Superskill Graphics Singapore

Printed by Biddles, Walnut Tree House,
Woodbridge Park, Guildford, Surrey U.K.

Apart from any fair dealing for the purposes of research
or private study, or criticism or review, as permitted
under the Copyright, Designs and Patents Act, 1988, this
publication may be reproduced, stored or transmitted, in
any forms or by any means, only with the prior
permission in writing of the publishers, or in the case of
reprographic reproduction in accordance with the terms
of licences issued by the Copyright Licensing Agency,
Inquiries concerning reproduction outside those terms
should be sent to the publishers.

ISBN 1 85264 053 7

CIP data for this book is available from the British Library

© B.A. Seaby Ltd.
7 Davies Street
London W1Y 1LL

BEXLEY LIBRARY SERVICE

LOC	CL No.		
ER	737·4942 RAY		
PRICE	ACC DATE		
19·95	4-12.92		ST
COLL C		GM LOAN TYPE	
	NF	ANF	
EYER		CH	PR

CONTENTS

PREFACE TO THE FIFTH EDITION

THE fourth edition of 'E.S.C.' as it is universally known, was published in early 1974, and has been out of print for some time.

The work, originally written by H. A. Seaby in 1949, has undergone many changes since it first appeared. I first co-operated with H.A.S. on the writing of the second edition in 1957; and in 1968 the book was practically re-written and it included large sections of my treatise 'Designers and Engravers of the English Milled Coinage', which was written as long ago as 1954. This third edition also featured, for the first time, photographs taken by Frank Purvey which made the work much more attractive in appearance and finally established it as the definitive standard work on the series. It sold out very rapidly, and in 1974 we re-wrote the book, adding much new material, including the Decimal Coinage to date. In the 1974 edition, it was also possible, for the first time, to publish details of the coinage of Edward VIII, as the Duke of Windsor had recently died: we were particularly grateful for the co-operation of the then Deputy Master of the Royal Mint and also for the help of Graham Dyer, the Mint Archivist.

Turning now to the present, fifth edition, I have included a considerable amount of new material—also many rarities have been changed, in the light of experience of numbers extant gleaned from collectors, sale catalogues etc. over the last fifteen years. I have always been aware that the minor denominations (fourpence to penny), required further study and I am indebted to one of our contributors who has now researched these coins for all reigns from Charles II to George II. As a result new types have been incorporated and illustrated for the first time. Particular mention can be made of the identification of several different busts for the fourpences and threepences of Queen Anne and of the threepences of Queen Victoria.

I have added a number of photographs, most of which illustrate fine detail, such as initials, lettering—sizes etc. and I hope these will be helpful. The Decimal Series has been brought up to date, and I have included the five pound, two pound and pound coins. Although not silver (or nickel!) coins *per se* they are our highest denominations, and are collected along with remaining coins.

As with previous editions, I was faced by the two major problems—firstly, whether or not to re-number, and secondly, what to include and what to leave out.

I know that many collectors (and museums also) catalogue their collections using E.S.C. references, and a re-numbering of the present edition would have caused untold problems. I have, therefore, admittedly with some reluctance, adhered to the old numbering, notwithstanding the unavoidable use of a, b, bi and so on. As before, I am not including uniface patterns and despite some protest, I am not giving separate numbers to all the proofs of the modern issues which are usually struck every year, apart from those issued with the sets.

I *am* including a number of the major varieties published by Peter Davies in his book 'British Silver Coins Since 1816'; but I think that to include all the minor varieties in such areas as beaded borders etc. would be counter-productive, and result in a large and cumbersome book. I feel that the two works are complementary, and the highly specialised collector of post 1816 material would probably have Davies in his library in any case.

This time I have given way to considerable lobbying on behalf of the so-called Hearn patterns of Edward VIII, dated 1936. I am listing these, as although they are really not contemporary patterns at all, it can be argued that they are collected as part of the series and that they fall into the same category as the Bonomi patterns of Victoria, whose inclusion has now been hallowed by the lapse of time.

I would like to thank the many collectors who have contributed to this volume. My particular thanks are due to Graham Dyer of the Royal Mint for his help in supplying coin photographs, to Roger Shuttlewood and Gerald Sommerville for contributing their specialised knowledge, to David Fletcher for rewriting the Decimal Section and to Harry Manville for invaluable proof-reading and suggestions for improving the text. I am most indebted to Brian Reeds who has devoted much of his time to the preparation of this edition.

P. A. RAYNER
HARPENDEN, 1992

INTRODUCTION

English silver coinage of the last three hundred years or so is certainly the most popular series of coins to have attracted the attention of coin collectors in Great Britain. This book has been compiled in order to provide collectors with a standard work of reference on the series, giving details of dates, varieties, comparative rarity, patterns and proofs, etc. It was thought best to use the title *English Silver Coinage* as it includes coins struck before the Act of Union 1707, but not coins made in Scotland prior to that date. To have used 'British' in the title might have implied that it covered coinage issued for British and Commonwealth territories overseas. Certain pieces of United Kingdom type which were struck in some years solely for use in the Colonies have been included.

Arrangement. The lists are arranged under denominations instead of by reigns. This may not be technically very sound, but it should be more useful, as it is becoming the practice of dealers to list their coins by denominations and for collectors to house their specimens in trays with holes of uniform size in each tray, thus keeping the coins of each denomination together; there are also some collectors who collect only one denomination. Furthermore, it seems more logical to describe the proofs and patterns with the ordinary coins than to list them in a separate section of the book.

Proofs and patterns with obverse and reverse similar to the current coins are included in the tabulated lists with an appropriate note in the Remarks column. Unadopted patterns are listed by themselves at the end of each reign.

Proofs are pieces struck from specially prepared dies as samples of a coin or coinage. In many cases they have a plain edge, instead of the normal inscribed or milled edge. They are usually found with a mirror-like field as they are from highly polished dies. The frosted effect on the bust or other raised parts of the design is produced by treating the corresponding incuse parts of the die with a weak acid solution. In a few cases, for instance the proofs of 1902, the whole coin has a matt surface. It has sometimes been the practice to supply proof sets in cases, usually prior to issuing a new coinage for circulation. The earlier sets, those of 1826, 1831, 1839 and 1853, were issued by the Engravers; whilst the later ones, 1887, 1893, 1902, 1911, 1927, 1937, 1950, 1951, 1953 and 1970 were issued officially by the Royal Mint. This last set, 1970, is of particular interest as it was to commemorate the end of the £.s.d. coinage. Proof sets of the first decimal coinage were issued in 1971 and have been struck every year subsequently.

Before the introduction of Decimal Coinage it was the practice of the Royal Mint to make a dozen or so proofs of each denomination every year. From time to time an odd specimen may come on the market; It has been thought best to omit them from the listings of George VI and Elizabeth II: they are all of roughly similar rarity. Since 1971 the Royal Mint has produced yearly proof sets in large numbers.

Patterns are pieces struck as suggestions for a new coinage, and most of them are not adopted. In theory it may seem easy to decide whether a piece is a pattern or a proof, but in practice it is not altogether simple. For instance, there are coins, such as the crowns of 1826 and 1831, which were issued in the proof sets of these years but were actually never struck for circulation. Should these be called proofs or patterns? There is also the coin which is of the normal type but bearing a date not struck for currency. In many instances this is the original pattern of the coin issued for circulation in the next year or later.

Both proofs and patterns of the silver coinage are sometimes found struck in a metal other than silver.

Trial pieces. These are mostly struck by an engraver to see how his work is progressing and have been omitted intentionally from this work, as have all uniface strikings which are really only trial pieces.

Varieties. In a work of this kind the question of how far one should go in including die varieties is one for serious consideration. In modern times working dies are made from a master die and so are identical, but this was not so before about 1770. The older dies were apparently made from a series of master punches, one for the head and one for each letter, etc., so that each working die was slightly different in some small detail. It is felt that it would make this work much too complicated to include the die variants and it would necessarily be incomplete, as there are no complete records of them. Grant R. Francis tried to do this in his fine work on the Tower coins of Charles I, but when one checks coins against his lists one finds, in the case of some denominations, nearly as many varieties omitted as are included. All the main minor varieties are given in the right hand column of the tables, with the estimated rarity in the preceding column, i.e., the same columns as for rarity of the normal coins. The varieties not included are:

Harp strings. The number of strings to the Irish harp varies considerably, especially in the early reigns, and particularly in the case of the crowns. In the case of worn coins they are difficult to count, and it is sometimes impossible to do so correctly when two or more overlap. Also dies wear and some strings are, therefore, not properly struck up, in fact some coins show no harp strings at all, especially in the reign of William III.[1]

---

[1] 'Wear' is not strictly accurate. In fact, on a die that has been in use for some time some of the minute detail, which on the die is incuse, may become filled up.

Stops. Variations in these have generally been left out, but when they are entirely lacking the fact is mentioned. In some cases the absence of a stop is due to wear of the die, or of the coin, and not to its being missing on the die in its original state.

Lions. The size of the lions on the halfcrowns and shillings of William III varies considerably and in the earlier work on this subject by H.A. Seaby, published in 1925, 'large' and 'small' lions were noted. This was not entirely satisfactory as there are also intermediate sizes and it is difficult to tell which is which.

Edge readings. The collars for the edge inscriptions are made in two or three sections which often slipped or were too long for a small blank, thus producing variations on the edge that were not intended. Many of these were included in the original *Milled Silver Coinage* published in 1925 but it is now realized that they are not really *die* varieties. For example in the variation 'NNO' on a crown of 1696 the 'A' must have slipped behind the end of the contiguous section and was not missing on the collar.

Another variation, perhaps the most common, is whether the edge reading is facing and clockwise, or reversed and anti-clockwise when the obverse is to the spectator. This variation occurs even on quite modern strikings, for instance the common 1935 Jubilee crown, but it is considered to have no significance.

Inscribed edges. Various devices have been used for this purpose. The *virole brisée* was one of the earliest and consisted of a segmented collar fitted to a second and unbroken collar. Blondeau's method, which was surrounded with secrecy, appears to have consisted of one or two thin strips of steel, bearing incuse inscriptions, placed inside a solid collar around the blank. Then there followed the Castaing machine which according to the few old prints which are available appears to have continued in use in the Royal Mint until the removal of the latter in 1810 from the Tower of London. This machine marked the edges by forcing the coin or blank to revolve between two inscribed steel bands. The modern method comprises a collar of three interlocking segments for raised inscriptions and a mechanical form of the Castaing machine for incuse inscriptions. This latter is used on the blank prior to striking.

It seems, therefore, that variations in edge markings, apart from clockwise or anti-clockwise, must fall generally into two classes: (a) incomplete or overlapping markings caused by the overlapping of the metal strips such as Blondeau used or incomplete and excessive evolutions by the castaing method; (b) incorrect order of the words of the inscription caused by the segments being misplaced.

Errors. Spelling errors and corrected errors have been included, but in this edition varieties where the error consists of an A unbarred, or an inverted V for A and so on, have been omitted because the majority of these 'errors' have been caused by worn dies.

Rarity, value and condition. Some numismatic works give the value of the coins being described at the time of publication. Even then, such prices can only be comparative as the value of each and every piece depends on its condition, i.e., state of preservation. Furthermore, some of these books are still standard works on their series but the values given are quite out of date and have been for many years. After careful consideration it has been decided not to include present value for each piece but to give instead twelve degrees of rarity as under:

R^7	Only one or two examples known.
R^6	Three or four examples known.
R^5	Five to ten examples known.
R^4	Eleven to twenty examples known.
R^3	Extremely rare.
R^2	Very rare.
R	Rare.
S	Scarce.
N	Normal, neither scarce nor common.
C	Common.
C^2	Very common.
C^3	Extremely common.

In many cases the indicated rarity is an estimate only and is not given from definite knowledge. In the case of the modern pre-decimal coins for the most part they have not been placed in the very highest categories, as probably more examples exist than have appeared to date; in the case of some of the patterns and proofs fairly accurate records are sometimes available.

With regard to values, all collectors can obtain a copy of Seaby's *Standard Catalogue of British Coins*, which is published every year and gives the approximate price a dealer would charge for the commonest coin of each type at the time of going to press. In this way values can be estimated for many pieces, which combined with the degrees of rarity given in this work will enable collectors to assess the value of most, if not all, of the coins listed here.

Corrections and Omissions. No doubt some inaccuracies, printers' errors and omissions have crept into this work and the publishers would be grateful if a record of any which are found could be sent to us.

HISTORY OF MILLED COINAGE

ELIZABETH I

First use of the mill and screw press in England

It is usual to refer to all coins struck by machinery as 'milled' but this is a misnomer. The term 'mill money' was originally applied to coins made at the Paris Mint about 1552. The metal was rolled to the required thickness, a cutting press stamped out the blanks, and a screw press used to strike the coins. The power for these operations was supplied by water or horse mills.

Despite the coins being technically and artistically superior to those made by hand, years of bitter opposition from mint workers who feared for their jobs finally drove the machine's inventor, Eloye Mestrelle, to seek employment at the Tower Mint in London in 1561. There he was allowed to set up and demonstrate his machinery, being paid the rather miserly salary of twenty-five pounds per annum. During the period from 1561 to 1572 he struck the following denominations. In gold: half-pound, crown and halfcrown: and in silver: shilling, sixpence, fourpence, threepence, twopence and three-farthings.

Elizabeth I Half Pound

The gold coins are extremely rare and it is doubtful if they circulated in any quantity. The silver shillings were struck only in small numbers, but the sixpences, struck nearly every year between 1561 and 1571, are relatively common and display such numerous variations in the style of portraiture, mint-mark and diameter that a considerable number of dies is indicated. The fourpence, threepence and halfgroat are considerably scarcer than the sixpences and only a very few specimens of the three-farthings are known. In all, a very considerable number of coins must have been struck. Also known are several superb patterns in gold and silver from dies engraved by Derick Anthony.

Despite the obvious superiority of his coins, Mestrelle fell foul of strenuous opposition to his machinery and in 1572 was deprived of his emoluments, probably because he was related to a certain Philip Mestrelle who was hanged at Tyburn in 1569 for forgery. An attempt to restore his position resulted in completely false accusations as to the speed and quality of striking being made by the Warden of the Mint, Richard Martin. Mestrelle was discharged, and six years later he was hanged at Norwich together with several accomplices for striking and passing false money.

CHARLES I

Further experiments with mill machinery by Nicholas Briot

It is to Charles' fine artistic taste and his intense desire to improve the poor quality of portraiture and striking of coins that we owe the employment in London of Nicholas Briot, one of the most brilliant artists and die cutters of his time.

Like Mestrelle, he was of French origin, having spent some years working at the Paris Mint amid continuous hostility towards mill and screw machinery, of which he was a staunch advocate. In 1628 he was allowed to set up machinery in the Tower Mint, and at once began to make a number of superb pattern pieces of an artistic and technical standard not previously achieved.

Apart from his outstanding qualities as an artist, his refinement over the machinery used by Mestrelle consisted of a circular collar which prevented the blank from spreading unevenly when struck, thus producing coins of a neater and rounder appearance bearing a fuller impression of the dies than had hitherto been possible. Portraiture on the hammered coins improved under his influence, although coins were still struck in a disgracefully shoddy fashion.

Briot's Crown Charles I

Briot's first milled issue consisted in gold of an angel, unite, double crown and crown, and in silver of a crown, halfcrown, shilling, sixpence, halfgroat and penny. These were struck between July 1631 and July 1632, some coins having in addition to the mint mark B, a flower or rose, the mark in use on the hammered coins at this time.

xiv ENGLISH SILVER COINAGE

In August 1635 he was appointed Master of the Scottish Mint, and although
he held this post until 1646, when he was succeeded by his son-in-law John
Falconer, most of the coins for which the Scottish series is justly proud were
struck in 1637. Doubtless under his influence, the use of the mill and screw
press in Scotland pre-dates the general use of this machinery in London by
several years. Briot's second milled issue in London, struck in 1638–9 with
the anchor mint mark consisted only of a silver halfcrown, shilling and sixpence, although hammered halfcrowns and shillings were also made from his
dies at this time. While continuing to work at the Tower Mint for the Par-
liamentary forces during the Civil War, he surreptitiously made dies for the
King's coins at York and Oxford. He died in 1646.

THE COMMONWEALTH, 1649–1660

In 1642, at the beginning of the Civil War, Parliament seized the Tower mint
but continued to strike coins in the name of Charles I and with his portrait.
After the king's execution Parliament ordered coins to be made in the name of
the Commonwealth and for the first time with the inscriptions in the English
tongue. The types of all the denominations were uniform, except for the half-
penny, and were very commonplace: the three smallest pieces bear no legend.
The only variation is a change in the mintmark: until 1657 it was a sun, after
that date an anchor; all pieces with this latter mark are rare.

The authorities having heard of the great advancements made in the manufacture of coins on the continent, sent to Paris for Peter Blondeau who had
invented a new machine. He came over and in a house in the Strand erected a
machine on the mill and screw principle, from which he struck the finely executed patterns of 1651. His halfcrown patterns were the first pieces made in
this country with an inscription on the edge. His position at the Mint was,
however, much opposed by the 'old brigade' and resulted in the issue of a
series of patterns by David Ramage to show that the foreigner was not
required. These pieces are of inferior workmanship to those of Blondeau.
However, he held on for a time, but by 1658 the opposition was so strong that
he was forced to resign leaving his machine behind. He retired to Paris with a
pension of £100.

Oliver Cromwell. A set of coins with the Protector's portrait was issued
by his order and with the consent of the Council. These pieces are of the finest
workmanship, the dies having been executed by that greatest of engravers,
Thomas Simon, and the striking done by means of Blondeau's machine. Most
authorities consider that these pieces were never put into circulation and must,
therefore, be classed as patterns. In the writer's view, however, the rare
halfcrowns of 1656 appear to have circulated as they nearly always turn up in
worn condition. The coins of 1658 were struck in large quantities, except for

the sixpence, and were probably intended for circulation: the majority were not issued owing to Cromwell's death in September of that year. Some of Simon's puncheons for the Cromwell coinage were sold in the Low Countries and an imitation crown was made there, known as the 'Dutch crown'. Other Dutch dies were prepared and some of these found their way back to the Mint, and in 1738 it was decided to strike a set of Cromwell's coins. Shillings and sixpences were struck from Dutch dies; and John Tanner, the Engraver at the Mint, made a crown from new dies.[1] Although not originals, these pieces always realize a good price as they are all rare.

CHARLES II, 1660–1685

At the beginning of this reign, Thomas Simon, who had been Chief Engraver at the Mint under the Commonwealth, applied for reinstatement, and although the King had already promised the position to Thomas Rawlins, he did in fact on May 31st, 1661, grant 'to Thomas Simon . . . the office of one of the engravers of the King's Arms shield and stamp'. It would appear that Simon shared the position with Rawlins, but most of the work devolved upon the former, although the two men may have co-operated to some extent in the production of dies for the three hammered coinages of 1660 to 1661[2]. These hammered coinages consist of three main issues, the first having no mark of value or inner circles. The second has the mark of value added behind the King's head, as instructed by a warrant of 28th November, 1661. The third issue, much the largest or at any rate the most common today, has an inner circle on both sides as well as the mark of value. There is practically no doubt that Simon was solely responsible for the dies of the undated Maundy and similar pieces, as in April 1665 he claims £35 in payment for 'altering the stamps of the fourpenny, threepenny, tuppeny and penny by way of the mill'. As this claim is of later date than that on which Simon was displaced by John Roettier, it shows clearly that he worked on dies for minor coins almost until his death during the Great Plague of 1665. John and Joseph Roettier, two brothers whose family had rendered services to Charles during his exile, were appointed engravers in 1661 and in January of the following year were directed to prepare all the necessary dies for the new 'milled' coinage. Shortly afterwards they were instructed to engrave a trial crown in competition with Simon, and all three men to cease all other work until the task be completed. The results were the famous 'petition crown' by Simon, and the pattern (E.S.C. 68-71) by the Roettiers: the sequel is of course well known; John Roettier was appointed Chief Engraver in May 1662 and was assisted by his brother Joseph in the production of dies for the milled coinage. Joseph left the

---

[1] D. F. Allen, *The Coinage of Cromwell and its Imitations.* B.N.J. xxiv page 191.
[2] The Indenture, dated 20 July 1660, authorizes silver crowns, but none is known.

Mint and went to France in 1672. In April 1662 Peter Blondeau was recalled from France, appointed Engineer, a new post, and was instructed 'to furnish all the mills, rollers, presses and other instruments, to cut, flatten, make round and size the pieces; the engine to make the edges of the money with letters and grainings, the great presses for coining of moneys and all other tools and engines for the new way of coining'.

George Bower was appointed an Engraver in Ordinary in 1664, but worked mainly on the production of medals. He is not known to have engraved any coin dies for Charles II or James II.

The first 'milled' halfcrowns and shillings were issued in 1663, the dated twopence in 1668, the dated fourpence, threepence and penny in 1670, and the sixpence in 1674. Thus four major and four minor denominations were struck in silver, the former having on their reverse four shields of arms in the form of a cross, and the small coins their value represented by one to four C's. The crown and halfcrown have an inscribed edge; on this are the words DECVS ET TVTAMEN which translated means 'An ornament and a safeguard', followed by the monarch's regnal year, which in this reign was reckoned from the death of Charles I. This practice was continued on the crown with a few breaks until 1935, and on the halfcrown until the end of the reign of George II. The regnal year does not correspond to the calendar year, and for this reason we usually find coins of the same date with two different regnal years on the edge. Another custom previously only adopted for Welsh silver was extended in this reign, that is, the custom of marking some of the coins with a symbol to denote the source of the metal from which they were struck:

Elephant, or *Elephant and Castle*, the African ('Guinea') Co., which had this symbol as its badge.

Plumes, silver from mines in Wales.

Rose, silver from mines in the West of England.

JAMES II, 1685–1688

There is little to be said about this reign, as the coinage continued with but few changes. The dies were again engraved by Roettier and the only variety is two slightly differing busts on the crown and halfcrown. The only difference in the larger denominations is that the interlinked C's for Carolus in the angles of the shields on the reverses are omitted. On the small coins, 4d to 1d, the former 'linked C's' design is replaced by one to four Roman I's: this serves both as an indication of denomination, and is also, by a useful coincidence, the initial letter of the King's name.

WILLIAM AND MARY, 1689–1694

Many engravers had a hand in the production of the various coinages for this interesting reign and it is a matter of no little difficulty accurately to attribute

certain coins to any particular artist, as some records, especially those apper-
taining to dies, are no longer in existence.

In 1688–9 John Roettier, still Chief Engraver, became ill with some kind of
muscular disease which affected him in both hands, thus causing him to dele-
gate most of his work to his two sons, James and Norbert, who were appointed
engravers about this time. Henry Harris, who had served at the Mint in a junior
capacity during the reign of Charles II, was appointed as one of the chief
engravers in August, 1689, but his work seems to have been concerned chiefly
with medals and seals, the Roettier brothers having carried out most of the
engraving of coin dies under their father's direction. Norbert Roettier was
reported to have stated that he engraved the Coronation Medal (which is usually attributed to John Roettier) 'without his assistance', and indeed this may be
so, as the elder Roettier was disabled at that time. Belonging to this year also
were the first and second issue halfcrowns and the fact that their high relief
busts are so very like those on the Coronation Medal leads one to suppose that
these also were the work of Norbert Roettier. The reverse design of the first
and second issue halfcrowns of 1689–90 was a crowned square-topped shield.
The third issue halfcrowns with the other silver were more likely to have been
the work of James Roettier who always appears to have preferred working in
lower relief than his brother. The reverse design of these coins consisted of
four crowned shields in the form of a cross with the monogram WM interlinked
in each angle. The sixpence however, seems to have some similarity to the
early halfcrown punches, but exact attribution is not possible. The reverse of
the small silver, from the fourpence down to the penny, now shows a crowned
modern numeral, a design which continues unchanged on the Maundy coins
until the present day.

WILLIAM III, 1694–1702

On the death of Mary no great change occurred in the silver coinage although
the designs of the four larger silver coins are more similar to those of James II.
The crown, shilling and sixpence were struck in 1695 although not in very
large quantities.

Up to this date the old hammered money was still in existence as it had
never been withdrawn from circulation. Owing to the rise in the value of silver, much of the full weight coinage had been exported to the Continent and
the hammered currency that still circulated here was worn out and much
clipped. Also, there was a large number of counterfeit hammered coins mixed
up with it. In 1695 the Government decided on a complete recoinage and laws
were passed for the prohibition of all clipped coins, for the prevention of clip-
ping and forgery and for the issue of a new coinage to replace the old and light
money. The old coins were mostly accepted at their face value and not by
weight so that the Government sustained the loss and not the owner. The

famous 'window' tax was levied on dwelling houses to raise £1,200,000 to make good this deficiency and to pay for the new coinage. In order to hasten this large undertaking, branch mints were opened at Bristol, Chester, Exeter, Norwich and York, the coins being marked B, C, E, N, y (or Y) below the bust. These mints operated for over two years with dies prepared mainly in London and dated 1696 and 1697. No crowns are known of these provincial mints. That there were millions of coins struck during this reign is obvious as today many of the pieces are still relatively common, especially the crowns and six-pences of the first of these years and the halfcrowns of 1698.

The King's bust was changed frequently during the reign and one of these needs a few words of comment. This is the one known as the 'second bust' on the higher denominations, and is readily distinguished by two large curls coming forward right across the chest. The sixpence of 1697 with this bust is only moderately rare, but all the other pieces are of exceptional rarity and must be patterns, but they have all been in circulation. Furthermore, there are two distinct varieties of this bust, one in lower relief of heavy style and the other with a rather narrower bust in higher relief, and with the hair more deeply engraved. At the time the first edition was written, the shilling of the second bust was still unknown, but was included in the table on the assumption that it might exist. A shilling with this bust in lower relief did eventually come to light and it is now in a private collection.

Once again, symbols are used to denote the source of the silver in the case of some of the coins of the later dates. Most of these are rare.

With regard to the engravers, Norbert Roettier, having been involved in some form of scandal, due possibly to his Jacobite sympathies, fled to France before the middle of the year 1695, thus leaving the entire responsibility for the engraving of coinage dies in the hands of his brother James; and it is to this artist that one can fairly certainly attribute all the early coins of the reign; the first bust on the halfcrown, shillings and sixpences in particular. James Roettier also fell into disgrace as he was found guilty at a Mint enquiry in 1697 of having smuggled dies of coinage for James II and Charles II out of the Tower to France; he was therefore dismissed from his post. Harris, who was still Chief Engraver, although not active on coinage dies, was directed to 'carry on the service', which he did with the help of John Croker. This latter, by far the most important of the engravers of the period, was a German who came to England in 1691 and was appointed an Engraver in 1697. After the death of Harris in 1705, Croker became Chief Engraver, and it was stated at that time that Harris was 'only a seal cutter and employed Mr. Croker to do the business of the mint'. To Croker then must be attributed most of the dies made after those engraved by James Roettier were worn out. He was later assisted by one James Bull, appointed Assistant Engraver or Probationer Engraver in Christmas 1698. Turning now to the coinage and the design of the coin, by far the most important event during this reign was the great re-coinage. Manuscript records at the Mint show the operating periods of the various provincial mints as follows:

EXETER	August	1696 to July 1698
YORK	September 1696 to April 1698	
BRISTOL	September 1696 to September 1698	
NORWICH	September 1696 to April 1698	
CHESTER	October	1696 to June 1698

It will thus be seen that even reckoning dates according to the old style, at any rate in the case of Bristol, Exeter and Chester, one would expect to see coins dated 1698. The fact that none is known to exist lends colour to T. B. Graham's theory that the late harp dies of 1697 were prepared so late in that year as to serve until the closing down of the mints in 1698.

There seems to be little doubt, due to the uniformity of design on the obverses, that Roettier was responsible for the engraving of most of the dies that were used in the provincial mints. In Treasury Papers of May 21st, 1697, appears a petition by Roettier, after his dismissal, for payment in respect of '500 pairs of Dyes for the Country Mints . . .' Later we see that 'Mr. Neale (the then Master) intends to pay him, his demand of sixty pounds tenn (*sic*) shillings, and with your Lordship's approbation, to give him fifty pounds more being the summ he desired for ye five hundred pair of Dyes for the Country Mints'. An Assistant Engraver was appointed for each mint 'to polish the Dyes in each country mint at a reasonable sallary to be allowed by ye K. (King) not exceeding forty (pounds) a year.'

Turning once more to the engravers Roettier and Croker, and the attribution to one or the other of the first and third bust coins, let us consider two possibilities. Firstly, as Roettier asserted that his designs, and only his, had been used until July 1697, did he produce the third bust coins for the provincial and Tower mints prior to his dismissal? If it could be proved that the third bust existed more frequently than only on rare coins (probably mules) dated 1696, then this could well be so, for as we have seen, he is known to have engraved five hundred pairs of dies for the provincial mints. However, it seems much more likely that Croker was responsible for the third bust silver coins as the shilling is almost identical with the second type guinea, usually ascribed to him. It is natural also that Croker would as nearly copy the general style of the Roettier coins as possible, particularly as the authorities desired uniformity of design for the provincial coinage. It is also almost certain that due to the length of time the country mints operated, Roettier's dies would have been exhausted before the mints ceased working.

It seems quite likely that after the provincial mints closed down, Croker adopted a more individual style, typified by the fourth bust or 'flaming hair' shilling of 1698.

The correct attribution of the 'fine work' gold and silver of 1700–1701 has presented a great problem. Let us first consider the existing contemporary records concerning this last period: In Mint MS. records appears an 'account of all dyes for gold and silver defaced and left good in the hands of ye Engravers April 13th 1700'. This account is an order for certain dies in stock at this time to be destroyed in the presence of the Warden and states eight heads, five 'armes', six 'paires' of Bull's dies for the shilling should be defaced with the exception of one reverse die which should be 'left good'. The dies for gold are not ascribed.

Another manuscript of January 7, 1701/2, gives 'tryall dyes of Mr. Bulls . . . armes left goode formerly 01'. This is most probably the reverse die referred to in 1700, and it is interesting to note that it was apparently only a trial die.

There is also a list of puncheons delivered into the Warden's custody on 13th January 1702, which includes puncheons for five guineas, guineas, half guineas, halfpence and farthing, all by Bull.

As to whom the fine work coinage may be attributed, there are three possibilities. Firstly, Croker and Bull may have each produced a series of dies for all denominations as there was a great demand for gold due to very large imports from the Continent. Secondly, Bull's dies may never have been used, and have all been defaced due to William's death. Thirdly, we can attribute the whole issue to Bull alone. It is interesting to note that no two guineas is shown in the list of puncheons by Bull, and if this coinage were his work, he could not have completed this puncheon before the list was made (January 1701/2). These puncheons cannot be for the gold issues of 1699 as they were not in stock in the earlier list of April 1700, where only the dies for a shilling were stated to be by Bull. Obviously therefore, Croker must have been responsible for the 1699 coinage. One can also see how nearly the bust on this gold resembles that on the fourth bust flaming hair shilling.

Returning to the 'fine work' coinage of 1700–01, it seems far more likely that these dies were the work of Croker than of Bull. Bull, although he must have been a very competent artist, as is shown by the reverses of some of Croker's medals of Queen Anne, had, at this time, been at the Mint only for about eighteen months, and it is not likely that such a large task as a completely new coinage would have been given to him; also the dies appearing in manuscript mint records are mentioned as being only trial dies. The style of the fine work coinage is also very typical of Croker's medallic work. the obverse of the State of Britain medal, and that of the fifth bust shilling are very similar in style. It would appear much more likely that this last issue of gold and silver represents Croker's later and more mature style, with the 'flaming hair' shilling and the 1699 gold coinage forming a transition in style between the 'Roettier copies' and these later coins. With regard to the second bust coins referred to earlier, it is possible that these were patterns made by Croker to obtain the post of Engraver when Roettier was dismissed in February 1696/7. The workmanship of the coins is far better than that shown on the other unique crown of the hair across the breast, which is much flatter relief and not such fine style. This coin is similar to the scarce second bust sixpence which occurs dated 1697 and very rarely 1696. The portraiture on these coins differs so greatly from the style of Roettier or Croker that one wonders if it could not be the work of Harris when he was working alone after Roettier's disgrace, or perhaps one of his junior assistants.

Finally, it is interesting to note that the portrait on the halfcrowns shows hardly any variation throughout the reign although new reverse designs or modifications are used from the beginning of 1698 onwards. It is quite likely that Roettier had made sufficient obverse dies for the whole reign before he quitted the Mint, as the reverse dies always tend to wear out more rapidly than do the obverses.

QUEEN ANNE, 1702–1714

No great change occurred in the coinage of this reign but the Union with Scotland in 1707 affected the design of the Royal arms on the shield. Heretofore the arms of England and Scotland had been placed in separate shields, but after the Act of Union they were impaled on two of the shields. Two new provenance marks appear on the coins of Anne. Some coins from the crown to the sixpence have VIGO below the queen's head—this commemorates the capture of the Spanish galleons at Vigo Bay in 1702 and it is from the metal captured that the coins were struck. Also we find for the first time the use of roses and plumes together on the same coin. An Order in Council of the 5th April 1706 directed that money coined from silver brought into the Mint by the 'Company for smelting down Lead with Pitcoale and Seacoale' should 'have the mark of distinction on each piece as represented in their petition.'

Before the Act of Union the coinage of Scotland was quite separate from that of England, the Scottish denominations being equivalent to only 1/12th of the English. For this reason the Anne 10 shilling piece struck in Scotland in 1705 weighed only 71 grains compared with the English shilling of 92 grains. As from the Union, the United Kingdom of England and Scotland used the same coinage, but during the years 1707–9, the Mint at Edinburgh continued to strike coins. These were of the same design as those struck in London and were for the most part from London made dies and puncheons, but had an E or E* below the queen's bust. As these coins were circulating in both countries it seems reasonable to include them in this book especially as some of them are almost the commonest coins of the reign.

At the beginning of the reign the engravers upon whom the work of engraving the coin dies rested were Croker and his apprentice Bull. James Roettier had been dismissed in 1697 as mentioned in the last chapter, and his brother

xxii   ENGLISH SILVER COINAGE

Norbert, who had been accused of 'playing tricks' with William III's portrait on the halfpence of William and Mary in 1694, had taken little active part in coinage ever since.

The sketches from which the coinage of Anne was engraved were probably the work of Sir Godfrey Kneller as a portrait in oils by this artist is very similar to that on the first coins. A newspaper of that period (*The Postman*) mentioned in April 1702 that ' . . . the Queen had lately had her picture drawn by Sir Godfrey Kneller in order to grave an impress for her coronation medals and coin'.

Croker was responsible for the engraving of most of the coinage dies, but his apprentice Bull and also one Gabriel Leclerk were appointed Assistant Engravers in 1705 and the former may have been responsible for some of the reverses as the task was often performed by an under-engraver at this time. Bull in fact engraved many of the reverses for Croker's medals of Anne. Little is known of Leclerk and he is not thought to have played an active part in the engraving of coinage dies—he left the Mint in 1709. It is, as in the previous reign, almost impossible to differentiate between the work of Bull and Croker due to the lack of contemporary records, but the former may have been responsible for the portrait on the 5 guineas of 1711, which differs in style from the other coins.

After the Union in 1707, it became the task of the Mint of Edinburgh to call in and convert into United Kingdom coin all the old Scottish money.

Puncheons for the making of dies were supplied by the Tower Mint and in a Warrant of June, the Master of the Edinburgh Mint was ordered to 'cause the . . . engraver to make new dyes' from these Tower Puncheons and ' . . . to make new puncheons and to use them for making dyes' which should be 'perfectly lyke the monies coyned in . . . the Tower'. Over half the bullion was coined into shillings and sixpences and this naturally caused more wear and tear on the dies for these denominations than those for the crown and halfcrown. This most probably accounts for the 'Edinburgh' bust on the small coins; this was undoubtedly an effort on the part of James Clerk, the then Scottish engraver, after Croker's puncheons for the second and third bust shillings and the ordinary sixpences had become exhausted.

An extract from Treasury papers of 1711 states that Clerk and his assistant Cave 'did . . . make one shilling head and reverse, one six pence head and reverse' and 'puncheons . . . for small coynes, viz. foure pence, three pence, two pence and one penny, etc.' They were asking for an increase in salary in respect of their 'extraordinary trouble during the great coinage' Little is known of the Maundy coins. There is however a slight change in portraiture on the small coins of 1706–7, but one cannot ascribe these with any certainty to the Mint at Edinburgh.

GEORGE I, 1714–1727

With the accession of the House of Brunswick the coinage remained the same except for the changes in the Royal titles and the Royal arms. The titles were abbreviated to D. G. M. BR . FR . ET . HIB . REX . F. D . BRVN . ET . L. DVX . S . R . I . A . TH . ET . EL, which stands for DEI GRATIA MAGNAE BRITANNIAE FRANCIAE ET HIBERNIAE REX FIDEI DEFENSOR BRUNSVICENSIS ET LUNEBURGENSIS DUX SACRI ROMANI IMPERII ARCHI-THESAURARIUS ET ELECTOR, or translated, 'By the Grace of God, King of Great Britain, France and Ireland, Defender of the Faith, Duke of Brunswick and Lüneburg, Arch-Treasurer and Elector of the Holy Roman Empire'. The *Fidei Defensor* title now appears on the coinage for the first time though it had been enjoyed by British sovereigns ever since it was conferred by the Pope on Henry VIII. We now find the arms of Brunswick Lüneburg in one of the shields. In this reign the bulk of the silver came from the importation of very large quantities from the South Sea Company, notorious for the 'Bubble'. Lesser amounts were supplied by the 'Company for smelting down Lead' and a very small amount by the Welsh Copper Company. All the silver obtained from this latter source was coined into shillings, which are fairly rare, and these pieces have the letters WCC below the king's bust and a Welsh plume and interlinked letter C's in the angles of the shields on the reverse.

With regard to the designers and engravers of this reign, Croker and Bull, who had together been responsible for the greater part of the coinage of Queen Anne, continued in office during this reign, although Bull may not have played a very large part in engraving the coinage dies.

Treasury papers of 1726 suggest that he may have been inactive for a number of years prior to this date, for in dealing with the appointment of John Rollo, an engraver of seals, they state that the Chief Engraver (Croker) had *'lacked the services of a skillful artist for many years'*. Bull must therefore have died some long time before 1726 and a petition by Croker dated January 30th, 1728–9 asking that Sigismund Tanner should serve as his apprentice states that Croker 'his Mat.s first engraver . . . being advanced in years' was 'the only one now living who has hitherto made puncheons for the heads on the coins'. The same document mentions that one Johann Rudolf Ochs, a Swiss engraver, also aged at that time, had been responsible for the reverse dies on the coins of George I. It seems therefore fairly reasonable, in view of these two pieces of contemporary evidence, to attribute the obverse dies of this coinage to Croker and the reverses to Ochs.

GEORGE II, 1727–1760

During the first part of this reign Croker, although very old, was still Chief Engraver, and was responsible for the young head portrait of this monarch. As mentioned previously, Johann Sigismund Tanner worked at the Mint as apprentice to Croker from January 1728–9 onwards, and on the death of Croker in March, 1741, succeeded him as Chief Engraver. The task of engraving the reverse dies of this coinage was now the duty of the assistant engraver; and from the beginning of 1729 until he became Chief Engraver this work probably occupied all Tanner's time. The name of Ochs, who had probably performed a similar task during the previous reign is again mentioned, but as he was an old man in 1728, according to Croker's petition mentioned in the last reign, it seems very unlikely that he, George II's engraver, was the same person who is mentioned by Hawkins as being on the Mint books in 1757 as Third Engraver. Hawkins even suggests that the same Ochs engraved for George III, but as Ochs senior had a son of the same name it seems almost certain that this son worked for George II and his successor and that Hawkins is in error.

We have definite documentary evidence that Tanner engraved some reverse dies in the form of an undated manuscript in the British Museum, which is an estimate by Croker of the expenses for making dies, etc. An extract reads as follows: 'In keeping accounts i doo propose to allow Mr. Tanner for making ye reverse Dyes . . . twelve shilling, and for ye remainder part of ye money I will make the dyes for ye heads . . .'

Tanner probably made the reverses for all the coins from 1729 until he became Chief Engraver, after which time they were probably engraved by Ochs junior. The old head coinage was undoubtedly Tanner's work, though the so-called intermediate head which appears on the gold may be Croker's work, as he did not die until 1741. Tanner, however, may have done the engraving under Croker's guidance.

Croker's dies for the obverse of the Maundy were used throughout the reign. Possibly there was no necessity for new dies to be made after Croker's death, as complete sets were issued during this time only in 1743, 1746 and 1760.

The source of the silver is still marked by provenance marks during this reign, as follows:

Roses—silver from mines in the west of England.
Plumes—silver from the Welsh Copper Company.
Roses and plumes—silver from the Company for Smelting Down Lead.
LIMA under the bust—Spanish treasure captured during Anson's voyage round the world, 1740–44.

GEORGE III, 1760–1820

Although this was a long reign, the number of silver coins issued by the Mint in the first 55 years was small, but it is nevertheless very interesting from a numismatic point of view. There was a small issue of shillings in 1763;

threepences in 1762 and 1763, and Maundy money. The issue of shillings in 1763 was a special one and it is said that £100 worth were struck for distribution by the Earl of Northumberland when he entered Dublin as Lord Lieutenant. These are therefore known as 'Northumberland' Shillings, though it seems certain that the total issue was considerably larger than the £100 worth required for the Earl. In 1787 a great quantity of shillings and sixpences were issued. These were the last shillings to be issued for general circulation prior to the recoinage of 1816, if we discount the rare Dorien and Magens shillings of 1798 (see page 126, note 1).

At this time Spain was mining vast quantities of bullion in her American colonies and coining from this silver 'pieces of eight' or eight reales, and also smaller denominations. These seem to have circulated in many parts of the world and as very considerable quantities were captured by the English, and owing to the shortage of regal silver in this country, they very readily passed as currency. This was technically illegal, but the government turned a blind eye and in fact legalised the position in 1797 by having them countermarked with the head of George III in a small oval. The puncheon used was that employed by the Assay Master at Goldsmith's Hall for stamping the duty mark on silver plate assayed after 1785. The dollars were then made current at 4/9d. and gave rise to the saying 'two Kings' heads not worth a crown'. These oval-countermarked dollars circulated at 4/9d from 9 March to 21 October 1797. They did not, as mentioned by some writers, circulate for a second period up to 1804. Early in 1804 the stamp was changed, the king's head being larger and in an octagon. The punch used for the head was that for the Maundy penny. These octagonal-countermarked dollars circulated from 11 January to 2 June 1804, and were current for five shillings.

In the same year, arrangements were made for Spanish dollars to be completely overstruck, thereby removing all but traces of the original design. This was made possible by Boulton's powerful machinery recently installed at the Soho Mint in Birmingham. These pieces were struck for The Bank of England, and were called Bank of England Dollars. They were really tokens but as they were an authorised issue, it appears proper that they should find a place in this work. The original patterns for the issue were engraved and dated as early as 1798. The dollars are all dated 1804, but they were struck until the year 1811, and occasionally on a coin restruck with insufficient pressure it is possible to detect dates later than 1804 of the original Spanish coin. There were three 'valuations' or periods of circulation for the Bank dollars, viz. 20 May 1804 to 10 March 1811 at five shillings; 11 March 1811 to 30 April 1817 at five shillings and sixpence (due to the shortage of silver prior to the recoinage); 1 May 1817 until demonetization on 25 March 1820 again at five shillings. Three shillings and 1/6 bank tokens were also issued: dies were prepared for a ninepence, but it was never put into circulation.

The Mint's old quarters in the Tower of London had been inadequate for many years past, and during the years 1810–12 the Royal Mint was built on Tower Hill and new steam-powered machinery was made and installed by Boulton and Watt. In 1816 it was resolved to issue a completely new coinage despite all difficulties and expense. Half-crowns, shillings and sixpences were struck during this year, Maundy in 1817 and the crown in 1818–20. The issue of silver is of reduced size and weight being now sixty-six shillings instead of sixty-two to the pound troy. All silver shillings from 1816 were still legally current until the withdrawal of the large five pence coin.

On the crown as well as on the larger gold denominations, we find the St. George and the Dragon device for the first time since the reign of Henry VIII. The head of the half-crown was changed in 1817, as the original design, showing the back of the shoulder to the spectator, was not popular. These early half-crowns are often colloquially known as 'Bull Heads'. The artist responsible for all these designs was Benedetto Pistrucci, an Italian gem-engraver who had come to find employment in London and whose work came to the notice of William Wellesley Pole, the Master of the Mint.

There were probably more changes of portraiture and design in this reign than in any other. Regarding the engravers, Tanner remained at the Mint holding the office of Chief Engraver until his death in 1775, but probably took little active part in preparing the new dies, as during his latter years he suffered from approaching blindness and other infirmities. Most of the work was carried out by his Chief Assistant, Richard Yeo, who succeeded to the post of Chief Engraver on Tanner's death. Yeo died only four years later in 1779.

Among the obverse dies attributed to Yeo are those for the first three issues of guineas and half-guineas, the quarter guinea and the famous Northumberland shilling referred to earlier. Thomas Pingo, who was the Assistant Engraver from 1771 until his death in 1776, produced the dies for the fourth issue of guineas and half guineas. He was succeeded by his son Louis, who was responsible for the design and engraving of many of the dies in George III's middle period. Among these are the well-known 'Spade' guineas, the 1787 shillings and sixpences etc. He engraved the obverses for the later gold coins from models supplied by Nathaniel Marchant, Assistant Engraver from 1792–1815.

J. R. Ochs junior remained as Third Engraver until his retirement in 1786. The dies for the first issue of Maundy are usually ascribed to him.

Thomas Wyon junior was appointed Assistant Engraver in 1811 and became Chief Engraver in 1815. He died two years later. Although active for so short a time, he left his stamp on the coinage. He was responsible for the design and engraving of the reverses for the first (Bull Head) halfcrown, the shilling and the sixpence. He engraved the obverses of these coins from a model by Benedetto Pistrucci. After Wyon's death Pistrucci engraved the dies himself. The crown is perhaps the most widely known as the reverse bears his renowned portrayal of St. George and the Dragon; the second halfcrown shows almost the same obverse as the crown and the modification of Wyon's reverse, which was used for the first halfcrown. William Wyon, cousin of Thomas Wyon junior, joined the Mint in 1816, and engraved the dies for the last issue of Maundy coins.

GEORGE IV, 1820–1830

Pistrucci and his assistant, Jean Baptiste Merlen, whom he introduced to the Mint in 1820, were together responsible for the greater part of the coinage of this reign. There are three main issues. The obverse, showing the King's laureate head, is combined with a reverse which shows a crowned floreate shield and emblems in the case of the first issue, and a square-topped shield crowned within the Garter on the second issue. The third issue consists of a bare head with, on the halfcrown, a coat-of-arms, and a crown surmounted by a crowned lion on the shilling and sixpence. The laureate King's head obverse was designed and engraved by Pistrucci. Merlen was responsible for the engraving of the reverse dies of all the silver coins. When the King's portrait was changed in 1825, Pistrucci was commissioned to engrave the obverse dies from a bust of George by Sir Francis Chantrey; but this he refused to do declaring that he would not degrade his art so far as to copy the work of another man. The result was that W. Wyon produced his fine, bare head portrait. William Wyon was appointed Chief Coinage Engraver in 1828, Pistrucci being given the post of Chief Medallist at the same time.

WILLIAM IV, 1830–37

The obverse of the coins of this reign was designed by W. Wyon who engraved the portrait from a bust by Sir Francis Chantrey. Merlen designed and engraved the reverses on the silver. There were no crowns struck for circulation during this reign, but proofs were issued in 1831 and 1834. These show the usual obverse portrait, and on the reverse a crowned shield on a mantle of ermine. The design for the halfcrown is similar, but the shilling and sixpence have a new coinage type, the value in words with a crown above.

An interesting innovation in this reign was the reintroduction, as a denomination, of the fourpence or groat. These were first struck in 1836 and were also issued the following year.

The three-halfpenny pieces, first struck in 1834, were never current in this country, but were a special issue for use in the West Indies and Ceylon. They are usually collected under the English series however, and we have therefore included them in the present work.

VICTORIA, 1837–1901

As is only natural with a reign of this length, there were several changes in the coinage. There were three main issues known as the 'Young' head, 'Jubilee' issue and 'Old' head issue respectively. There was also the so-called 'Gothic' issue of crowns and florins.

Young Head. This is the first issue and shows the Queen with a young head, usually with a fillet. The smaller denominations were issued in 1838. Crowns and halfcrowns were issued in the 1839 proof sets, a few of the latter being put into circulation, but crowns were not generally issued until 1844, and were again struck in 1845 and 1847. The 'Britannia' groat was continued up to 1855, and was recalled from circulation in 1887. Threepences of the same type as the Maundy coin were issued for general circulation in 1845 and continued to be struck for nearly 100 years except for 1847 and 1848. Prior to 1845 however, they had sometimes been struck in quantities (as well as the twopences) for sending to some of the Colonies which used the British coinage. Wyon designed and engraved the so-called 'Young' head of the Queen, and the reverse designs were produced by Merlen, who retired in 1844. These designs, however, were engraved by Leonard Charles Wyon, who entered the service of the Mint on Merlen's retirement. He later succeeded W. Wyon, his father, as Chief Engraver, and is probably best known for his portrait of Victoria on the early bronze 'bun' pennies.

'Godless' Florin. In the early part of this reign, there was a strong agitation that the country should change over to a decimal coinage. A motion in favour of silver pieces of the value of one-tenth and one-hundredth of a pound was placed before Parliament, but was, however, withdrawn, on the understanding that the former piece be issued. Hence, the florin became a new denomination, and was first issued in 1849 with the Queen shown wearing a crown. Because DG or Dei Gratia was omitted from the Queen's titles it has become popularly known as the 'Godless' Florin. The Queen's portrait was designed and engraved by W. Wyon, and the reverse design for this and also for the Gothic florin, which superseded it, was by William Dyce.

Gothic Issue. We have never been able to ascertain the reason for the issue of the Gothic crown in 1847 and 1853. Certainly large numbers of this fine coin were struck of the first date and some undoubtedly did get into circulation, although it is somewhat unusual to find a worn piece.

A revised design for the florin was made and first used in 1851. This was copied from the Gothic crown issued in 1847. The date on these pieces is in small Roman numerals in Gothic script at the end of the obverse legend.

Jubilee Issue. In 1887 it was decided to issue a new coinage on the occasion of the Queen's Golden Jubilee. The well-known Jubilee type head was engraved by L. C. Wyon from designs by Sir Joseph Boehm. Wyon designed the reverses himself, except of course for that of the crown, which shows Pistrucci's famous treatment of St. George and the Dragon. An innovation in this coinage was the issue of a double florin or four shilling piece, which did not prove popular, probably due to its being readily confused with the crown: this was discontinued in 1890. L. C. Wyon died in 1891 and was succeeded by George William de Saulles, who was appointed Chief Engraver in 1893.

Old Head. The design of the coins was again changed in 1893 and the new portrait of the Queen wearing a coronet and veil was designed by Sir Thomas Brock and engraved by De Saulles. The reverse designs of the old head coins were by various artists. The crown still showed Pistrucci's St. George, the halfcrown was designed by Brock and the 'three shields' reverses of the florin and shilling by Sir Edward Poynter; the sixpence and threepence were modifications of Merlen's original designs.

EDWARD VII, 1901–1910

There was only one issue of coins during this reign, the obverse portrait of the King being engraved by De Saulles, as also were the new reverse designs for the half crown, florin and shilling. The florin of this reign is notable in that it shows a standing figure of Britannia. It was also during this reign that the practice of using a reducing machine was generally adopted and for this reason it would probably be more correct to refer to the engraver as a designer.

GEORGE V, 1910–1936

The coinage of this reign is usually considered to fall into four distinct issues, the first two being almost identical apart from fineness. The obverse portrait of George V used throughout the reign with small modifications was prepared from plaster casts made by Sir Bertram MacKennal and his initials B. M. appear on the truncation of the bust. The reverse designs for the halfcrown and shilling were modifications of de Saulles's design for Edward VII, but the sixpence no longer has the words SIX PENCE on the reverse and is a smaller version of the shilling, showing the crown surmounted by a lion crowned. The florin was designed after the style of the 1887 Jubilee issue piece, but was somewhat modified. The designer is not known and it was probably carried out by a staff engraver at the Royal Mint.

In 1920, after the First World War, for a few months the price of silver rose above 5/6d per ounce. It was, therefore, possible to melt the ordinary currency and make a profit on it. Also it would have meant a big loss to the Mint to strike good silver of the same size as usual. It was, therefore, resolved to debase the silver coinage for the first time since the reign of Edward VI: this was a most unfortunate decision as the price of silver soon dropped below the danger point. The new (second) issue was struck in metal of which 50 per cent was silver and 50 per cent alloy. At first great difficulty was experienced in finding a suitable alloy and the early coins in worn condition soon turned dull, almost a brownish colour. The authorities quickly improved the mixture and later coins do not become so discoloured.

It has been pointed out to us that the second (debased) coinage appears to have been struck from new dies with the king's bust in lower relief. The Mint informs us that the same bust was used, but that as the coins were in a different metal the resistance to the dies would be different. This would account for the apparent lower relief. Furthermore the engineers may have varied the striking pressure according to the alloy used and the rate of wear on the dies. Different dies do exist: there are a large number of minor varieties.

In 1926 the effigy of the king was slightly altered, the initials of the engraver's name were moved toward the rear of the truncation and the whole head slightly reduced in size; also a new beaded border was added. This type is often known as the 'modified effigy' type or more correctly 'third coinage'.

In 1927 it was decided to change again the reverse types of the silver coins and two innovations occur. Up to this issue no crown had been struck for this reign, but through the efforts of Sir Charles Oman, then President of the Royal Numismatic Society and an M.P. for Oxford, this denomination was included. However, there was so little demand for it that very few were issued each year. The threepenny piece now had a reverse design of three acorns and can therefore be easily distinguished from the Maundy threepence. In 1930 the reverse dies of the Maundy were re-engraved but the design was not changed. All the new reverse types for the fourth coinage were designed by Kruger Gray.

In the Royal Mint Museum are many patterns for this and later reigns, but we have decided not to include them here as they are not available to collectors.

In 1935 the first true British commemorative coin was issued to mark the King's Silver Jubilee. The modernistic St George reverse was designed by Percy Metcalfe. Twenty-five special Jubilee crowns were made in gold and two thousand five hundred were struck in sterling silver and as the Mint received far more orders than they could supply, they were distributed by ballot. These pieces had an edge inscription in relief whereas on the normal coins it is incuse.

EDWARD VIII, 1936

George V died in January of this year and Edward VIII reigned until his abdication in December. New dies were prepared for the reign; these were dated 1937 and coins were struck in fairly large quantities. Almost all the coins were melted down, and only very few specimens survived. The 'commonest' of these is the 12-sided threepence, some of which were sent to vending-machine manufacturers before the abdication, and were not returned when the pieces were recalled: a very few of this denomination found their way into circulation. A number of uniface trial pieces were publicly auctioned and I have seen a trial reverse for the florin which was found in circulation in the 1960's.

Coins of all denominations exist, except for half sovereigns and Maundy money of Edward VIII, but few are in private hands. The portrait on all these pieces, at the King's special request, was turned to the spectator's left, which if precedent had been followed, would have been the other way round.

During 1936 a full series of silver pieces was struck with the portrait and name of George V and many numismatists regard these as posthumous coins of George V struck during the reign of Edward VIII. A monograph 'The proposed coinage of King Edward VIII' by Graham P. Dyer, Librarian and Curator, Royal Mint, has been published by H. M. Stationery Office, and gives full historical details of the background to the proposed coinage, describing all the patterns, trial pieces etc. which were submitted for consideration. In *English Silver Coinage* (E.S.C) I have restricted mention to the finally accepted coinage, and in line with our previous policy with regard to uniface patterns, have omitted them from the book.

GEORGE VI, 1936–1952

A full complement of silver coins was issued in 1937 with new designs. There were two innovations. Shillings were issued concurrently with two reverse designs, one of these bearing the crest of the English and the other the crest of the Scottish version of the Royal Arms. The other change was the issue of a new 12-sided nickel-brass threepenny piece in addition to the small silver coin which was retained. This latter piece circulated chiefly in Scotland and the colonies; in fact complete issues of some years were sent overseas, hence their rarity in this country. The coin was not struck for circulation in the U.K. after 1941 and the last date of the denomination to appear was 1944.

A revolutionary change took place in 1947, when the silver coinage ceased to be issued and was replaced with a coinage in cupro-nickel. The designs were not changed, but the milling on the edge was made much closer. The change of metal was made in order to repay silver borrowed during the war from the United States. The Maundy coins were again struck in fine silver.

When India became independent in 1947 the King relinquished his title of Emperor (IND : IMP) and these titles were therefore omitted from 1949 onwards. This did not necessitate any major changes in design apart from re-spacing of words, with the exception of the sixpence, where the royal cipher GRI was modified to GVIR. On the occasion of the National Exhibition in 1951 known as the Festival of Britain, a commemorative crown in cupro-nickel was struck. This year also marked the quatercentenary of the issue of the first silver crown by Edward VI in 1551. The dies for the reverse of this 1951 crown, which shows Pistrucci's St. George and the Dragon, were made from a punch manufactured for a crown of 1899, the date being added by hand. Over two million of these coins were struck, all from polished dies, but owing to the comparatively short time in which the Mint had to make them, the finish of the normal coins was not up to what we normally understand as proof standard. A very few crowns were struck from specially prepared dies and these pieces have a more highly frosted portrait and a more brilliantly polished field. They have come to be known as 'VIP' proofs.

ELIZABETH II, 1952 –

Although Her Majesty ascended the throne in February, 1952, following usual practice no coins were issued bearing her portrait until about the time of the coronation in June 1953. Although striking of the new coins began late in 1952, denominations urgently needed were struck bearing a portrait of George VI exactly as his last coinage, and in fact sixpences, threepences, halfpennies and farthings were also struck early in 1953, but still dated 1952. A halfcrown with George VI's portrait dated 1952 turned up in the North of England in the late 1960's.

The only unusual feature of design which occurred on the new 'silver' coinage for Elizabeth II was the equestrian figure for the crown, and this was the first such representation since the reign of Charles I. The obverse, designed by Gilbert Ledward, shows Her Majesty, in uniform, seated on the police horse Winston. The reverse is also unorthodox in that it bears no legend—the design consists of the national emblems radiating from a central crown, with uncrowned shields of England, Scotland, Ireland and England in saltire. It was designed by D. G. Fuller.

The portrait of the Queen chosen for the coinage was by Mrs. Mary Gillick but the Mint found that it did not strike very well owing to its delicate treatment. A number of experiments was carried out late in 1953 in an attempt to sharpen the design and to ensure better wearing characteristics of the obverse. The Queen's portrait, especially when reduced to the size of the smaller denominations, appeared in very low relief and with insufficient detail. A number of different re-cut obverse dies were used for the later 1953 pieces and then for 1954 onwards: on these the portrait is shown in somewhat higher relief and much finer detail is visible.

The reverse design of the halfcrown is reminiscent of that of the pound-sovereign of Elizabeth I, a crowned garnished shield between E R. The florin and sixpence both show different treatments of the national emblems, with the leek of Wales appearing for the first time on a British coin. The tradition, dating from 1937, of striking two types of shilling, one English and one Scottish, was maintained, the two coins depicting on the reverse the respective quarterings of the royal arms, crowned.

In 1954, the Queen declared by proclamation a change in the royal style and titles. It was thought that the title 'Britt : Omn :' (= of all the Britains, i.e., overseas possessions) was no longer in keeping with the status of the British Commonwealth, and the words were accordingly omitted from the legend on coins struck from that year onwards.

In 1960, on the occasion of the British Trade Exposition held in New York, the Royal Mint, who had a stand at the exhibition, struck commemorative medals at the site. A special crown was also issued at this time, but as U.K. coin may only be struck in this country, the crowns were struck at the Royal Mint. The pieces destined for sale in New York were struck from polished dies, the finish of the coin being somewhat similar to that of the 1951 Festival piece, though not of such high quality. The polished-die crowns were sold in special plastic cases at the Exhibition. When the Exhibition closed, surplus stocks were returned to the U.K. in bags, and most of the specimens from polished dies now on the market in the U.K. are more or less defaced by bag scratches. As it was thought desirable to make crowns available to collectors here, a limited quantity was struck from ordinary dies; these also are hard to obtain in perfect state, as they were supplied to dealers and banks in bags. The obverse of this crown is the normal coinage portrait of the Queen by Mary Gillick, and the reverse is identical with that of the 1953 crown apart from the date; the edge is grained. The value FIVE SHILLINGS appears below the head.

On the death of Sir Winston Churchill in 1965, it was decided to issue a commemorative crown. These coins have been widely criticised due to their poor standard of workmanship, which probably resulted from their having to be produced in very large quantities in as short a time as possible. This crown has the Gillick portrait with the date 1965 below the bust; the reverse shows the head of Churchill by the sculptor Oscar Nemon and the inscription CHURCHILL; the edge is grained. An unusual feature for a modern crown is that no mark of denomination appears.[1]

---

[1] For background notes on decimal coinage, see Part II.

NOTE FOR COLLECTORS

For the purpose of clarity we have adopted the convention that a single dash — means 'as above' i.e. following the description of the coin immediately before. All coins are in silver unless otherwise stated.

Except for a very few cases we have kept the same numbering as the earlier editions, additional material being numbered A, B, etc.

ABBREVIATIONS

O. or *obv*.	= Obverse	R or *rev*.	= Reverse
r.	= right	l.	= left
dr.	= draped	laur.	= laureate.
cuir.	= cuirassed	ex.	= exergue
mm.	= mintmark	mon.	= monogram
Cu.-ni.	= cupro-nickel	BU	= brilliant uncirculated
Mule	= accidental use of an incorrect die for one side.		

N.B. In giving the edge years (i.e., regnal years), when they are in more than one word, only the initial of the first word (D= DECIMO, V= VICESIMO, T= TRICESIMO) is entered in the table. Hence Nos. 38 to 54 should read VICESIMO PRIMO, etc., and Nos. 56 to 67 should read TRICESIMO PRIMO, etc.

PART ONE

PRE-DECIMAL CURRENCY
1649–1971

CROWNS

THE COMMONWEALTH

Only one type.   As illustration.   *Edge*, plain.

No.	Date	R	Varieties
1	**1649**	R^4	
2	—	R^5	Thin wire-line inner circle and inverted N in ENGLAND.
3	**1651**	R^4	
4	**1652**	R	
5	—	R^3	Very large 2 of date over 1
6	**1653**	N	
6A	—	R^3	V for V in VS
7	**1654**	R^3	
8	**1656**	R^2	
9	—	S	Small 6 of date over 4
9A	—	R	Large 6 of date over small 6 over 4

CROMWELL

10 11

10   By Simon, 1658[1]. As illustration, with top leaf of laurel wreath to l. of r.
     foot of A[2].   *Edge*, HAS . NISI . PERITVRVS . MIHI . ADIMAT . NEMO *[3]   *S*
10A   — *In gold*   *R*[7]
11   *Dutch copy.*   Similar, but top leaf of laurel to first limb of N, which
     letter is upside down.   *Edge*, as before   *R*[3]
11A   — *On silver gilt flan*[4]   *R*[7]
13   *Tanner's copy.*   Similar, but slightly different features, top leaf of laurel
     between A and N, the latter not upside down, leaf not so pointed; the
     beading of the border is wider; stops after HIB and PRO. Flaw in all P's.
     Edge, as before   *R*[4]
14   — *Edge*, plain   *R*[4]
14A   Simon's obv. muled with Tanner's rev. *Edge*, plain; on thick flan   *R*[7]
14B   As 14A but muling reversed   *R*[7]

---

[1] The date is always 1658 altered from 1657.
[2] At a very early stage a flaw started in the die near the O of OLIVAR and slowly stretched right
across the bust. We have never seen a specimen without a minute sign of this flaw. They can be
obtained with all the stages of the flaw showing. Some of the later strikings from this die show
that an attempt was made to repair the flaw.
[3] The translation of this legend is 'Let no one remove these (letters) from me under penalty of
death'.
[4] In previous editions 11B, in pewter and 12, in lead with plain edge were included. These are now
considered to be spurious.

CHARLES II

Type A

Type **A**   First bust, rose below, as illustration. *Edge*, DECVS . ET . TVTAMEN
          ⋆ + ⋆ (or without the stops or all the ornaments).[1]
B   Similar, but edge dated, DECVS . ET . TVTAMEN . ⋆ + ⋆ . 1662 . ⋆ + ⋆.
C   *O*. CAROLVS . II . DEI . GRATIA. The bust is a variety of the first bust;
          it is slightly broader, of less fine style, and the ties to the back hair
          are straight and without rose below. R. and edge similar.
D   As last but without date on edge.
E   *O*. As last. R. Similar, but none of the shields quartered, shield of
          England at top, France at bottom, as illustration below. *Edge*, DECVS
          ET TVTAMEN ⋆ ANNO REGNI XV + +

Type C

---

[1] On coins of type A (rose below bust) there are a large number of varieties in the length and style
   of the ties behind the head. For recent research see A. J. Broad, 'Rosa Sine Causa', *Seaby Coin
   and Medal Bulletin* March 1989, 38–41 and notes.

Type F   G   Type F

F   Second bust; smaller than last and with curving tie to wreath.[1] R. As
        last. *Edge*, date still in Roman numerals.
G   Similar, but with Elephant below bust.
H   Second bust. *Edge*, as before, but the years of the king's reign in
        words instead of in Roman numerals[2].

Type I   Type J

I   Third bust; much larger and broader than the second, tie nearly
        straight. From end of tie to tip of nose is 20 mm.
J   Fourth bust; still larger, with older features and more pointed nose.
        From end of tie to tip of nose is 21 mm.
K   Similar, but with Elephant and castle below bust.

---

[1] The coins of 1662 and 1664 are from two or three different working punches and they are again
slightly different from that used for the other dates. The main style is the same and the differences are not sufficient to warrant their inclusion as major varieties.
[2] In 1667 the edge reads AN REG instead of ANNO REGNI.

No.	Type	Date	Edge Year	R	Varieties, Remarks, etc.
15	**A. First bust, rose below**	**1662**	none	C^2	See note[1]
15A	—	—	—	C^2	Edge lettering more closely spaced
16	—	—	—	R^5	*Proof*
17	**B.** —	—	**1662**	S	
18	**C.** — **no rose**	—	—	R^2	
18A	—	—	—	R^3	Cloak frosted, curl on neck and extra curl below c. (See Lingford lot 282)
19	**D.** —	—	none	S	
20	—	—	—	R^3	Cloak frosted, curl on neck
20A	—	—	—	R^3	— and as 18A
21	—	—	—	R^6	— *proof*, plain edge[2]
22	**E.** — **new reverse**	**1663**	XV	N	
22A	—	—	none	R^5	No date on edge
23	—	—	XV	R^2	Cloak and C's frosted
24	—	—	—	R^6	— *proof*
25	—	—	—	R^6	— *proof in gold*
26	—	—	—	S	Cloak only frosted
27	—	—	—	R	— extra curl below c
27A	—	—	—	R	— No stops on rev.
28	**F. Second bust**	**1664**	XVI	N	See note[1] on page 5
29	—	—	—	R^6	Proof
30	—	**1665**	—	R^5	
31	—	—	XVII	R^3	
31A	—	—	—	R^3	5 of date over 4
32	—	**1666**	XVIII	S	
32A	—	—	—	R^4	RE.X instead of REX.
33	**G.** — **Elephant below**	—	—	R	
34	—	—	—	R^2	RE.X instead of REX.
34A	**H. Second bust**	—	—	R^7	
35	—	**1667**	DECIMO NONO	S	AN. REG. on edge
35A	—	—	—	S	AN .˙ REG .˙ on edge
36	—	**1668**	VICESIMO	N	ANNO . REGNI . on edge
36A	—	—	—	R^4	TVTAMEN . ET . DECVS inverted[3]

[1] Although this is a very common coin, no crowns of Charles II are common in first class condition.
[2] The reverse is the same for the pattern die for E.S.C. 71.
[3] On this variety, a section of the collar has been used inverted.

No.	Type	Date	Edge Year	R	Varieties, Remarks, etc.
37	**H. Second bust**	**1668**	VICESIMO	R^2	8 of date over 7
37A	—	—	—	R^4	8 of date over 5
38	—	**1669**	V. PRIMO	R^3	
39	—	—	—	R^3	9 of date over 8
40	—	**1670**	V. SECVNDO	R	
41	—	—	—	R^2	70 of date over 69
42	—	**1671**	V. TERTIO	N	
42A	—	—	—	R^4	T of ET struck over R
42B	—	—	—	R^6	ET struck over FR
43	**I. Third bust**	**1671**	V. TERTIO	N	
44	—	—	V. QVARTO	R^5	See note[1]
45	—	**1672**	—	N	See note[2]
46	—	**1673**	—	R^5	
47	—	—	V. QVINTO	N	
48	—	—	—	R	3 of date over 2
49	—	**1674**	V. SEXTO	R^6	
50	—	**1675**	V. SEPTIMO	R^4	
50A	—	—	—	R^3	5 of date over 3
50B	—	—	—	R^5	— error, edge EGNI
51	—	**1676**	V. OCTAVO	C	
52	—	**1677**	V. NONO	S	
53	—	—	—	R^2	7 of date over 6
54	—	—	—	R	— 'boar's head' flaw above the head on *obv.*
55	—	**1678**	TRICESIMO	R^2	8 of date over 7
56	—	**1679**	T. PRIMO	C	
57	**J. Fourth bust**	—	—	N	
57A	—	—	—	R	HIBR . EX error
58	**I. Third bust**	**1680**	T. SECVNDO	R^2	
59	—	—	—	R	80 of date over 79
60	**J. Fourth bust**	—	—	S	
61	—	—	—	R^2	80 of date over 79
63	**K. — Elephant & Castle**	**1681**	T. TERTIO	R^4	See note[3]

[1] An example is in the B.M. (ex. Clark Thornhill collection) and is rather interesting as it has the wrong edge for this year. The other edge if there were two, should be VICESIMO SECVNDO.

[2] In the years 1664, 1671 and 1672 the dies are not all made from the same working-punches so there are two or three slight varieties of busts.

[3] The coin of 1680 with 'E & C' was originally published from a very worn specimen. There is a coin in VF condition in the B.M. fourth bust 1680 with a flaw below the bust which could be mistaken on a worn coin for an elephant or 'E & C' mark. There is a similar piece in worn state in the Museum at Manchester. I am therefore of the opinion that E.S.C. 62, 1968 edition, does not exist.

No.	Type	Date	Edge Year	R	Varieties, Remarks, etc.
64	**J.** —	—	—	S	
65	—	1682	T. QVARTO	R^4	
65A	—	—	—	N	2 of date over 1
65B	—	—	—	R^2	Appears as QVRRTO due to QVARTO being struck over TERTIO
66	—	1683	T. QVINTO	R^2	
67	—	1684	T. SEXTO	R^2	

Patterns

68

68 As the coin of type D, without edge date or rose below bust which is
without drapery. Edge, DECVS ET TVTAMEN * + * R^6
69 — *In gold* R^6
70 — *Edge, plain* R^6
71 — *In gold* R^6

These four pieces do not all have the same reverse die: there are minor
differences.

72

72 By Simon, 1663. As illustration. *Edge*, in two lines
THOMAS SIMON. MOST . HVMBLY . PRAYS . YOVR . *MAJESTY* TO .
COMPARE . THIS . HIS . TRYALL . PIECE . WITH . THE . DVTCH . AND . IF .
MORE (second line) TRVLY . DRAWN &. EMBOSS'D . MORE . GRACE : FVLLY
. ORDER'D . AND . MORE . ACCVRATELY . ENGRAVEN . TO . RELIEVE . HIM.,
two C's interlinked between palm branch and a branch of laurel, with a
crown above, separate the end of the lines from the beginning. *This is
known as the 'Petition crown'.* R^4

73 — *Edge*, REDDITE . QVÆ . CÆSARIS . CÆSARI & CT. POST, followed by sun appearing out of cloud. *This is known as the 'Reddite crown'* R^5

74 — *In pewter* R^6

74A — *Edge*, RENDER . TO . CÆSAR . THE . THINGS . WHICH . ARE . CÆSARS &c.* R^6

74B — *In pewter* R^6

75 — *Edge*, plain. *In pewter* R^6

JAMES II

Type A *O.* IACOBVS . II . DEI . GRATIA, first bust laureate and draped l., short lock of hair curls outwards towards the chin. R. As illustration below. *Edge*, as before, DECVS, etc.

A   B

B Similar, but second bust, narrower than last and the short lock curls towards back of head.

No.	Type	Date	Edge Year	R	Varieties, Remarks, etc.
76	**A. First bust**	**1686**	SECVNDO	*S*	See note[1]
77	—	—	—	*R²*	No stops on *obv.*
78	**B. Second bust**	**1687**	TERTIO	*C²*	See note[2]
79	—	—	—	*R*	Smaller lettering on edge
80	—	**1688**	QVARTO	*C*	See note[2]
81	—	—	—	*N*	Last 8 of date over 7[3]

[1] This piece is not really quite as rare as is sometimes thought, but it is a difficult coin to obtain in first class condition.
[2] Crowns with the second bust are very often found with the hair above the the the forehead not properly struck up.
[3] Unbarred As occurring in the legends of some coins, particularly in 1688 are almost certainly due to die-filling.

WILLIAM AND MARY

83

Only one type. *Edge*, as before, DECVS, etc.

No.	Date	Edge Year	R	Varieties, Remarks, etc.
82	**1691**	TERTIO	N	
82A	—	—	R^4	Reads TERTTIO
83	**1692**	QVARTO	N	
84	—	—	R^3	2 of date over 2 upside down
85	—	QVINTO	S	—

WILLIAM III

A

First harp

Type A As illustration. *O*. First bust with curved breastplate or drapery. R. as James II, but with Nassau lion in centre; first harp with large female bust on l. well above the r. end of the harp. *Edge*, as before.

B

Second harp

Type B *O*. Second bust, with two locks of hair across the bust and no hair below the truncation. R. with second harp which has a smaller female bust level with right end.[1]

---

[1] There are only two known examples with the second bust, both in the British Museum, from completely different *obverse* dies, but both with two locks of hair across the bust. One is like the comparatively common second bust sixpences of 1697 of rather heavy style in low relief; the other has a narrower bust in high relief with the hair more deeply engraved; this is illustrated as type B above. Both these coins are patterns.

Type C

C   *O*. Third bust, easily distinguished by the straight breastplate or drapery. R. with first harp.

D   *O*. Third bust. R. with second harp.

Type E   Third harp

E   *O*. Third bust variety, same general style but dies have been recut and hair varied a little. Tie slightly longer and thinner than on the third bust R. New reverse of same general design but with third harp with scroll front and back.

No.	Type	Date	Edge Year	R	Varieties, Remarks, etc.
86	A. First bust, first harp	1695	SEPTIMO	N	
87	—	—	OCTAVO	C	
87A	—	—	—	R^3	Reads TVTA·EN
88	—	—	NONE	R^4	*Proof*, plain edge
89	—	1696	OCTAVO	C	
89A	—	—	—	R^2	No stops on *obv.*
89B	—	—	—	R^3	G of GRA over D
89C	—	—	—	R^3	As 89B but no stops on *obv.*
90	—	—	—	R^3	Last 6 of date over 5
91	—	—	—	R^2	GEI instead of DEI
92	—	—	NONE	R^4	*Proof*, plain edge[1]
93	B. Second bust, second harp	—	OCTAVO	R^7	See note[1] on p. 13
94	C. Third bust, first harp	—	—	C	
94A	—	—	TRICESIMO	R^5	Error edge of 1678
95	—	—	NONE	R^4	*Proof*, plain edge[1,2]
96	D. — second harp	1697	NONO	R^3	
97	E. Third bust var., third harp	1700	DVODECIMO	N	
98	—	—	D. TERTIO	R	

[1] The harp on these two proofs is a variety, not quite like the first or second. The shields are of the same design as that shown containing the third harp. Perhaps we should class them as patterns rather than proofs.

[2] It is now thought that the Third Bust type may not exist.

ANNE

A

B   C

Before Union with Scotland

Type **A**   *O.* First bust, the two stray curls on top are low, VIGO. below. R. .MAG BR. FRA ET. HIB REG, single cruciform shields as before but with the star of the Garter in the centre. *Known as the 'Before Union' reverse. Edge,* as before.

B   *O.* First bust, without VIGO. R. Similar, but with plumes in the angles.

C   Similar, but with roses and plumes alternately in the angles.

After Union with Scotland

D   F

D *O*. Second bust, the two stray curls are taller, the head is also at least 1 mm. broader, **E** (for *Edinburgh*) below bust. **R**. .MAG : BRI : FR : ET. HIB : REG :, similar, but the top and bottom shields have the English and Scottish arms impaled, and the shield on the r. has the French arms. *This is known as the 'After Union' reverse.*

E Similar, but *without* the E.

F As last, with plumes in the angles of the reverse.

G

G *O*. Third bust, hair much more wiry. **R**. as before, but roses and plumes alternately in the angles.

No.	Type	Date	Edge Year	R	Varieties, etc.
	Before Union Reverse				
99	A. VIGO **below first bust** ...	1703	TERTIO	*N*	
100	B. **First bust, plumes on** *rev*.	1705	QVINTO	*R²*	
101	C. — **roses and plumes on** *rev*.	1706	—	*R*	
102	—	1707	SEXTO	*C*	
	After Union Reverse				
103	D. **Second bust, E below** ..	—	—	*C²*	
104	E. **Second bust**	—	SEPTIMO	*N*	
105	—	1708	—	*N*	
106	D. **Second bust, E below**	—	—	*N*	
107	—	—	—	*S*	8 of date over 7
108	F. **Second bust, plumes on** *rev*.	—	—	*S*	
108A	—	—	—	*R⁴*	Reading BR . FRA as on Before Union coins
109	G. **Third bust, roses and plumes**	1713	DVODECIMO	*N*	

GEORGE I

Type **A** As illustration below with roses and plumes alternately in the angles
of reverse. Note that the arms have changed, the bottom shield now
bears the arms of Ireland and that on the l. has the arms of
Brunswick-Lüneburg. *Edge*, as before.

A   B

B Similar, but with **SS C** (for South Sea Company) alternately in the
angles.

No.	Type	Date	Edge Year	R	Variety, etc.
110	**A. Roses and plumes**	**1716**	SECVNDO	*S*	
111	—	**1718**	QVINTO	*R⁴*	
111A	—	—	—	*R*	8 of date over 6
112	—	**1720**	SEXTO	*R²*	
113	—	—	—	*R*	20 of date over 18
114	**B. SS C on** *rev.*	**1723**	DECIMO	*S*	
115	**A. Roses and plumes**	**1726**	D. TERTIO	*R²*	

GEORGE II

Type **A**   *O*. Young-head bust. **R**. As illustration below, but plain in the angles.

B

B *O*. Young-head bust. **R**. Roses and plumes in angles.
C *O*. Young-head bust. **R**. Roses in angles.
D *O*. Old-head bust.   **R**. As last, with roses in angles.

D   E

E *O*. **LIMA** below old-head bust.   **R**. Plain in the angles.
F *O*. Old-head bust, nothing below.   **R**. As type **E**.

No.	Type	Date	Edge Year	R	Variety, etc.
116	**A. Young head (plain)**	**1731**	none		*Pattern*, plain edge[1]
117	**B. — roses and plumes**	**1732**	SEXTO	R	
118	—	—	none	R³	*Proof*, plain edge. *Obv.* convex
119	—	**1734**	SEPTIMO	R	
120	—	**1735**	OCTAVO	S	
121	—	**1736**	NONO	S	
122	**C. — roses**	**1739**	DVODECIMO	N	
123	—	**1741**	D. QVARTO	N	
124	**D. Old head, roses**	**1743**	D. SEPTIMO	N	
125	**E. LIMA below old head**	**1746**	D. NONO	N	
126	**F. Old head (plain)**	—	VICESIMO	R	*Proof only*
127	—	**1750**	V. QVARTO	S	
128	—	**1751**	—	R	

GEORGE III

Countermarked Spanish Dollars

A   B

Type **A**   A Spanish, or more often a Spanish-American dollar (8 reales) or
occasionally some other large coin, countermarked on the centre of
the obverse with the head of George III in small oval (a punch similar to that used for hallmarking large silver articles).

B   A similar coin countermarked with a larger head of George III
(taken from the Maundy penny) in an octagonal stamp.

---

[1] This piece is illustrated by Folkes in his 1763 book, even giving the weight, but it appears to be
unknown today, and it was not known to Ruding in 1840.

No.	Type of Counterstamp	Overstruck Coins		Mintmarks	R	
		Country and Mint				
129	A. Oval	Mexico, *Mexico City* ...		M̊	C	
131	—	Bolivia, *Potosi*		PTS mon.	S	
132	—	Guatemala, *Guatemala*		NG	R²	
133	—	Peru, *Lima*		LIMÆ mon.	N	
134	—	Chile, *Santiago*		S̊	R³	
135	—	Spain........................			R³	
136	—	France.......................			R⁴	
137	—	U.S.A........................			R⁷	See note[1]
138	B. Octagonal	Mexico, *Mexico City* ...		M̊	S	
139	—	Bolivia, *Potosi*		PTS mon.	R	
140	—	Guatemala, *Guatemala*		NG	R³	
140A	—	Peru, *Lima*		LIMÆ mon.	R²	
141	—	Spain........................			R²	
142	—	France.......................			R⁷	See note[1]
143	—	U.S.A........................			R⁵	See note[2]

Note   A small number of non portrait 'pillar' dollars countermarked with an oval stamp exist. These appear to be genuine countermarks and have been stamped in error.

[1] Believed to be unique (in Bank of England collection).
[2] Five genuine specimens are known; also 3 forgeries.
Note. Collectors should be most wary of paying high prices for unusual countermarked coins: many very dangerous forgeries exist, also a number of countermarks from genuine punches are found on coins which are believed never to have circulated as countermarked pieces.

Bank of England Dollars

Type A   Reverse 2

Obverse A   As illustration. Stop after REX, first leaf of laurel points to the
upright of E in DEI; on truncation, . : C . H . K . or : C . H . K; the
stops before the C are not always clear.

     B   Similar, but no stops between C H K (i.e. : C H K).

     C   As **A** but leaf to centre of E.

     D   As **A** but leaf to end of E, C.H.K. close.

     E   No stop after REX, leaf to centre of E.

Patterns only

     F   Leaf to centre of E, · · K on truncation.

     G   Leaf to upright of E, · · K on truncation.

     H   GEORGIUS III . DEI GRATIA (no REX); bust as before, first leaf to D;
on truncation, : . C.H.K.

     I   Similar, but · : C. H. K. on truncation.

     J   Similar, but · : K or . . : K. on truncation.

     K   GEORGIUS III DEI GRATIA REX; smaller laur. and dr. bust **left**; first
leaf to upright of D; ★ · ★ on truncation; five berries in wreath.

     L   Similar, but six berries.

H/Reverse 3·   Reverse 1

Type K

Reverse 1 Shield dollar, 1798. *Pattern only*. M . B . F . ET . H . REX . F . D . B . ET . L . D . S . R . I . A . T . ET . E . 1798, royal arms surmounted by crown which divides date.

2 Britannia dollar, 1804. As illustration, K in relief under shield.

2a Similar, but K inverted thus ꓘ.

2b Similar, but the inverted ꓘ is incuse.

3 Garter dollar, 1804. *Pattern only*. BRITANNIARUM REX FIDEI DEFENSOR, the royal arms within Garter, surmounted by crown which divides date, DOLLAR below.

4 Five shillings and sixpence, 1811. *Pattern only*. BANK OF ENGLAND TOKEN, Britannia seated left holding spear and resting l. arm on shield, in exergue, FIVE SHILLINGS / & SIXPENCE / 1811.

5 Five shillings and sixpence, 1811. *Pattern only*. BANK / TOKEN / 5S. 6D. / 1811 within an oakwreath, stem slightly downwards, I.P. under tie.

5a Similar, but stem slightly upwards, I · P. under tie.

Reverse 4   Reverse 5a

The column headed Davis No. is a reference to 'The Nineteenth Century
Token Coinage' by W. J. Davis.

No.	Type			Date	R	Varieties, Remarks, etc.
	Obv.	Rev.	Davis No.			
144	A	2	D. 17	1804	C^2	
145	—	—		—	R	Proof
146	—	—	D. 18	—	R	Proof in copper
147	—	2b		—	R^2	
148	B	2	D. 16	—	R	
148A	—	—		—	R	Proof
149	C	—	D. 10	—	S	
150	—	—		—	S	Proof
151	—	—		—	R^5	Proof in silver gilt
152	—	—	D. 11	—	S	Proof in copper
153	—	2a	D. 19	—	R	
154	—	—		—	R	Proof
155	—	—		—	R	Proof in copper
156	—	2b	D. 6	—	S	
157	—	—	D. 7	—	R^3	Proof in copper
158	D	2		—	R^3	
159	—	2a	D. 8	—	R^2	
160	—	—	—	—	R	Proof
160A	—	—	—	—	R^5	Proof in silver gilt
161	—	—	D. 9	—	R^2	Proof in copper
162	—	2b	D. 12	—	R^2	
163	—	—	D. 13	—	R^2	Proof in copper
164	E	2	D. 14	—	C	
164A	—	—		—	R^3	Proof in copper; thicker flan
165	—	—		—	R	Proof
166	—	—	D. 15	—	R	Proof in copper
167	—	—		—	R^4	c.h.k. recut. Proof in copper on very thick flan

Patterns

No.	Type and Date		Davis No.	R	Varieties, Remarks, etc.
	Obverse	Reverse			
168	C. Bust r.	1. Shield, 1798.......	D. 1	R^4	
169	—	—		R^7	In Gold
170	—	—	D. 2	R^2	In copper
171	A. —	—	D. 3	R^4	
172	—	—	D. 4	R^2	In copper

No.	Type and Date Obverse	Type and Date Reverse	Davis No.	R	Varieties, Remarks, etc.
173	F. —	—	D. 5	R^4	
174	—	—		R^3	In copper
175	G. —	—		R^6	
175A	—	—		R^6	In copper
175B	—	—		R^6	In copper gilt
176	H. —	—		R^7	In white metal
177	I. —	—		R^4	
178	—	—		R^4	In copper
178A	J. —	—		R^6	In copper on very thick flan, wt 28.3 gm
179	K. Bust 1.	—		R^4	
180	—	—	D. 29	R^4	In copper
181	H. Bust r.	3. Garter, 1804	D. 20	R	
182	I. —	—	D. 21	R	
183	—	—	D. 22	R^4	In copper
184	—	—		R^5	In white metal
185	J. —	—	D. 23	R^3	
186	—	—		R^6	Struck over octagonal cmkd. dollar
187	—	—		R^4	In copper
188	G. —	—	D. 24	R^3	
189	—	—	D. 25	R^5	In copper
190	I. —	2. Britannia, 1804		R^5	
191	J. —	—		R^5	
192	L. Bust 1.	—	D. 41	R^3	In copper[1]
193	K. —	—		R^3	In copper[1]
194	C. Bust. r.	4. Britannia, 1811	D. 30	R^4	See note[1]
194A	—	—		R^7	Thick flan, 36.667 gm
195	—	—	D. 31	R^3	In copper
195A	—	—		R^6	In copper gilt
196	D. —	—	D. 32	R^4	See note[1]
197	—	—	D. 33	R^4	In copper
198	K. Bust 1.	—	D. 26	R^3	
199	—	—	D. 27	R^2	In copper
200	L. —	—	D. 28	R^4	
201	—	—		R^3	In copper
202	—	—		R^7	In white metal
203	—	5. Wreath, 1811 ...	D. 34	R^4	
204	—	—	D. 35	R^4	In copper
205	K. —	5a. —	D. 36	R^3	

[1] These coins are probably mules.

No.	Type and Date		Davis No.	R	Varieties, Remarks, etc.
	Obverse	Reverse			
206	—	—	D. 37	S	In copper
207	—	—	D. 38	R⁶	In brass
208	C. Bust r.	—	D. 42	R³	See note¹ on page 25
209	—	—	D. 43	R²	In copper
210	D. —	—	D. 44	R⁴	See note¹ on page 25

George III, Last or New Coinage

Type as illustration. *Edge*, DECUS ET TUTAMEN . ANNO REGNI followed by
regnal year in Roman numerals, all in high relief and occupying the whole
width of the edge.

No.	Date	Edge Year	R	Varieties, Remarks, etc.
211	1818	LVIII	C	
212	—	—	R^2	Proof[1]
213	—	—	R^6	Edge incusely inscribed. Pattern
213A	—	—	R^5	DECUS ANNO REGNI ET TUTAMEN. LVIII.
214	—	LIX	C	
215	1819	—	C^2	See note[2] below
215A	—	—	R^3	Without stops on edge
215B	—	—	R^3	9 of date altered from 8
216	—	LX	N	
217	—	—	R^2	Proof[1]
218	—	none	R^7	Proof, plain edge
219	1820	LX	C	See note[3] below
220	—	—	R^3	Proof[1]
220A	—	—	R^3	20 of date altered from 19

[1] With some hesitancy these inscribed edge proofs have been included as they have been published previously and are generally considered to have been struck. This is confirmed by the other denominations of which there are undoubted proofs. The standard of the striking of these crowns was so high and they were issued, and are still found, in such perfect preservation that it is almost impossible to distinguish a proof from a perfect ordinary specimen.

[2] This coin exists with the date crudely re-engraved.

[3] We have seen photographs of the reverse of a crown dated 1820, which clearly showed traces of certain letters in the Garter legend having been re-engraved on the die.

Patterns

221

221 By Webb and Mills for Mudie, undated. *O*. GEORGIUS III DEI GRATIA, laur.
     bust. r.; beneath, JM. D and TW. F. in script. R. Four shields cruciformly
     arranged, with rose, thistle, shamrock and horse disposed in the angles;
     at sides, MILLS FECIT in script. *Edge*, plain   *S*
222 — *In lead* R^5

223

223 By W. Wyon, 1817. *O*. GEORGIUS III D : G : BRITANNIARUM REX F : D : —
     1817 his laur. head r., W. WYON below truncation. R. FOEDUS
     INVIOLABILE, three figures emblematical of the three kingdoms (the
     'Three Graces') with emblems and shield; W. WYON on left; palm-branch
     and quiver in exergue. *Edge*, plain R^2
224 — *In gold* R^7
225 — *In copper* R^6
226 — *In white metal* R^5
227 — Somewhat similar, but larger lettering on obverse, no F : D : , signa-
     ture in script capitals. R. Legend smaller and Œ for OE, lion's head over
     thistle, artist's name in exergue in place of ornament, *Edge*, plain. *In
     lead, very thick flan* R^7
228 Similar, but lion's head and thistle smaller. *In lead, thick flan* R^7

229

229 By W. Wyon, 1817. *O.* GEORGIUS III D : G : BRITANNIARUM REX — 1817, his laur. bust dr. r., W. WYON below truncation. R. INCORRUPTA FIDES VERITASQUE, large crowned shield (somewhat similar in design to that on Simon's Cromwell crown). *Edge*, plain. See note[2] on page 30 R^4

230 — *In gold* R^5

231 By Pistrucci, 1817. *O.* GEORGIUS III DEI GRATIA BRITANNIARUM REX F : D : — 1817, his laur. head r., tie with bow and two ends, rather like the adopted coin but broader and with slightly shorter neck (there is a slight flaw on the obverse die which caused it to be destroyed). No beaded border either side. R. St. George and dragon within the Garter, the latter with usual legend and ruled with fine horizontal lines, a minute pellet upon the horse's body. *Edge*, plain; thick flan R^6

232 As last, legend ends BRITANNIAR : REX F : D. and the laurel-wreath has three leaves at top instead of four, beaded border both sides. R. Similar, but narrower Garter, not ruled, W.W.P. on buckle. *Edge*, incusely inscribed on a sunken band, DECUS ET TUTAMEN ANNO REGNI QUINQUAGESIMO ꓤ SEPTIMO. Flan of usual size and thickness R^7

233 — GEORGIUS III D : G : BRITANNIARUM REX F : D — 1817, laur. head as last. R. Similar, but wider Garter and without initials on buckle. *Edge*, inscribed in raised letters between two fine cord borders, DECUS ET TUTAMEN ANNO REGNI LVIII R^7

234

234 By Pistrucci, 1818. *O.* GEORGIUS III D : G BRITANNIARUM REX F : D : —
1818, **large** laur. head r., two ties (no bow) to wreath, PISTRUCCI below
truncation. Toothed border each side. R. St. George and dragon within
Garter, with usual legend, which is ruled with fine horizontal lines;
PISTRUCCI in exergue. *Edge*, plain R^5

234A — *In gold* R^7

234B — *In white metal* R^7

235 — *In lead, large flan* R^7

236 — *Edge*, inscribed in large letters, as current coin R^5

237 — *Edge*, inscribed in letters which do not occupy the whole width of the
flan R^6

238 — *Edge*, incusely inscribed R^5

239 Similar, but very heavy toothed border on reverse. *Edge*, incusely
inscribed. *In lead* R^7

240 Similar, but die is not polished; toothed border is coarser on obverse and
altogether missing on reverse. The Garter is broader and has larger
lettering. *Edge*, plain R^7

241 Similar to 211, but lettering on obverse much larger, head is from slightly differing punch and the Garter is ruled with fine horizontal lines.
Edge, inscribed as usual in raised letters, rose stops R^6

241A — *Edge*, incusely inscribed; star stops R^7

242 — *Edge*, plain R^7

242A As currency issue but head as last. *Edge*, plain. *In white metal* R^7

243 By Droz, 1820, after Monneron's pattern by Dupré (1792). *O.* VIS VNI-
TATE FORTIOR, Hercules seated by a column, endeavouring to break a
bundle of sticks across his knee; in exergue, 1820 above branches. R.
DECVS ET TVTAMEN, crowned shield. *Edge*, plain[1] R^5

244 — *In copper* R^2

245 — *In copper gilt* R^6

---

[1] This has been left under the reign of George III, where it is usually put, but Brooke gives it to
George IV, as he had found it assigned to that reign in a sale catalogue of 1828. The type is
hardly applicable to either reign, but one would not expect to find it as a suggestion for a new
reign, as the king would naturally expect his portrait to be used: maybe it should be classified as
a medal rather than a coin.
The first public offering of this piece was in the J.T. Brockett sale in June 1823 (H & R 1823.8)
lot 1199, where it says: 'No more than 25 having been struck in silver.' However, an MS note in
one copy of this catalogue says: 'Only 18 copies of no. 1199 were struck in silver—7 were
struck in gold, making the 25 above mentioned.'

GEORGE IV

Type **A**   As illustration. *Edge,* DECUS etc., followed by regnal year in words, all in large raised letters.

B   As illustration. *Edge,* usually inscribed in rather small raised lettering.

No.	Type	Date	Edge Year	R	Varieties, etc.
246	A. Laur. head; St. George	1821	SECUNDO	C^2	
247	—	—	—	R	Proof
248	—	—	—	R^6	Proof in copper
249	—	—	none	R^6	Proof in copper with plain edge[1]
250	—	—	TERTIO	R^3	Proof. Error edge
251	—	1822	SECUNDO	S	
251A	—	—	—	R^4	Proof
252	—	—	TERTIO	N	
253	—	—	—	R	Proof
254	—	1823	none	R^6	Proof with plain edge
254A	—	—	—	R^7	Proof in white metal
255	B. Bare head; shield rev.	1825	none	R^3	Pattern only, with plain edge
256	—	—	—	R^6	— in Barton's metal[2]
257	—	1826	SEPTIMO	R	Proof only, issued in the sets
258	—	—	none	R^7	Proof with plain edge
258A	—	—	LVIII	R^7	Proof, with edge of last reign, incusely inscribed
258B	—	none	none	R^7	Pattern in copper, undated, edge reads DECUS ET TUTAMEN in large lettering
258C	—	182?	OCTAVO	R^7	In copper, edge . . . OCTAVO . . . (defaced at the mint)

[1] This coin may be E.S.C. 248 with the edge removed.
[2] Barton's metal is a copper sheet on to which is rolled and pressed a thin sheet of gold; it is quite a different process to gilding, being more like Sheffield plating, and more gold is used. The copper core shows on the edge, but the process of cutting the blanks presses a little of the gold down over the edge.

259

Patterns

259 By Mills for Whiteaves, 1820. GEORGIUS IV DEI GRATIA, his very large head l. with little neck, G. MILLS . F on truncation, MDCCCXX below. ℞. BRITANNIARUM ET HAN : REX FIDEI DEFENSOR, royal arms on square shield within Garter, crowned and with supporters, helmet, crest, scroll, etc., PUB . BY R . WHITEAVES below. *Edge*, plain R^3

260 — *In gold* R^7

261 Similar, but king wears collar and necktie, MDCCCXX and MILLS F below R^5

262 By Pistrucci, 1820. As the current crown, but there is a long streamer of hair floating behind from beneath St. George's helmet; the initials w. w. P. are differently written, and the small dot on the horse's body has not yet been removed. *Edge*, plain R^6

263 By W. Wyon and J. B. Merlen, 1828. As the proof crown of 1826, but **larger** head of king, W. W. incuse on truncation. *Edge*, usual legend, dated NONO R^7

264 — *O.* GEORGIUS IV D : G : BRITANNIAR : REX F : D :, **large** head, no initials on truncation. ℞. and edge as the proof crown of 1826, i.e., dated SEPTIMO, which is incorrect for a coin of 1828. *In copper* R^7

265 — *Edge*, dated OCTAVO, two arrows and a rosette dividing words. *In copper* R^7

265A By ?, undated (1828 or 29). In white metal, laureate bust to left, similar to that of the currency crowns. GEORGIUS IIII D : G : BRITANNIAR : REX F : D : ℞. Royal arms with supporters, similar to those of the Whiteaves patterns, no legend. A letter M (Merlen) appears in Gothic script in the centre below the motto. *Edge*, plain R^6

265B Similar, but no letter M below the motto. R^7

266 By Pistrucci and Merlen, undated (1829). *O.* As the crowns of the first issue, laureate head left. ℞. BRITANNIARUM REX FID : DEF : , square-topped shield of the royal arms heraldically shaded, encircled by the collar of the Garter with the George pendant hanging below, all upon an ermine mantle, crown above. *Edge*, DECUS, etc., NONO. *In copper* R^7

267 By Wyon and Merlen, 1829. *O*. Very similar to proof crown of 1826, but initials on truncation in relief and there is a slight difference in the arrangement of the hair. R. As last. *Edge*, plain   *R*[6]

268 — *Edge*, DECUS, etc., NONO   *R*[6]

269 — *In copper*   *R*[7]

270 *O*. As last. R. as type B (pattern of 1825/6)   *R*[7]

265A

265B

WILLIAM IV

271   276

Proofs or Patterns only. As illustration.

No.	ENGRAVER'S SIGNATURE	DATE	EDGE YEAR	R	VARIETIES, Remarks, etc.
271	**W.W.**	**1831**	none	R^2	Plain edge; issued in sets
272	—	—	—	R^5	— *in gold*
273	**W. WYON**.........................	—	—	R^4	—
274	**W.W.**	**1832**	TERTIO	R^7	*In lead*[1]
275	—	**1834**	none	R^5	*Plain edge*

Patterns

276 By W. Wyon and J. B. Merlen, undated. *O.* As before with w. w. incuse
on truncation. R. BRITANNIARUM REX FID : DEF : , type as before, except
that the top of the collar of the Garter is shown above the shield, and
beneath the pendant are the initials J. B. M., and the George itself is
turned to right instead of to left; the mantle is more richly decorated and
the collar is more circular in design. *Edge*, plain R^6

277 — *In lead* R^7

278 *O.* As before, but w. WYON in relief on truncation. R. As last, except that
fewer links are visible in the collar which is almost circular. The initials
below the George are omitted. *Edge*, plain R^6

---

[1] On this edge a spray divides the motto from the date which is followed by a lion passant; all
between two narrow ornate borders.

VICTORIA

A

Type **A** Young head. *O.* VICTORIA DEI GRATIA, her young head l., W. WYON .
R A on truncation, date below. R. BRITANNIARUM REGINA FID : DEF : ,
square-topped shield, crowned, within branches, floral ornament
below. *Edge*, DECUS, etc., incusely inscribed with ornament after
TUTAMEN and the regnal year in Roman numerals.

B

B Gothic. *O.* 𝔙𝔦𝔠𝔱𝔬𝔯𝔦𝔞 𝔡𝔢𝔦 𝔤𝔯𝔞𝔱𝔦𝔞 𝔟𝔯𝔦𝔱𝔞𝔫𝔫𝔦𝔞𝔯 . 𝔯𝔢𝔤 : 𝔣 : 𝔡., her
crowned bust draped l. with richly embroidered bodice. R. 𝔱𝔲𝔢𝔞𝔱𝔲𝔯
𝔲𝔫𝔦𝔱𝔞 𝔡𝔢𝔲𝔰 𝔞𝔫𝔫𝔬 𝔡𝔬𝔪 𝔪𝔡𝔠𝔠𝔠𝔵𝔩𝔟𝔦𝔦 (or 𝔪𝔡𝔠𝔠𝔠𝔩𝔦𝔦𝔦), cruciform shields
crowned, star of the Garter in centre; rose, thistle, shamrock and
rose in the angles within tressure of arcs. *Edge*, as usual, but in
small raised Gothic characters, rose and crown stops.
C Jubilee. *O.* VICTORIA D : G : BRITT : REG : F : D : , her bust veiled and
dr. l., wearing small crown, two orders and necklace. R. No legend,
Pistrucci's St. George and dragon, date in ex. *Edge*, milled.
D Old head. *O.* VICTORIA . DEI . GRA BRITT . REGINA . FID . DEF . IND .
IMP., her coronetted bust veiled and dr. l., wearing star and necklace.
R. as last. *Edge*, usual legend in raised letters, with the regnal year
in Roman numerals.

C   D

No.	Type	Date	Edge Year	R	Varieties Remarks, etc.
279	**A. Young head**	**1839**	none	R	*Proof only*, plain edge; issued in the sets[1]
280	—	**1844**	VIII	C	Edge stops are stars[2]
280A	—	—	—	R[6]	*Proof*, edge stops are cinquefoils
281	—	—	—	C	Edge stops are cinquefoils
282	—	**1845**	—	C[2]	Edge stops are cinquefoils[2]
282A	—	—	—	C	Edge stops are stars
283	—	—	—	R[6]	*Proof*
286	—	**1847**	XI	C	See note[2]
287	—	—	Milled	R[7]	*Pattern or trial piece*[3]
288	**B. Gothic**	—	UNDECIMO	S	*Proof only*[4], 8000 were struck
290	—	—	SEPTIMO	R[7]	*Proof* with error edge
291	—	—	none	R	*Proof* with plain edge
291A	—	—	—	R[6]	Struck in pure silver (for presentation to 'VIP's')
292	—	—	—	R[6]	As last. *In gold*
292A	—	—	—	R[7]	As last. *In white metal*
293	—	**1853**	SEPTIMO	R[3]	*Proof only*, issued in the sets
294	—	—	none	R[5]	*Proof only*, with plain edge
295	**A. Young head**	**1879**	none	R[7]	*Proof or Pattern* with plain edge

[1] The obverse lettering is smaller than on the later coins and starts at 8 o'clock instead of 7 o'clock.

[2] Young head crowns are common in worn to average condition (F and below) but are very difficult to obtain **EF**—the rarity of an uncirculated specimen would perhaps be R[3].

[3] This piece, which is in the British Museum, does not have the appearance of a proof or pattern and is therefore possibly in the nature of a trial piece made from the old 1847 dies when the authorities were considering a milled edge for the 1887 issue.

[4] Mr. Stride, formerly Chief Clerk of the Royal Mint, says that the Gothic crowns were never issued for ordinary circulation and that all were struck in proof state. Some appear with the raised design heavily frosted, apparently early strikings.

No.	Type	Date	Edge Year	R	Varieties Remarks, etc.
296	**C. Jubilee**.........	**1887**	Milled	C^3	
297	—	—	—	R	*Proof*, issued in the sets
298	—	**1888**	—	S	
299	—	**1889**	—	C^2	
300	—	**1890**	—	N	
301	—	**1891**	—	N	
302	—	**1892**	—	N	
303	**D. Old head**	**1893**	LVI	C	
304	—	—	—	S	*Proof*, issued in the sets
305	—	—	LVII	R	
306	—	**1894**	—	S	
307	—	—	LVIII	S	
308	—	**1895**	—	S	
309	—	—	LIX	N	
310	—	**1896**	—	R	
311	—	—	LX	N	
312	—	**1897**	—	N	
313	—	—	LXI	C	
314	—	**1898**	—	R	
315	—	—	LXII	S	
316	—	**1899**	—	S	
317	—	—	LXIII	S	
318	—	**1900**	—	S	
319	—	—	LXIV	N	

320

Patterns

320 By Bonomi, 1837 (issued by J. Rochelle Thomas in 1887). *O.* VICTORIA
REG DEI GRA 1837 incuse, her coronetted head l. sunken; ornate border.
R. Britannia standing r. with trident and shield, holding Victory, all
sunken; BRITT / MINERVA on l., VICTRIX / FID DEF on r. incuse; ornate border. *Edge,* plain but for T followed by a number (1 to 150) R^2
320A — *In gold* (6 struck) R^5
321 — *In copper or bronze* (20 struck) R^4
321a — *In copper,* plain edge. No ornament on coronet and no earring. Hair
unfinished. R No ornamental border except three stars by trident.
Inverted As for Vs in DECUS etc R^6
322 — *In hard white metal* R^3
323 — *In white metal.* No number on edge R^3
323A — *In aluminium* R^3
324 — *In lead* R^3
325 — *Edge,* milled R^5
326 — *In copper* R^3
327 — *In white metal* R^3
327A — *In lead* R^3
328 — *O.* Similar. R. Royal arms with supporters, motto beneath. *Edge,*
plain R^6
328A — *In white metal* R^4

329

329 By W. Wyon, 1839. As illustration. VICTORIA D : G : BRITANNIARUM REGI-
NA F : D : , her young head l., hair bound with two fillets, the front one
ornate, W. WYON. R . A . on truncation. R. DIRIGIT DEUS GRESSUS MEOS, the
Queen, as Una, guiding the British lion l.; in ex., MDCCCXXXIX / W.
WYON. R . A . As the five-pound piece of this date but on a thicker and
slightly wider flan. *Edge,* DECUS, etc., TERTIO in large letters[1] R^6

---

[1] There are other 'Una' patterns in silver, some with small letters on edge and some with plain
edge, from varying obverse dies, which are left out as they are probably proofs of the five-pound
piece struck in silver.

330   — *In gold* (weight 823 grains) R^7
331   — *Edge*, plain. *In gold* R^7
332   By W. Wyon, 1839. *O*. As the proof crown of 1839. R. As last, but
       DIRIGE. *Edge*, faintly inscribed R^7
333   — *Edge*, plain R^6
334   — *In gold* R^7
335   — *O*. VICTORIA DEI GRATIA . — 1839, small bust of the queen l. with two
       plain fillets, W. WYON. R . A . on truncation, legend starts opposite the
       queen's chin. R. As adopted coin. *Edge*, plain R^7
336   — As the proof of 1839, No. 279, but head much larger R^7
337   By W. Wyon, 1844. As current piece, but smaller lettering, date in large
       figures, very small bust, W. W. in relief below. *Edge*, plain R^7
338   — As current coin, but the die is unfinished where the hair falls below
       the knot at the back of the queen's head. *Edge*, inscribed as usual R^2
338A   By W. Wyon, 1845. As the current coin, but the obverse lettering is
       smaller. *Edge*, plain R^6
339   — As last, but there is a broad margin at the edge of the coin thus mak-
       ing the piece slightly larger in diameter. *Edge*, plain R^4
339A   — *In gold* R^7
340   — *Edge*, faintly inscribed DECUS, etc., VIII R^6
340A   — *Edge*, faintly inscribed DECUS, etc., IX R^7
341   By W. Wyon, 1846. As the 'Gothic' crown of 1847, but the Queen's
       bodice is plain below the border. *Edge*, plain R^4
342   By W. Wyon, 1847. As the current 'Gothic' crown, but the edge is
       inscribed between two narrow grained borders R^6
342A   undated, unsigned. *O*. VICTORIA . D : G : BRITANNIAR . REG : F : D : Young
       head l., similar to young head issue of 1844, but larger. R. Crowned
       arms with lion and unicorn supporters within wreath of oak and laurel.
       Edge, plain R^7

343

343 By J. R. Thomas, for Spink and Son, 1887. O. VICTORIA . BY . THE .
     GRACE. OF. GOD. QUEEN. OF. GREAT. BRITAIN. EMP : OF. INDIA, her old bust,
     crowned, veiled and draped left, J.R.T. on truncation. R. FIVE SHILLINGS
     above royal arms with supporters, MDCCCLXXXVII and spray below;
     ornate border each side. *Edge*, plain[1] R^5
344 — But SPINK & SON on truncation. *Edge*, plain (32 struck) R^3
345 — Plain on truncation. *Edge*, plain R^4
346 — SPINK & SON added at bottom of *rev*. *Edge*, plain R^2
347 — *In gold* (6 struck) R^5
348 — *In copper* (5 struck) R^5
349 — *In aluminium* (10 struck) R^5
351 — *In lead* R^4
351A — *In cupro-nickel* R^5
352 — *Edge*, milled R^4
353 — *In gold* (6 struck) R^5

357

357 By L. C. Wyon, 1888. VICTORIA D : G : BRITT : REG : F : D : , large cor-
     onetted bust dr. and veiled l., wearing necklace, L.C.W. on truncation.
     R. Pistrucci's St. George and dragon, date in ex. *Edge*, milled R^6
357A — Plain on truncation R^7
358 By L. C. Wyon, 1890. O. As last. R. FIVE SHILLINGS, Pistrucci's St.
     George but occupying less of the field than the last. *Edge*, milled R^7
359 — O. As current coin. R. as last. *Edge*, milled R^7
360 By T. Brock, 1892. As the current coins of 1893 but reading REG instead
     of REGINA, only IMP (instead of IND IMP) comes below the truncation; also
     artist's initials T.B. are omitted. Three crowns divide the inscription on
     the edge R^7

---

[1] Some of nos. 343–351 have MADE IN BAVARIA incuse on the edge.

EDWARD VII

362

O. EDWARDVS VII DEI GRA : BRITT : OMN : REX FID : DEF : IND : IMP : , his head r., Dᴱ S. below. R. Pistrucci's St. George and dragon, 1902 in ex. *Edge,* normal inscription, raised letters.

361   The current coin, 1902 (the only date)   C
362   *Proof*, 1902, matt surface; issued in the sets   N

Patterns
363   By Spink and Son, 1902, after the Tower crowns of Charles I. *O*.
      EDWARD : VII D : G : BRITT : ET TERRAR : TRANSMARIN : 1902, the king,
      crowned, in coronation robes and holding sword, on horseback l.,
      ground below horse, monogram of Londonia behind the King. R. Q : I :
      D : S : BRITANNICA . REX . FID : DEF : IND : IMP : followed by mintmark,
      sun; oval garnished shield. *Edge*, plain R^3
364   — *In gold* R^5
365   — Struck on thick flan of double weight to represent a half-pound or
      ten-shilling piece R^5
366   — Struck on thicker flan to represent a pound R^4

GEORGE V

A

Type **A** As illustration. *O*. GEORGIVS V DEI GRA : BRITT : OMN : REX, bare head l., BM on truncation. ℞. . FID . . DEF . . IND . . IMP . —. CROWN ., large crown and date within wreath ornate with three roses and three thistles, K . G . below. *Edge*, milled (.500 silver)

B

B *O*. GEORGIVS V . D G . BRITT : OMN : REX . F D. IND : IMP., head as last. ℞. CROWN 1935, St. George and dragon of modernistic style, P M below. *Edge*, incusely inscribed DECUS, etc., XXV (.500 silver)

No.	Type	Date	Edge Year	R	Varieties, Remarks, etc.
367	**A. Crown** *rev*...	1927	Milled	*N*	*Proof only*, in the sets. 15,030 struck
367A	—	—	—	*R*[7]	Matt, sandblasted flan
368	—	1928	—	*N*	Only 9034 pieces struck
369	—	1929	—	*S*	Only 4994 pieces struck
370	—	1930	—	*S*	Only 4847 pieces struck

Note. Proofs exist of dates other than 1927; they are all about *R*[5] and should not be confused with the brilliant so called 'early strikings'. (See L. A. Lawrence sale, 1954).

No.	Type	Date	Edge Year	R	Varieties, Remarks, etc.
371	—	1931	—	S	Only 4056 pieces struck
372	—	1932	—	S	Only 2395 pieces struck
373	—	1933	—	N	Only 7132 pieces struck
374	—	1934	—	R^2	Only 932 pieces struck
375	**B. St. George** *rev.*	1935	XXV	C^3	714,769 pieces struck
375A	—	—	—	R^6	Error edge, — MEN. ANNO— REGNI XXV.
376	—	—	—	N	Specimen issued in box[1]
377	—	—	—	R^5	*Proof* in good silver (.925)[1]
377A	—	—	—	R^6	*Proof* in silver (.500)
378	—	—	—	R	*Proof or pattern* with raised lettering on edge; 2500 issued in boxes. (.925)[1]
379	—	—	—	R^3	— *In gold* (30 struck)
380	—	—	—	R^5	— Error edge, as 378, but DECUS ANNO REGNI ET TUTAMEN . XXV .
381	**A. Crown** *rev.*...	1936	Milled	R	Issued during the reign of Edward VIII. Only 2473 pieces struck

[1] The mint had many more applications for the raised edge pattern than the 2,500 they had struck. The unlucky applicants were offered a specimen of the ordinary crown in a box; these were carefully struck and are superior to the ordinary coins. There are, however, a few very rare proofs of the incuse edge issue, No. 377, with a highly polished field, actually better finished and more mirror-like than the pattern.

382   387

Patterns

382 By A. G. Wyon, 1910. *O.* GEORGIUS V D : G : BRITT : OMN : REX MDCDX,
     bare head l. R. No legend or exergue, a fine conception of St. George
     and the dragon left, filling the whole of the field. *Edge*, plain R^5
383 — *In gold* R^7
384 — *Edge*, milled R^5
385 — *In gold* R^7
386 — Matt surface. *Edge*, plain R^6
386A — *In copper; plated* R^6
386B — *Edge*, milled. Struck in pure silver R^7
387 — *O.* GEORGIVS V D : G : BRITANNIARVM OMNIVM REX, similar, but rather
     larger head. R. At last, but rather smaller design with straight ground
     line, 1910 in ex. *Edge*, plain R^5
388 — *In gold* R^7
389 — *Edge*, milled R^5
390 — *In gold* R^7
391 — On smaller thinner flan. *Edge*, milled R^5
391A — Matt surface all over R^7

391B — By B. MacKennal and Kruger Gray. *O.* As current type. R. St.
     George with lance piercing dragon; he is mounted on a very finely exe-
     cuted horse, quite unlike that on the current coin; on l. above, 1935, on r.
     above, CROWN. *Edge*, as current coin but in relief R^6

EDWARD VIII

391C

391C *O.* EDWARDVS VIII D : G : BR : OMN : REX, his bare head left, HP below. R.
As 1937 crown of George VI *R*[6]

391D By G. Hearn. Many varieties. Two examples illustrated below. These
fantasy pieces have continued to be struck over many years, with reverses for various dominions and colonies, e.g. Australia, Bermuda,
Ceylon, Hong Kong, and New Zealand, as well as Great Britain, in the
original series, and others in more recent strikings.

391D

391D

GEORGE VI

Type A

Type A *O.* GEORGIVS VI D : G : BR : OMN : REX, his bare head left, HP below. R̩. FID : DEF : : IND : IMP — CROWN : 1937., royal arms crowned with supporters, motto on scroll on ground below, KG in field. *Edge,* milled (*.500 silver*).

No.	Type	Date	R	Varieties, Remarks, etc.
392	**A. Royal arms** *rev...*	**1937**	C^3	
393	—	—	N	*Proof* from the sets
393A	—	—	R^5	*Proof* with more frosting on *rev.*
393B	—	—	R^7	*Matt proof*

Type B

Type B *O.* GEORGIVS VI D : G : BR : OMN : REX F : D : above his bare head left, HP below truncation, FIVE SHILLINGS below. R̩. Pistrucci's St. George, date in exergue. *Edge,* ★ MDCCCLI CIVIUM INDUSTRIA FLORET CIVITAS MCMLI (1851 By the industry of its people the state flourishes 1951). Struck in *cupro-nickel.*

No.	Type	Date	R	Varieties, Remarks, etc.
393c	B. Cu.-Ni. St. George	1951	C^2	Struck for the Festival of Britain and issued in small cardboard box, also in the proof sets.[1]
393d	—	—	R^4	*Proof or Pattern* with design frosted and field more brilliant
393e	—	—	R^7	Sandblasted dies.

ELIZABETH II

Type A   Type B

Type A   Coronation issue. *O*. ELIZABETH . II . DEI . GRATIA . BRITT OMN . REGI-NA . FID . DEFENSOR rose FIVE SHILLINGS rose. Queen on horseback l., horse on pedestal, small wreath below; crowned royal cypher each side of horse; GL behind near hind hoof. R. Crown in centre, rose above, thistle on l., shamrock on r., leek and 1953 below, four shields in saltire in the angles; EF above Irish shield and CT above English shield. *Edge*, + FAITH AND TRUTH I WILL BEAR UNTO YOU.

   B   Issued on the occasion of the British Trade Fair in New York. *O*. · ELIZABETH II DEI GRATIA REGINA F · D · FIVE SHILLINGS. bust r. R. As type A, but dated 1960. *Edge*, milled.

[1] The very rare pieces with plain edge were unintentional strikings on un-edged blanks.

Type C

Type C Sir Winston Churchill commemorative issue. *O*. ELIZABETH II DEI GRATIA REGINA F . D . 1965. Bust r. R. CHURCHILL, bust of Churchill in 'Siren Suit' r. *Edge*, milled.

No.	TYPE	DATE	R	VARIETIES, Remarks, etc.
393F	A. Cu.-Ni. Equestrian figure...................	1953	C^3	Ordinary coin, 5,962,621 issued in plastic case
393G	—	—	N	*Proof* issued in the sets and at Maundy ceremony in 1953 and succeeding years
393H	—	—	R^3	*Proof or Pattern*, design frosted, highly polished field
393J	—	—	R^7	Pattern, whole coin very dull, from sandblasted dies
393K	B. Cu.-Ni. Bust r.	1960	N	Ordinary coin[2]
393L	—	—	S	Struck from polished dies[1]
393M	—	—	R^4	'VIP' *proof*, frosted design, highly polished field.
393N	C. Cu.-Ni. Bust r.	1965	C^3	Ordinary coin[2]
393O	—	—	R^6	Specimen, struck with 'satin' finish

[1] The coins sold at the Exhibition site were struck in the U.K. from polished dies, and exported in special blue plastic cases. After the closing of the Exhibition unsold pieces were shipped back to the U.K. in bags, having been removed from the cases which were destroyed or disposed of in the U.S.A. In consequence polished die crowns are very difficult to obtain in perfect state, and the rarity of a perfect piece would be greater than indicated.

[2] Specimens with plain edge were unintentional strikings without a collar.

Pattern Crown

393N

393P *O.* As the current coin.
   R. Basically as the current coin but in higher relief. The crown is
   superimposed on a cross and the emblems are larger. *Edge,* as current
   coin R^7
393Q By Anthony Foley. *O.* PHILIP : DUKE : OF : EDINBURGH ∴ *O.* ELIZABETH :
   II : D : G : REGINA : F : D : + their conjoined busts l. R. GREAT BRITAIN.
   Britannia riding in biga 1, hurling thunderbolts. In Exergue 1966. One
   hundred struck in .925 *silver* R^2

DOUBLE FLORINS

VICTORIA

395

Roman   Arabic
  I   1

O. VICTORIA DEI GRATIA, 'Jubilee' bust l. **R.** FID : DEF : BRITT : REG : and
date, cruciform crowned shields, star of the Garter in centre, four sceptres in
the angles. *Edge*, milled.

No.	TYPE	DATE	R	VARIETIES, Remarks, etc.
394	**Roman I in date**	**1887**	*C*	
394A	—	—	*R*	*Proof*
395	**Arabic 1 in date**	—	*C²*	
396	—	—	*S*	*Proof*, issued in the sets
397	—	**1888**	*N*	
397A	—	—	*R²*	Second I in Queen's name is an inverted 1[1]
398	—	**1889**	*C*	
398A	—	—	*R³*	Second I in Queen's name is an inverted 1[1]
399	—	**1890**	*N*	

Patterns
400   By L. C. Wyon, 1890, *O.* As the current coin. **R.** DOUBLE FLORIN —
1890 between two sprigs; shields and sceptres as before but lined. *Edge,*
milled   *R⁷*

---

[1] Actually from a broken I punch.

GEORGE V

402

Patterns

401 By Reginald Huth, 1911. (*Struck by Messrs. John Pinches*). *O.* GEOR-
GIVS. V . DEI . GRATIA, his bare-headed bust dr. l. R. BRITANNIARVM REX
1911. crowned cruciform shields of England, Scotland, Ireland and
Wales, the latter with dragon rampant; in centre, star with the 'legs of
Man' in the middle; rose, thistle, shamrock and leek in the angles. *Edge*,
plain[1] R^2

401A *Edge*, milled R^2

402 *O.* Similar. R. BRI . 1911 . REX – DOUBLE FLORIN, similar. *Edge*, plain[1] R^2

402A *Edge*, milled. (Huth sale, lot 735) R^4

403 — 1914. *O.* Similar. R. BRI . 1914 . REX . – TWELVE GROATS, similar.
Edge, plain[1] R^2

404 — *In platinum* R^6

405 — *Edge*, milled R^2

406 — *In gold* R^6

406A — *O.* as *rev.* of 402. R. as last R^5

---

[1] These patterns were also struck in all sorts of other metals, iron, copper, zinc, etc., and the name
of the metal was stamped on the obverse under the chin or on the edge. They are all rare.

GEORGE VI

Pattern

406B *O*. Bust to l., 1950 below. R. Pistrucci's St. George and the Dragon
within Garter. *Edge*, milled R^5

406C Similar, but FOUR SHILLINGS stamped incuse into the milled edge R^7

THREE SHILLINGS
GEORGE III
Bank of England Tokens

A¹   B¹   2

Obv. **A¹** Draped **bust** in armour, front leaf of laurel points to end of E in DEI, five berries in wreath. Plain edge

      A² Similar, but leaf between D and E.

      A³ Similar, but leaf to upright of E.

      A⁴ Similar, but leaf to end of E, four berries in wreath.

      B¹ Laureate **head**, leaf between I and G.

      B² Similar, but leaf to centre of D.

Rev. **1¹** BANK TOKEN 3 SHILL. and date within oakwreath with twenty-seven acorns.

      1² Similar, but twenty-six acorns.

      1³ Similar, but twenty-five acorns.

      1⁴ Similar, but twenty-four acorns.

      2 BANK TOKEN 3 SHILL. and date within wreath of oak and olive, as illustration.

No.	OBVERSE	REV.	DAVIS No.	DATE	R	VARIETIES, Remarks, etc.
407	**A¹ Bust**............	**1¹**	*D*. 49	**1811**	*R*	
408	—	**1²**	*D*. 48	—	*C²*	
409	—	—		—	*R*	*Proof*
409A	**A²** —	**1¹**		—	*R⁴*	*Proof*
410	—	**1²**	*D*. 47	—	*R²*	
411	—	**1³**	*D*. 46	—	*R²*	
412	—	—		—	*R²*	*Proof*
413	**A³** —	**1⁴**	*D*. 45	—	*R²*	
414	—	—		—	*R²*	*Proof*

No.	OBVERSE	REV.	DAVIS No.	DATE	R	VARIETIES, Remarks, etc.
		TYPE				
414A	—	1¹		—	R^4	*Proof*
414B	—	1²		—	R^4	*Proof*
415	A^4 —	—	D. 50	1812	C	
416	B^1 **Head**	2	D. 52	1812	C	
417	—	—		—	R	*Proof*
418	—	—	D. 53	—	R^7	*Proof in gold*
419	B^2 —	—	D. 55	—	R^3	
420	—	—	D. 56	—	R^6	*Proof in platinum*
421	B^1 —	—	D. 57	1813	C	
422	—	—	D. 58	1814	C	
423	—	—	D. 59	1815	C	
424	—	—	D. 60	1816	R^3	

HALFCROWNS

THE COMMONWEALTH

Type A

Type **A**   As illustration, with *mm.* sun.[1] **B**   Similar, but with *mm.* anchor.

No.	Type	Date	R	Varieties, Remarks, etc.
425	**A. *Mm.* sun**	**1649**	R^2	
426	—	**1651**	R^2	
426A	—	—	R^4	Reads GOD WITH · VS
426B	—	—	R^4	Reads COMMON · WEALTH
427	—	—	R^5	*Proof*, see note 1 on page 57
428	—	—	R^7	On shilling flan. See note[2] on page 57
429	—	**1652**	R	
430	—	—	R^2	2 of date over 1
430A	—	—	R^4	Reads THE COMMON . WEALTH . OF ENGLAND, error
431	—	**1653**	N	
431A	—	—	S	No stop after THE
431B	—	—	R	Only stop on rev. is after date
432	—	—	R	3 of date over 1
433	—	—	R	3 of date over 2
433A	—	—	R^4	65 of date over 56 (i.e. altered from 1563)
434	—	**1654**	S	
434A	—	—	R^3	Reads COMMONWEATTH
435	—	—	R	4 of date over 3
435A	—	—	R^3	First O in COMMONWEALTH struck over M
436	—	**1655**	R^5	
437	—	**1656**	S	
437A	—	—	R^4	Reads TH·E·COMMONWEALTH, *etc.*
437B	—	—	R^6	As 437 but of proof-like appearance
437C	—	—	R^3	Reads COMMON · WEALTH
438	—	—	R	6 of date over 5
438A	—	—	R^4	— TH·E
439	**B. *Mm.* anchor** ..	**1658**	R^5	
440	—	—	R^4	8 of date over 7
441	—	**1659**	R^7	
442	—	**1660**	R^4	

[1] On some coins of 1651 and 1656 the value appears as · II VI · or · II · VI · .

443

Patterns

443 By Blondeau, 1651. Type as illustration, similar to the current half-crown, but much neater workmanship and struck in a mill. *Edge,* IN . THE . THIRD . YEARE . OF . FREEDOME . BY . GODS . BLESSING . RESTORED . 1651 R^3

444 Similar. *Edge,* TRVTH : AND : PEACE : 1651 olive-branch : PETRVS : BLONDÆVS : INVENTOR : FECIT . palm-branch R^2

444A Similar. *In copper,* on thin flan, edge plain R^7

444B By Simon or Blondeau (?), 1651. Similar in design to the current coin, but with hair-line within a beaded border both sides, and leaves on the inside of palm branch; probably not machine-made.[3] R^5

445

445 By Ramage, 1651. As illustration. *Edge,* TRVTH ★ AND ★ PEACE ★ 1651 ★ between two beaded lines R^5

445A Similar. On thin flan, edge beaded[4] R^6

445B Similar. Edge, plain R^7

445C Similar. On thin flan[4] R^7

---

[1] This, in the British Museum, may be just an exceptionally well struck ordinary coin. Also in the B.M. is a halfcrown of this date with a milled edge; it is not as well struck as might be expected of a proof, so may be an experimental piece or have had the milling added unofficially.

[2] Really a shilling struck from a halfcrown reverse die and a shilling obv. die—2 known, 1 in B.M.

[3] This coin appears in some earlier editions as no. 428A; described as a proof. It is obviously a pattern and was therefore transferred accordingly.

[4] Some authorities consider these to be shillings but I am still inclined to regard them as halfcrowns struck on a thin flan.

445D

445D By Ramage (?), 1651. *Obv.* similar to the current coin, but of finer style. R. The shields are square-shaped and smaller, very similar to No. 445, but no mark of value : reads GOD . VVITH . VS . (i.e. VV for W.)
Edge, plain R^7

CROMWELL

446

446   As illustration, but reading HI and dated 1656. *Edge*, HAS . NISI . PER-
ITVRVS . MIHI . ADIMAT . NEMO + R^3
447   Similar, but 1658 and reading HIB   S
447A *Proof in gold* R^6

CHARLES II

Type A   Type B

Hammered Coinage

Type A   first hammered coinage. As illustration, without mark of value or
          inner circles.

    B   second hammered coinage. Similar, but with mark of value behind
          the head; legend varies.

Type C

    C   third hammered coinage. Similar to last, with mark of value, but
          also with inner circle both sides; legend varies.

Milled Coinage

Type D   *O*. CAROLVS . II . DEI . GRATIA; first bust. R. MAG . BR . FRA . ET. HIB .
          REX date, cruciform shields, with interlinked C's in angles. *Edge*,
          DECVS, etc., followed by regnal year in Roman numerals.

    E   Similar, but second bust; rather broader.

    F   Similar, but third bust; smaller than the two previous busts and with
          curved ties to wreath.

    G   Elephant below third bust.

First bust

Second bust

Elephant below
third bust

Plume in centre

Fourth bust

Elephant & castle below
fourth bust

H Third bust. *Edge*, as before but the regnal years, from now on, are put in words; the coins of 1671 and 1672 have a very slight variety of the bust.

I Fourth bust; much larger.

J Plume below fourth bust.

K As last, but a plume also in centre of the reverse in place of the star of the Garter.

L Elephant and castle below fourth bust.

No.	Type	Date	Edge Year	R	Varieties, Remarks, etc.
	Hammered				
448	A. No value or circles...	None	None	R^3	
449	B. Value, no circles......	—	—	R^4	BRIT FRAN
450	—	—	—	R^5	BRIT FRA
451	—	—	—	R^4	BRI FRA with small xxx
451A	—	—	—	R^4	BRI FRA with large xxx
452	C. Value and circles.....	—	—	S	BRIT FRA
453	—	—	—	S	BRI FRA
454	—	—	—	R	— CAROLV
455	—	—	—	R	BRI FR
456	—	—	—	N	MAG BR FR
456A	—	—	—	R^2	MA BR FR
456B	C. Bust to lower edge of coin.....................	—	—	R^5	MAG : BR : FR :
	Milled				
457	D. First bust................	1663	XV	N	
457A	—	—	—	R^2	V of CAROLVS over S
458	—	—	—	R^6	*Proof*
459	—	—	—	R	No stops on *obv.*
460	E. Second bust.............	1664	XVI	R^2	
461	F. Third bust...............	1666	XVIII	R^5	Last 6 of date over 3, possibly 4. See note[1]
462	G. — Elephant below..	—	—	R^3	—
463	H. —	1667	DECIMO NONO	R^6	7 of date over 4. Edge, AN REG
464	—	1668	VICESIMO	R^2	8 of date over 4
465	—	1669	V. PRIMO	R^5	
465A	—	—	—	R^5	R of PRIMO over I
466	—	—	—	R^3	9 of date over 4
467	—	1670	V. SECVNDO	N	
467A	—	—	—	R^3	MRG instead of MAG
468	Third bust variety........	1671	V. TERTIO	N	
469	—	—	—	R	1 of date over 0
470	—	1672	—	R^5	
471	—	—	V. QVARTO	R	
472	I. Fourth bust	—	—	R^3	
473	—	1673	V. QVINTO	N	
473A	—	—	—	R^3	A of FRA over R
473B	—	—	—	R^3	B of BR over R

[1] H.E. Manville says that the final figure is not 3. I have examined three specimens and have not been able to determine the figure accurately so this may well be the case. I have reduced the rarity from R^6 to R^5.

No.	Type	Date	Edge Year	R	Varieties, Remarks, etc.
474	**J. — plume below**.......	—	—	R^5	
475	**K. — plume both sides**	—	—	R^6	
476	**I. —**	**1674**	V. SEXTO	R^2	
476A	—	—	—	R^4	4 of date over 3
477	—	**1675**	V. SEPTIMO	R	
477A	—	—	—	R^2	1 of date retrograde
478	—	**1676**	V. OCTAVO	S	
478A	—	—	—	N	1 of date retrograde
479	—	**1677**	V. NONO	N	
480	—	**1678**	TRICESIMO	R^4	
481	—	**1679**	T. PRIMO	C	
481A	—	—	—	R^3	Reads GRATTA in error
482	—	—	—	R^3	Reads REGᴙI in error
483	—	—	—	R	Reads DECNS in error
483A	—	—	—	R^2	Reads DNCVS in error
484	—	—	—	R^3	Reads PRICESIMO in error[1]
484A	—	—	—	R^3	Reads DECVS ET TVTAMEN
485	—	**1680**	T. SECVNDO	R^3	
485A	—	—	—	R^3	D in SECUNDO reversed
486	—	**1681**	T. TERTIO	R	
487	—	—	—	R	1 of date over 0
488	**L. — Elephant & Castle**	—	—	R^4	
489	**I. —**	**1682**	T. QVARTO	R^2	
489A	—	—	—	R^3	2 of date over 1
489B	—	—	—	R^3	82 of date over 79
490	—	**1683**	T. QVINTO	S	
491	**J. — plume below**........	—	—	R^7	
492	**I. —**	**1684**	T. SEXTO	R^4	4 of date over 3

[1] The 'P' could be a flawed 'T'.

JAMES II

Type A *O.* IACOBVS . II . DEI . GRATIA, first bust laur. and dr. l., curl below
ear curls towards neck. R. and edge as before, but plain in angles.

First Bust   Tie of 1st Bust   Tie of 2nd Bust

B Similar, but second bust, curl below ear curls backward, rather older
features.

493	A. First bust	1685	PRIMO	*N*	
494	—	1686	SECVNDO	*N*	See note below[1]
495	—	—	—	*R³*	Last 6 of date over 5
496	—	—	TERTIO	*R*	
496A	—	—	—	*R³*	V of IACOBVS struck over S
497	—	—	—	*R²*	V of IACOBVS over B
498	—	1687	—	*N*	
499	—	—	—	*R*	7 of date over 6
499A	—	—	—	*R⁴*	6 of date over 8
500	B. Second bust	—	—	*R²*	
501	—	—	—	*R⁶*	*Proof*
502	—	1688	QVARTO	*S*	

[1] All James II halfcrowns are scarce in first class condition.

WILLIAM AND MARY

First busts   First shield   Second shield

Type **A**   *O*. First busts. R. First type, crowned shield with arms quarterly, and arms of Orange-Nassau on inescutcheon.

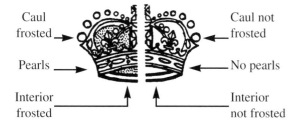

Caul frosted →   ← Caul not frosted

Pearls →   ← No pearls

Interior frosted   Interior not frosted

B   *O*. First busts. R. Second type, with arms of England and France quarterly in first and fourth main quarters.

Type C

C   *O*. Second busts, finer style portraits. R. Third type, with cruciform crowned shields, with arms of Orange-Nassau in centre, WM cypher in angles.

No.	Type	Date	Edge Year	R	Varieties, Remarks, etc.
503	A. First busts, first shield	1689	PRIMO	C^2	Caul and interior frosted, pearls[1]
503A	—	—	—	R	2nd L of GVLIELMVS over M
503B	—	—	—	R	1st V of GVLIELMVS over A (or A) Caul only frosted
504	—	—	—	S	— as 503, but no pearls
505	—	—	—	C^2	Caul only frosted, pearls
505A	—	—	—	R	1st V of GVLIELMVS over A
506	—	—	—	N	Caul only, no pearls
507	—	—	—	N	No frosting, pearls
507A	—	—	—	R	No stops on obv
507B	—	—	—	R^2	As 503, but FRA
508	B. — second shield	—	—	N	Caul and interior frosted, pearls
509	—	—	—	N	— no pearls
509A	—	—	—	R^4	Caul and interior frosted, pearls, inverted F in place of E in ET. HIB
509B	—	—	—	R^3	Caul only frosted, pearls, inverted F in place of E in GVLIELMVS
510	—	—	—	N	Caul only frosted, pearls
510A	—	—	—	R	Interior only frosted, no pearls
510B	—	—	—	R	Caul only frosted, no pearls
511	—	—	—	N	No frosting, pearls
512	—	—	—	N	No frosting, no pearls
513	—	1690	SECVNDO	R	—
514	—	—	—	R^3	— reads GRETIA in error 2nd V of GVLIELMVS struck over S
515	—	—	TERTIO	R^2	No frosting, no pearls
516	C. Second busts, third shields	1691	—	N	See note[2]
517	—	1692	QVARTO	N	See note[3]

[1] The caul is the velvet cap showing through in the upper part of the crown; the interior is the part of the inside of the crown showing between the outer and inner band. The pearls are the dots between the rectangles on the band of the crown.
[2] The halfcrown of 1691 with the first shield which was published in the 'Milled Silver Coinage', without being seen, has since proved to be a contemporary forgery.
[3] The date, 1692, reads clockwise as in the illustration, whereas the other dates of this type read in two lines from left to right.

No.	Type	Date	Edge Year	R	Varieties, Remarks, etc.
517A	—	—	—	R^3	R of REGINA struck over G
518	—	—	QVINTO	R^4	
519	—	**1693**	—	C	
520	—	—	—	R^2	3 of date upside down
521	—	—	—	N	3 of date over 3 upside down

WILLIAM III

Type **i**   *O.* As illustration below. **R.** Cruciform shields as last issue of last reign, but plain in the angles, shields are large and bear the early harp which has the woman's bust well above the right hand end. *Edge*, as before.

ii   Similar, but ordinary harp, the woman's head being almost in line with the right hand end. There are two or three slight variations of this harp, and from 1698 there is a slight modification of the shield.

First bust   C below first bust   Second bust

iii   Similar, but small shields of slightly different shape.

    B   (for *Bristol*)   below bust[1] ⎫

    C   (for *Chester*)   below bust ⎪

    E   (for *Exeter*)   below bust ⎬ combined with each of the plain reverses illustrated on page 68

    N   (for *Norwich*)   below bust[1] ⎪

    y   (for *York*)   below bust ⎭

iv   Second bust with wiry hair and two curls across the breast, hair does not go below truncation. **R.** as last.

v   Elephant and castle below first bust. **R.** as ii.

vi   First bust. **R.** As ii, but with plumes in the angles.

---

[1] Coins of type iii of these mints dated 1696 exist with the shields slightly larger than normal for the 'small shields' type.

Large shields
early harp

Small shields

Large shields
ordinary harp

Mod. large shields
plumes in angles

These illustrations show the reverses 90° offset to right in order to facilitate identification of the different types of Irish harp.

No.	Type	Date	Edge Year	R	Varieties, Remarks, etc.
522	i. **Large shields, early harp**	**1696**	OCTAVO	N	See note[1]
523	—	—	none	R^4	*Proof*, plain edge, thick flan
523A	—	—	—	R^4	— wide thick flan
524	— **B below bust**	—	OCTAVO	S	
524A	—	—	—	R^6	On thick flan, wt. 328.5 grs.
525	— **C below bust**	—	—	R	
526	— **E below bust**	—	—	R^2	
527	— **N below bust**	—	—	R^4	
528	— **y below bust**	—	—	R	
528A	—	—	—	R^5	Arms of Scotland at date
529	—	—	—	R^4	y over E (looks like inverted A)
530	ii. **Large shields, ordinary harp**	—	—	R^3	
530A	— **B below bust**	—	—	R^4	
531	— **C below bust**	—	—	R^3	
532	— **E below bust**	—	—	R^3	
532A	—	—	NONO	R^5	
533	— **N below bust**	—	OCTAVO	R^4	
534	iii. **Small shields**	—	—	C	
534A	—	—	—	R^3	Reads DECVS
535	— **B below bust**	—	—	R	
535A	—	—	—	R^3	See note[1] on page 67
535B	—	—	—	R^6	— *proof*
536	— **C below bust**	—	—	R^2	
537	— **E below bust**	—	—	R^4	
538	— **N below bust**	—	—	R	
538A	—	—	—	R^4	See note[1] on page 67
539	— **y below bust**	—	—	R^2	
540	iv. **Second bust**	—	—	R^7	
541	ii. **First bust, large shields**	**1697**	NONO	C	See note[2]
541A	—	—	—	R^2	7 of date over 6
541B	—	—	—	R^5	Reads GRR for GRA
541C	—	—	—	R^5	Blundered edge : DECVS . EMEN . AMEN . ANNO REGNINONO

[1] Some of the halfcrowns of this date have a slight variety of bust. This is most noticeable in the curl nearest to the front of the neck.

[2] The size of the lions on the English shield varies very considerably on coins of this year. Some could be called 'large lions' and some 'small lions'. Also there are differences in the size of the harp.

No.	Type	Date	Edge Year	R	Varieties, Remarks, etc.
542	—	—	none	R^5	*Proof* with plain edge
543	— **B below bust**	—	NONO	N	
543A	—	—	—	R^6	*Proof* on thick flan, 328.7 grs., B below bust partly erased on die
544	—	—	—	R	No stops on *rev.*
545	— **C below bust**	—	—	S	
546	ii. **First bust, large shields E below bust**	1697	OCTAVO	R^4	See note[1]
547	—	—	NONO	N	
547A	—	—	—	R^3	Reads TVTAMEN
548	—	—	—	R^4	E under bust over C
548A	—	—	—	R^4	— reads TVTAMEN
548B	—	—	—	R^4	E under bust over B
548C	—	—	—	R^4	— reads TVTAMEN
549	— **N below bust**	—	OCTAVO	R^6	See note[1]
550	—	—	NONO	S	
550A	—	—	—	R^5	Arms of Scotland at date
550B	— **y below bust**	—	OCTAVO	R^6	See note[1]
551	—	—	NONO	N	
552	—	—	—	R	A different **y**. See note[2]
553	— **First bust modified large shield**	1698	OCTAVO	R^6	See note[3]
554	—	—	DECIMO	C^2	
554A	—	—	—	R^3	8 of date over 7
555	—	—	UNDECIMO	R^5	
556	—	1699	—	R	
557	—	—	—	R^3	DECVS ET TVTAMEN
559	—	—	—	R^4	Arms of Scotland at date
560	—	—	—	R^3	Lion of Nassau inverted
561	—	1700	DVODECIMO	N	

[1] Undoubtedly a wrong edge has been used accidentally; the second edge for 1697 should be DECIMO.

[2] This 'y' is sometimes called a capital Y, as it is without the usual tail of the normal small y, but it is not such a definite capital Y as is found on the shillings and sixpences and is probably a badly cut small y.

[3] Undoubtedly a wrong edge has been used accidentally; the two correct regnal years for this date are DECIMO and UNDECIMO.

No.	Type	Date	Edge Year	R	Varieties, Remarks, etc.
562	—	—	D. TERTIO	N	See note[1]
563	—	—	—	R[2]	DECVS for DECVS, error
564	—	1701	—	N	See note[1]
565	—	—	—	R	No stops on *rev.*
566	v. — **Elephant and castle**	—	—	R[4]	See note[2]
567	vi. — **Plumes on reverse**	—	—	R	

[1] Some of these have slightly larger lettering on reverse and larger harps.
[2] There is a variety with the provenance mark larger, i.e. the castle is much taller, and the elephant broader and of different style (R[5]).

ANNE

Type **A** As illustration **B** below, but without VIGO.[1]
    B As illustration below, VIGO below bust.

               Type B   Type D

    C Plumes in angles of reverse.
    D Similar, but roses and plumes alternately in the angles[2].

After Union with Scotland

               Type C   Type F

    E Similar to type **A** but reading BRI FR, and the top and bottom shields
        have arms of England and Scotland impaled, nothing in the angles.
    F Similar, but **E** for Edinburgh below bust.
    G Similar, but plumes in the angles on the reverse.
    H Similar, but roses and plumes in the angles.

---

[1] The Queen's bust varies very slightly during the reign, but nothing like so much as on the
crowns and shillings. There are two slight varieties of bust on the 1708 plumes halfcrowns, one
like the early coins and one like the later ones; there are also perhaps two on 1707 roses and
plumes.
[2] The style of the crowns above the shields on 1706 and 1707 roses and plumes coins varies.

Type G   Type E and F   Type H

No.	Type	Date	Edge Year	R	Varieties, Remarks, etc.
568	**A. Before Union** *rev.,* **plain**	1703	TERTIO	R^4	
569	**B.** — VIGO **below bust**........	—	—	N	
570	**C.** — **plumes in angles**	1704	—	R^2	
571	—	1705	QVINTO	R	
572	**D.** — **roses and plumes**	1706	—	S	See note² on p. 72
573	—	1707	SEXTO	N	See note² on p. 72
574	**E. After Union** *rev.,* **plain**	—	SEPTIMO	N	
574A	—	—	—	R^4	Edge reads ET . T . TVTAMEN
574B	—	—	—	R^6	Piedfort on thick flan, 318.3 grs
575	**F.** — E **below bust**	—	SEXTO	C^2	See note¹ below
575A	—	—	SEPTIMO	R^5	
576	**F.** — E **below bust**	1708	—	S	See note¹ below
577	**E.** —	—	—	C	
578	**G.** — **plumes in angles**	—	—	R	Two busts, see note²
579	**E.** —	1709	OCTAVO	N	
580	**F.** — E **below bust**	—	—	R^3	
581	**H.** — **roses and plumes**	1710	NONO	S	
582	—	1712	UNDECIMO	C	
583	**E.** —	1713	DVODECIMO	S	
584	**H.** — **roses and plumes**	—	—	N	
585	—	1714	D. TERTIO	N	
585A	—	—	—	R^2	4 of date over 3

¹ On Edinburgh halfcrowns of 1707 the figure 1 in date is always a 'J', as on all coins of the London mint. Edinburgh coins of 1708 usually have a local rev. die with a 'Z' type figure 1. Rarely, however, one sees a Tower die with a J type figure 1 on coins of 1708.

² These coins are rarer than 'S' would indicate, but not as rare as the 1705 plumes coins—I have nevertheless rated them as 'R'. [See also note¹ on page 72].

GEORGE I

Type **A** As illustration below but plain in angles of reverse.
    B Roses and plumes in angles.

Type B

Type C   Type D

C With SS C (for South Sea Company) in angles of reverse.
D Similar to **B**, but the roses and plumes are smaller in size.

No.	Type	Date	Edge Year	R	Varieties, Remarks, etc.
586	**A. Plain**.............................	1715	none	R^5	*Pattern only*, plain edge
587	**B. Roses and plumes**.........	—	SECVNDO	R	
588	—	—	—	R^2	Words in wrong order on edge
588A	—	—	none	R^6	Plain edge in error
589	—	1717	TIRTIO	S	TIRTIO instead of TERTIO
590	—	1720	SEXTO	S	20 of date over 17
591	—	—	—	R^3	Date not altered
592	**C. SS C**............................	1723	DECIMO	S	
593	**D. Small roses and plumes**	1726	D. TERTIO	R^5	

GEORGE II

A to C

Plain   Roses   Roses and Plumes

Type **A**   *O*. 'Young head'. R. Cruciform shields, plain in the angles.
    B   Similar, but roses and plumes alternately in the angles.
    C   Similar, but roses only in the angles.

D and F   E

D   *O*. 'Old head'. R. As last with roses.
E   LIMA below bust. R. Plain in angles.
F   As **D**, but plain in angles.

No.	Type	Date	Edge Year	R	Varieties, Remarks, etc.
594	**A. Young head, plain**	**1731**	none	R^4	*Pattern only*, plain edge[1]
595	**B.** — **roses and plumes**	—	QVINTO	*N*	
596	—	**1732**	SEXTO	*N*	
597	—	**1734**	SEPTIMO	*S*	
598	—	**1735**	OCTAVO	*S*	
599	—	**1736**	NONO	*R*	
600	**C.** — **roses**	**1739**	DVODECIMO	*N*	
601	—	**1741**	D. QVARTO	R^3	
601A	—	—	—	*N*	41 of date struck over 39
602	—	—	—	*R*	— Larger lettering on *obv.*
603	**D. Old head, roses**	**1743**	D. SEPTIMO	*N*	
603A	—	—	—	R^2	U for V in GEORGIUS
604	—	**1745**	D. NONO	*N*	See note[3]
604A	—	—	—	R^2	5 of date struck over 3
605	**E.** LIMA **below bust**	—	—	C^2	See notes[2] and [3]
606	—	**1746**	—	C^3	See note[2]
607	—	—	—	*R*	6 of date over 5
608	**F. Old head, plain**	—	VICESIMO	*R*	*Proof only*
609	—	**1750**	V. QVARTO	*S*	
610	—	**1751**	—	R^2	

---

[1] This pattern has obverse slightly convex.
[2] The design of the Scottish arms varies slightly on different specimens of 1745 and 1746 with the LIMA *obverse*; we have noted at least three varieties.
[3] On coins dated 1745, either LIMA or 'Roses', the king's name is spelt GEORGIUS, i.e. U for the usual V.

GEORGE III

Countermarked Spanish half dollars

611

611 A Spanish 4 reales countermarked on the centre of the obverse with the bust of George III in small oval.[1]   *S*

Last or new coinage

Type A

Type **A**   As illustration, large or 'bull' head. *Edge*, milled.[2]

Type B

B   Second type; smaller head, new reverse.

---

[1] These usually turn up on pure Spanish coins of Madrid mint. These pieces, unlike the 8 reales, are much commoner than the 4 reales of the Spanish-American mints. The countermark may, however, occasionally be found on other foreign coins.

[2] This is the normal edge for the halfcrown from this issue onwards.

No.	Type	Date	R	Varieties, Remarks, etc.
613	**A. Large head**......................	**1816**	C	
614	—	—	R^2	*Proof*
615	—	—	R^2	*Proof* with plain edge
616	—	**1817**	C	
616A	—	—	R	D of DEI over T
617	—	—	R^2	*Proof*
617A	—	—	R^6	*Proof in copper*
617B	—	—	R^3	*Proof* with plain edge
618	**B. Small head**......................	—	C^2	
618A	—	—	R^3	Reversed S's in Garter motto
619	—	—	R^2	*Proof*
620	—	—	R	*Proof* with plain edge
621	—	**1818**	C	
622	—	—	R^4	*Proof*
623	—	**1819**	C	
624	—	—	R^3	*Proof*
625	—	**1820**	S	
626	—	—	R^3	*Proof* with plain edge
626A	—	—	R^5	*Proof* with milled edge

Pattern

627 By T. Wyon, 1817. *O.* As the 'small head' but slightly different features. R. The 'new reverse', but shield is of a different shape and garnished, the garnishing overlapping the Garter. R^4

GEORGE IV

Type A

Type A   *O*. GEORGIUS IIII D : G : BRITANNIAR : REX F : D : as illustration above. R. Crowned garnished shield and emblems, as illustration.

Type B

B   *O*. As last. R. As illustration above. Crowned shield within Garter and collar of the Garter.

C   *O*. GEORGIUS IV DEI GRATIA, *bare* head l., date below. R. As illustration. BRITANNIARUM REX FID : DEF, square-topped shield garnished, surmounted by helmet crowned and with lambrequins, motto, DIEU etc., on scroll below.

No.	Type	Date	R	Varieties, Remarks, etc.
628	**A. First head, first** *rev.*	1820	C^2	
629	—	—	R	*Proof*
630	—	—	R^3	*Proof* with plain edge
631	—	1821	C	See note[1]
632	—	—	R^2	*Proof*
633	—	1823	R^3	Heavier garnishing. See note[2]
634	**B. Second** *rev.*	—	C	
635	—	—	R^3	*Proof*
636	—	1824	S	
637	—	—	R^4	*Proof*
638	—	—	R^3	*Proof in copper*, plain edge
639	**C. Second head, third** *rev.* ..	—	R^6	
639A	—	—	R^4	*Pattern*, from polished dies
639B	—	—	R^4	— plain edge
640	—	—	R^7	— *In gold*
641	—	—	R^4	— *In copper*
642	—	1825	C	See note[3]
643	—	—	S	*Proof*
644	—	—	R^2	*Proof* with plain edge
645	—	—	R^4	— *In Barton's metal*[4]
646	—	1826	C^2	
647	—	—	S	*Proof*, issued in the sets
648	—	1828	S	
649	—	1829	N	

Patterns

649A By Pistrucci and Merlen, 1820. Almost as type A, but no engraver's initials (B.P.) below bust, and tie ends straighter. R^5

650 By Pistrucci and Wyon, 1822. As type B but there is straight ground under the dragon and the Garter is narrower with beaded borders. *Edge*, milled R^7

651 — *Edge*, plain R^7

652 — 1823. As type A, but new and more deeply cut dies. *Edge*, milled
                          R^6

653 — 1824. Similar, but for date R^6

---

[1] On some of these the garnishing is heavier, as the type A halfcrowns of 1823.
[2] The so-called proof of this date is probably the pattern No. 652.
[3] In M.S.C by H.A. Seaby, a halfcrown of the second coinage appears with the note, 'possibly a pattern'. I have not traced this coin and have, therefore, omitted it.
[4] For description of Barton's metal see page 32.

654 By W. Binfield, undated. *O.* GEORGIUS IIII D : G ; BRITANNIAR : REX F :
D : , large laureate head l., artist's name in full beneath. R. 2ˢ . 6ᴰ.
divided by caduceus, surmounted by trident, the whole within laurel-
branches. *Edge,* plain   *R*⁷
655 — *In bronze or copper*   *R*⁶

650

WILLIAM IV

Type A

Type A   *O.* GULIELMUS IIII D : G : BRITANNIAR : REX F : D : , his bare head r., w
w incuse on truncation. R. Shield on mantle crowned, ANNO and
date below.
B   Similar, but *W W* in script, incuse.

No.	Type	Date	R	Varieties, Remarks, etc.
656	**A. With WW**........................	**1831**	R^5	See note[1]
657	—	—	*S*	*Proof,* plain edge, issued in sets
658	**B. WW in script**..................	—	*R*	*Proof only,* plain edge
659	—	—	R^2	— milled edge
660	**A. With WW**........................	**1834**	*R*	
661	—	—	R^2	*Proof*
662	**B. W W in script**..................	—	*C*	
663	—	—	*R*	*Proof*
664	—	—	R^4	*Proof,* plain edge
665	—	**1835**	*R*	
666	—	**1836**	*C*	
666A	—	—	R^3	6 of date over 5
666B	—	—	R^4	*Proof,* plain edge
667	—	**1837**	*S*	

---

[1] Although ordinary halfcrowns of this date were struck and a few are known, they were never put
into general circulation.

VICTORIA

Type A¹   Type A⁴

Type **A**¹ Young head. *O*. VICTORIA DEI GRATIA, young head left, with one plain and one ornate fillet in hair, w w in relief on truncation. **R**. REGINA FID : DEF : BRITANNIARUM, square-topped shield, crowned, in branches, ornament below.

A² Similar, but two ornate fillets.

A²ᐟ³ Similar, but two plain fillets.

A³ Similar, as last, but w w incuse.

A⁴ Similar to last but no initials.

A⁵ Similar, but slightly coarser workmanship. (See note¹).

Type A⁵   Type B

B Jubilee. *O*. VICTORIA DEI GRATIA, tall bust l., dr. and veiled, with small crown. **R**. REGINA FID : DEF : BRITANNIARUM, shield in Garter and collar of the Order of the Garter, crowned, date below.

---

¹ Dr G. Bullmore pointed out that there are really two types of A⁵. The early coins show a narrower space between DEI and GRATIA and REGINA and FID; also the crown over shield is narrower. The back hair is slightly finer style. Dr Bullmore also indicates that the 1868 coins show all the features of post 1879 A⁵ coins and suggests they were unofficial coins made perhaps in 1887 when dies became obsolete on the introduction of the 1887 Jubilee issue. The official view expressed by the Royal Mint now is that the coins are all very clever forgeries, struck from false dies, probably around the turn of the century; they are all light weight and struck in silver around .915 fine instead of .925. (See also notes on p. 85).

Type **C**

C   Old head. *O.* VICTORIA . DEI GRA . BRITT . REG., her coronetted bust
l., veiled and draped. **R.** FID . DEF . IND . IMP. — . HALF CROWN.,
spade-shaped shield within collar of the Garter crowned, inner circle, date below.

No.	TYPE	DATE	R	VARIETIES, Remarks, etc.
668	**A¹ Young head, 1 plain and 1 ornate fillet, W W in rel.**	**1839**	R^4	
669	—	—	R^3	*Proof*
670	—	—	*S*	*Proof*, plain edge, issued in sets
671	**A² Young head, 2 ornate fil., W W in rel.**	—	R^2	*Proof or Pattern* with plain edge
671A	**A²ᐟ³ — 2 plain fil., W W in rel.**	—	R^5	*Proof*, plain edge
672	**A³ — 2 plain fil., W W incuse**	—	R^4	
672A	—	—	R^4	*Proof*
672B	—	—	R^3	*Proof* with plain edge
673	—	**1840**	*S*	
674	**A⁴ — no initials**	**1841**	R^3	
675	—	**1842**	*N*	
676	—	**1843**	*R*	
677	—	**1844**	*N*	
678	—	—	R^4	Struck without collar on large flan
679	—	**1845**	*N*	
680	—	**1846**	*S*	
681	—	**1848**	R^3	Date not altered from 1846[1]
681A	—	—	R^2	Last 8 of date over 6
682	—	**1849**	*S*	Large date
683	—	—	*R*	Small date
684	—	**1850**	*S*	
685	—	—	R^4	*Proof*
686	—	**1851**		*Proof* (?) Does this date exist?
687	—	**1853**	R^2	*Proof only*, issued in sets

[1] The obverse lettering on this die is irregularly spaced.

No.	Type	Date	R	Varieties, Remarks, etc.
688	A¹ **Young head 1 orn. fil., W W in rel.**	1862	R^5	*Proof or Pattern only*
689	—	—	R^2	— plain edge
690	—	1864	R^2	— milled edge[1]
691	—	—	R^2	— plain edge[1]
692	A⁵ **Young head, no initials, inferior work**	1874	N	See note[2]
693	—	—	R^2	*Proof*
694	—	—	R^5	*Proof* with plain edge
695	—	—	R^7	*In gold*
696	—	1875	N	
697	—	—	R^3	*Proof*
698	—	—	R^7	*Proof or Pattern* with plain edge[3]
699	—	1876	S	
699A	—	—	R^2	6 of date struck over 5
700	—	1877	S	
701	—	1878	S	
702	—	—	R^4	*Proof*
703	—	1879	R	
704	—	—	R^4	*Proof*
704A	—	—	R^5	*Proof* with plain edge
705	—	1880	S	
706	—	—	R^4	*Proof*
707	—	1881	N	
708	—	—	R^3	*Proof*
709	—	—	R^7	*Proof* with plain edge
710	—	1882	N	
711	—	1883	N	

[1] Struck for the foundation ceremony of the Albert Memorial.
[2] No halfcrowns for the U.K. were struck between 1850 and 1874. At various times, however, examples have been seen dated 1866, 1868 and 1871. A specimen dated 1861 brought £115 at a sale in the North in 1967, in about 'fair' condition.
Also a coin sent in from Eire, although in very poor condition clearly showed the date, 1861. This was almost certainly a coin of type A⁵.
Three specimens dated 1868 have been seen. One of these had a very broad second 8 in date, but the owner has a letter from the Mint authenticating the coin as a genuine mint production.
One specimen of 1871 was also seen. It would seem that 1861, 1866 and 1871 coins are extremely rare, but coins of 1868 are less rare that was at first thought. (See note on p. 83.)
Further research on these coins has led me to believe that they are probably contemporary forgeries. They are all of type A⁵, and if the dates were genuine, they should be of type A⁴. Although at various times semi-official opinions have been expressed that the pieces were genuine, there are no mint records of these dates having been issued, and the most likely source is that of a counterfeiter operating in the 1890's who was not aware that these dates had not been officially struck at the Royal mint. (See note on p. 83)
[3] A piece in the 'Nobleman' (Ferrari) Sale, ex Murdoch coll. which H. A. Seaby catalogued as 'As the current coin but from a different die; believed to be a unique pattern from a die which fractured and was discarded'.

No.	Type	Date	R	Varieties, Remarks, etc.
712	—	**1884**	*S*	
713	—	**1885**	*N*	
714	—	—	*R³*	*Proof*
715	—	**1886**	*N*	
716	—	—	*R⁷*	*Proof*
717	—	**1887**	*N*	
718	—	—	*R⁵*	*Proof*
719	**B. Jubilee issue**	**1887**	*C³*	
720	—	—	*S*	*Proof*, issued in the sets
721	—	**1888**	*N*	
722	—	**1889**	*S*	
723	—	**1890**	*S*	
724	—	**1891**	*S*	
725	—	**1892**	*S*	
726	**C. Old head**	**1893**	*C*	
727	—	—	*N*	*Proof*, issued in the sets
728	—	**1894**	*S*	
729	—	**1895**	*N*	
730	—	**1896**	*S*	
731	—	**1897**	*N*	
732	—	**1898**	*S*	
733	—	**1899**	*N*	
734	—	**1900**	*C*	
735	—	**1901**	*N*	

Patterns
736 By W. Wyon, 1839. As current coin, but much smaller head with plain
     fillets, large date below; perhaps from the punch made for the halfpenny.
     Edge, plain R^6
736A Similar, but one ornamented fillet only R^7
737 Similar. *Edge*, milled R^6
738 By W. Wyon and Pistrucci, 1875 (date both sides). *O.* As type A⁵. R.
     Pistrucci's St. George and Dragon, date in ex. *Edge*, plain R^7
739 By L. C. Wyon (?) and Pistrucci, 1875. *O.* VICTORIA DEI GRATIA BRITAN-
     NIAR : REG : F : D :, her coronetted head l. R. As last. *Edge*, plain R^6

740

740 By L. C. Wyon, 1876. *O.* VICTORIA D : G : BRITANNIAR : REG : F : D :
     1876, her coronetted head l., L.C.W. below. R. A fine large equestrian
     figure of St. George in crested helmet about to transfix the dragon,
     which is depicted unusually large, ground beneath, no legend, L.C.W.
     below. *Edge*, plain R^5
741 Similar. *In gold* R^7
742 By L. C. Wyon (?) 1884. *O.* Legend, crowned and veiled bust. R. BRI-
     TANNIARUM REGINA FID : DEF 1884, shield encircled by Garter and also
     collar of the order. *Edge*, milled R^7
743 By Boehm and L. C. Wyon (?), 1890. *O.* As ordinary Jubilee issue. R.
     HALF CROWN 1890, square shield, crowned and heraldically shaded with-
     in the Garter and also the collar of the order. *Edge*, milled R^7
744 Similar, but diademed head of the queen R^7
745 By P. T. E., 1890. *O.* VICTORIA REGINA DEI GRATIA, head rather like
     Jubilee type, but bust viewed more from the front, P.T.E. below. R.
     . DEI . . GRAT : FID : DEF . 1890, four shields divided by sceptre and
     MODEL $\frac{1}{2}$ CROWN, crown above. *Edge*, plain. *In copper silvered* (full
     halfcrown size) R^4
745A As 745, on thick flan. *In copper* R^4
745B 1890 by F.B. Obv. Similar to 745 but F.B to r. of ribbon. Plain edge, *in*
     silvered copper R^5

EDWARD VII

O. EDWARDVS VII DEI GRA : BRITT : OMN : REX, bare head r. **R.** FID : DEF IND :
IMP : – HALF . DATE . CROWN, crowned shield in Garter.

No.	DATE	R	VARIETIES, Remarks, etc.	No.	DATE	R	VARIETY Remarks, etc.
746	1902	*N*	See note[1]	751	1906	*S*	
747	—	*N*	*Proof,* matt surface	752	1907	*R*	
748	1903	*R²*	See note[2]	753	1908	*R*	
749	1904	*R*		754	1909	*R*	
750	1905	*R²*	See note[2]	755	1910	*S*	

---

[1] During World War II, I received in change a very worn halfcrown mule—*obv.* Edward VII; *rev.*
Victoria old head issue, dated 1901.
[2] Halfcrowns of 1903, 1904 and 1905 are rare in any condition, particularly the last date. Other
dates are only as rare as marked if in EF state. This rule applies also to later reigns.

GEORGE V

A   A and B

Type A   *O.* GEORGIVS V DEI GRA : BRITT : OMN : REX, his bare head l., B.M. on
truncation. **R.** FID : DEF : IND : IMP : – HALF . date . CROWN, crowned
shield in Garter.

B   Similar, but only 50% silver and 50% alloy.

C   *O.* Modified effigy, distinguishable by the B.M. being nearer to back
of neck and without stops; beading is more pronounced (See illustration on left below). **R.** Similar to **B**, but beading more pronounced.

C   D

D   *O.* Similar. **R.** New type. Thistle FID . DEF rose IND . IMP shamrock
— HALF . CROWN . date, two interlinked Gs crowned either side of
shield; beading more pronounced like obverse.

757	**A. .925 silver**..................	1911	*N*	See note[2] on page 88
758	—..............................	—	*S*	*Proof*
759	—..............................	1912	*S*	
760	—..............................	1913	*R*	
761	—..............................	1914	*S*	
762	—..............................	1915	*N*	
763	—..............................	1916	*N*	
764	—..............................	1917	*N*	
765	—..............................	1918	*N*	
766	—..............................	1919	*S*	

No.	Type	Date	R	Varieties, Remarks, etc.
767	**B. 'Debased' .500**............	**1920**	*S*	
768	—	**1921**	*S*	
769	—	**1922**	*S*	
770	—	**1923**	*S*	
771	—	**1924**	*S*	
772	—	**1925**	*S*	
773	—	**1926**	*R*	
773A	—	—	R^2	No colon after OMN. (See note[1])
774	**C. Modified effigy**............	—	*S*	See note[2]
775	—	**1927**	*N*	
776	**D. New type**....................	—	*N*	*Proof only.* From 776D proofs of many dates were struck
776A	—	—	R^7	Matt proof
777	—	**1928**	*N*	
778	—	**1929**	*N*	
779	—	**1930**	R^2	
780	—	**1931**	*S*	
781	—	**1932**	*S*	
782	—	**1933**	*S*	
783	—	**1934**	*S*	
784	—	**1935**	*N*	
785	—	**1936**	*N*	

EDWARD VIII

785A

785A *O.* As the crown, **R.** FID : DEF : IND : IMP HALF . CROWN . 1937. The Royal arms as a Standard flag, crowned 'E8' mgr. either side R^6

---

[1] Mr. F. W. Curry has shown me a coin which quite clearly has one stop of the colon thus OMN· and this leads one to suppose that these coins were struck from defective dies, both dots becoming erased at a later stage. Mr. C. Cooke reported seeing a coin without colon after GRA, of the same date, which seems to confirm my views.
[2] Although the rarity has been reduced from *R* to *S* it is rarer than the 1927 coin: the 2nd coinage piece of 1926 *E.S.C.* 773 is rarer than the 3rd coinage piece of the same date, and the rarity has been increased to *R*.

GEORGE VI

A   C

Type A *O*. As crown. R̥. FID : DEF : IND : IMP — HALF CROWN and date, shield
hanging from hook. On each side, two interlinked Gs crowned, K G
below.

B Similar, but struck in cupro-nickel, closer milling on edge.

C New type, without IND IMP. Engraver's initials K.G. omitted.

786	**A. .500 Æ**	**1937**	*N*	
787	—	—	*S*	*Proof*
787A	—	—	*R⁷*	Matt *proof*
788	—	**1938**	*S*	See note ³ below
789	—	**1939**	*S*	
790	—	**1940**	*C*	
791	—	**1941**	*C*	
792	—	**1942**	*C*	
793	—	**1943**	*C*	
794	—	**1944**	*C*	
795	—	**1945**	*C²*	
796	—	**1946**	*C²*	
796A	**B. Cu.-Ni.**	—	*R⁶*	*Proof or Pattern.* See note¹
797	—	**1947**	*N*	
798	—	**1948**	*N*	
798A	**C. — New type**	**1949**	*N*	
798B	—	**1950**	*N*	
798C	—	—	*S*	*Proof.* Sand blasted dies exist
798D	—	**1951**	*N*	
798E	—	—	*R*	*Proof.* Sand blasted dies exist
798F	—	**1952**	*R⁷*	Note²

¹ These coins were patterns, or trials in cupro-nickel for the 1947 coinage, struck before 1947 dies
  were prepared.
² Not issued for general circulation.
³ So called 'V.I.P.' proofs exist for most of these dates.

798f

ELIZABETH II

Type A   Type B

Type A   + ELIZABETH II DEI GRATIA BRITT : OMN : REGINA, her laureate bust
draped right. R. Crown above square-topped garnished shield
between E R, + FID . . DEF + above, HALF CROWN 1953 below.

   B   As before but + ELIZABETH . II . DEI . GRATIA . REGINA

No.	Type	Date	R	Remarks, etc.	No.	Type	Date	R	Remarks, etc.
798G	A. Cu.-ni.	1953	N	See note[3]	798R	—	—	R	From polished
798H	—	—	S	*Proof*					banks[2]
798I	B. —	1954	C		798S	—	1962	C^3	
798J	—	1955	C		798T	—	1963	C^3	
798K	—	1956	C		798U	—	1964	C^3	
798L	—	1957	C		798V	—	1965	C^3	
798M	—	1958	C^2		798W	—	1966	C^3	
798N	—	1959	C^2		798X	—	1967	C^3	
798O	—	1960	C^2		798Y	—	1970	S	*Proof*
798P	—	1961	C^3	See note[1]					

[1] The coin listed in previous editions as '798Q. Engraver's initials E.F. omitted' has been deleted.
I have seen many styles of this die, and the 'variety' is due to die wear and 'filling up' of these
small initials.

[2] Presumably these coins were struck on blanks originally prepared for striking the proof halfcrowns of 1953. They were not struck from polished dies.

[3] Sand blasted dies exist for 1953. 'V.I.P.' proofs were struck from 1954–1963.

FLORINS

VICTORIA

Type A   Type B

Type A   'Godless'. *O.* VICTORIA REGINA date, her crowned bust draped l., ww below. R. ONE FLORIN — ONE TENTH OF A POUND; cruciform shields; rose, thistle, rose and shamrock in the angles. *Edge,* milled, *as are all florins.*

B¹   'Gothic'. *O.* 𝕭𝖎𝖈𝖙𝖔𝖗𝖎𝖆 𝖉 : 𝖌 : 𝖇𝖗𝖎𝖙 : 𝖗𝖊𝖌 : 𝖋 : 𝖉 : followed by the date in Roman numerals in the same script, bust very similar to last, w w below, ornamentation of 48 arcs and trefoils around. R. 𝕺𝖓𝖊 𝖋𝖑𝖔𝖗𝖎𝖓 — 𝖔𝖓𝖊 𝖙𝖊𝖓𝖙𝖍 𝖔𝖋 𝖆 𝖕𝖔𝖚𝖓𝖉 type very similar to last but not quite so ornate and with a floriated cross in centre instead of a rose.

B²   Similar, but with die number also below bust.

B³   As last, but reading 𝖇𝖗𝖎𝖙𝖙: and queen with more aquiline nose and slightly different hair style.

B⁴   As last, with die number, but without w w

B⁵   As last, with no w w, but only 42 arcs.

B⁵ᐟ⁶   As **B⁵**, but no die number.

B⁶   As **B³**, with w w, but no die number.

B⁷   As last, but no w w and only 38 arcs; new portrait of queen with older features.

B⁸   As last, but only 33 arcs.

B³ᐟ⁸   As type **B⁸**, with 33 arcs, but portrait as **B³**.

B⁹   As last, but 46 arcs, and portrait as **B³**.

C and **D**. See page 97.

---

[1] Roger Shuttlewood has noted that the number of arcs can be calculated quickly by counting the number of arcs under the bust and multiplying by five.

No.	Type	Max. Die No.[1]	Date[2]		R	Varieties, etc.
802	**A. Godless**	none	**1849**	—	C^2	
802A	—	—	—	—	N	WW partly obliterated by fine line. See note [3]
803	**B[1]. Gothic, 𝔟𝔯𝔦𝔱:, WW**	—	mdcccli	(1851)	R^4	
804	—	—	—	—	R^5	Proof
805	—	—	—	—	R^6	Plain edge
806	—	—	mdccclii	(1852)	C	
807	—	—	—	—	R^2	Proof
807A	—	—	—	—	R^2	[ii. over i]
807B	—	—	mdcccliii	(1853)	N	See note [4]
808	—	—	—	—	N	No stop after date
809	—	—	—	—	R^2	Proof, issued in the sets
811	—	—	mdcccliv	(1854)	R^3	
811A	—	—	—	—	R^3	No stop after date
812	—	—	mdccclv	(1855)	S	
813	—	—	mdccclvi	(1856)	R	
813A	—	—	—	—	S	No stop after date
814	—	—	mdccclvii	(1857)	S	
815	—	—	—	—	R^3	Proof
816	—	—	mdccclviii	(1858)	N	
816A	—	—	—	—	R^4	Proof
816B	—	—	—	—	N	No stop after date
817	—	—	mdccclix	(1859)	N	
818	—	—	—	—	R	No stop after date
819	—	—	mdccclx	(1860)	R	
820	— 𝔟𝔯𝔦𝔱., WW	—	mdccclxii	(1862)	R^2	
821	—	—	—	—	R^5	Proof, plain edge
822	— 𝔟𝔯𝔦𝔱:, WW	—	mdccclxiii	(1863)	R^3	
823	—	—	—	—	R^4	Proof, plain edge

[1] Highest die number noted, but there may be higher.
[2] For type B this is on the coin in Roman numerals in Gothic type with stops when indicated. The Arabic date is not shown on the coin.
[3] In the 1968 edition I included here a note to the effect that the late Harvey Shulman and I thought this variety to be due to filling in of the initials on the die. Mr. David Seeley has pointed out convincingly that these coins were made from an altered 1848 matrix, and the additional inner circle has erased the letters.
[4] Coins of this and some other dates are known with reverses struck from the proof die. They are very rare, but are not of sufficient significance numismatically to give them a separate number.

No.	Type	Max. Die No.[1]	Date[2]		R	Varieties, etc.
824	B². Gothic, brit:, WW	73	mdccclxiv	(1864)	N	
824A	—	⎫ 47 ⎧	—	—	R⁴	On heavy flan (228 grs.)
825	—	⎭ ⎩	—	—	R⁴	Proof on heavy flan
826	—	⎫ 65 ⎧	mdccclxv	(1865)	S	
827	—	⎭ ⎩	—	—	R³	Colon after date
828	—	⎫ 31 ⎧	mdccclxvi	(1866)	R	
829	—	⎭ ⎩	—	—	R³	Colon after date
830	—	9	mdccclxvii	(1867)	R²	
831	B³. .britt, WW	none	—	—	R⁵	Proof or Pattern only
832	—	none	—	—	R⁵	— with plain edge
832A	B⁵. — 42 arcs	32	—	—	R⁴	No WW
833	B³. — 48 arcs	30	mdccclxviii	(1868)	R	With WW
834	—	⎫ 18 ⎧	mdccclxix	(1869)	S	
835	—	⎭ ⎩	—	—	R³	Proof
836	—	35	mdccclxx	(1870)	S	
836A	—	?	—	—	R⁵	Proof
837	—	68	mdccclxxi	(1871)	S	
838	—	?	—	—	R⁴	Proof
839	—	43	—	—	R⁴	— with plain edge
840	—	154	mdccclxxii	(1872)	C	
841	—	262	mdccclxxiii	(1873)	C	
842	—	?	—	—	R⁵	Proof
843	—	62	mdccclxxiv	(1874)	N	
843A	—	30	—	—	R²	iv of date over iii
844	—	88	mdccclxxv	(1875)	N	
845	—	47	mdccclxxvi	(1876)	S	
846	—	61	mdccclxxvii	(1877)	R	
847	B⁴. — no WW	62	—	—	R³	Stop after date
848	B⁵. — 42 arcs	68	—	—	R	Stop after date
848A	—	none	—	—	R	
849	—	95	mdccclxxviii	(1878)	N	
849A	—	73	—	—	R⁶	Proof
849B	B³. — WW, 48 arcs	?	mdccclxxix	(1879)	R⁴	
850	B⁵/⁶. — no WW, 42 arcs	none	—	—	R³	
851	B⁶. — WW, 48 arcs	—	—	—	R	
852	B⁷. — no WW, 38 arcs	—	—	—	R	New portrait

[1] Highest die number noted but there may be higher.

No.	Type	Max. Die No.	Date		R	Varieties, etc.
853	—	—	mdccclxxix		R^5	Proof
853A	—	—	—	—	R^5	— with plain edge
854	B^8. — no WW, 33 arcs	—	mdccclxxx	(1880)	S	New portrait
854A	$B^{3/8}$. As last but portrait as types B^3 and B^9	—	—	—	R^4	
855	B^8. No WW, 33 arcs	—	—	—	R^4	Proof
856	—	—	mdccclxxxi	(1881)	C	
857	—	—	—	—	R^5	Proof
858	—	—	—	—	R^6	— with plain edge
858A	—	—	—	—	S	End of date appears to read xxri[1]
859	—	—	mdccclxxxiii	(1883)	C	
860	—	—	mdccclxxxiv	(1884)	C	
861	—	—	mdccclxxxv	(1885)	C	
862	—	—	—	—	R^6	Proof
863	—	—	mdccclxxxvi	(1886)	N	
864	—	—	—	—	R^6	Proof
865	—	—	mdccclxxxvii	(1887)	S	
866	B^9. — WW, 46 arcs	—	—	—	R	Old portrait
867	—	—	—	—	R^6	Proof

[1] This variety is struck from an imperfect die—the 'r' is caused by a broken 'x' punch.

C

D

C Jubilee head. *O*. VICTORIA DEI GRATIA, veiled and draped bust l.
wearing small crown. **R.** FID : DEF : BRITT : REG : and date, cruciform
crowned shields, star of Garter in centre, sceptre in each angle.

D Old head. *O*. VICTORIA DEI . GRA . BRITT . REGINA . FID . DEF . IND .
IMP., old coronetted bust dr. and veiled l. R. TWO SHILLINGS . ONE .
FLORIN, three shields of England, Scotland and Ireland, rose, shamrock and thistle between, over two sceptres, within Garter, crown
above, date below.

868	**C. Jubilee**	1887	C^3	
869	—	—	S	*Proof*, issued in the sets
870	—	1888	S	
871	—	1889	S	
872	—	1890	R	
873	—	1891	R^2	
874	—	1892	R^2	
875	—	—	R^6	*Proof*
876	**D. Old head**	1893	N	
877	—	—	N	*Proof*, issued in the sets
878	—	1894	S	
879	—	1895	S	
880	—	1896	S	
881	—	1897	N	
882	—	1898	S	
883	—	1899	S	
884	—	1900	N	
885	—	1901	N	

a   b   c

Ai   Biv   Cvi

By W. Wyon, 1848. A series of 27 patterns and three reverse mules.

Obverse   **a.**   As the adopted 'Godless' florin, i.e., crowned bust l.

              b.   Similar, but large laureate head of Queen l.

              c.   Similar, but Queen's head l. with plain fillet.

Reverse type **A.**   Cruciform shields, as the adopted florin.

              B.   Royal cypher VR, interlinked with rose, thistle and sham-rock, Prince of Wales's plumes with motto, all within quatrefoil.

              C.   Oak-wreath and trident.

Reverse legend **i.**   ONE FLORIN   — ONE TENTH OF A POUND.

              ii.   ONE FLORIN   — TWO SHILLINGS.

              iii.   ONE CENTUM — ONE TENTH OF A POUND.

              iv.   ONE DECADE — ONE TENTH OF A POUND.

              v.   ONE DIME   — ONE TENTH OF A POUND.

              vi.   ONE DECADE — 100 MILLES — ONE TENTH OF A POUND.

              vii.   ONE CENTUM — 100 MILLES — ONE TENTH OF A POUND.

No.	TYPE OBV.	REV	EDGE	R	Remarks
886	a	Ai	Plain	R^2	
886A	—	—	—	R^7	*In gold*
886B	—	—	Milled	R^4	
887	b	—	—	R^2	
888	c	—	—	R^2	
889	a	Av	—	R^2	
890	b	—	—	R^2	
891	c	—	—	R^2	
892	a	Bi	—	R^2	
893	b	—	—	R^2	
894	c	—	—	R^2	
895	a	Bii	—	R^2	
896	b	—	—	R^2	
897	c	—	—	R^2	
898	a	Biii	—	R^2	
899	b	—	—	R^2	
900	c	—	—	R^2	
901	a	Biv	—	R^2	
902	b	—	—	R^2	
903	c	—	—	R^2	
904	a	Ci	—	R^2	
905	b	—	—	R^2	
906	c	—	—	R^2	
907	a	Cvi	—	R^2	
908	b	—	—	R^2	
909	c	—	—	R^2	
910	a	Cvii	—	R^2	
911	b	—	—	R^2	
912	c	—	—	R^2	
913	Bi	Bii	SEPTIMO	R^5	
914	Biii	Cvii	—	R^5	Each is a mule of two reverses
915	Biv	Cvi	—	R^5	

916 By L. C. Wyon (?) and Pistrucci, 1875. *O.* VICTORIA DEI GRATIA BRITAN-NIAR : REG : F : D : , coronetted head l. R. Pistrucci's St. George and dragon. *Edge*, plain. As the pattern halfcrown no. 739 R^6

917 By L. C. Wyon, 1876. As the pattern halfcrown of this date, no. 740, but on a much lighter blank R^6

918 By L. C. Wyon, 1891. As the current Jubilee florin, but FLORIN, date between two sprigs, and the shields lined. Edge, milled R^7

EDWARD VII

O.   EDWARDVS VII D : G : BRITT : OMN : REX F : D : IND : IMP : , his head r., DE S below.

R.   ONE FLORIN TWO SHILLINGS, Britannia standing facing on prow of vessel, on which appears the date.

No.	DATE	R	VARIETIES, Remarks, etc.	No.	DATE	R	VARIETIES, Remarks etc.
919	1902	C		924	1906	S	
920	—	N	*Proof*, matt surface	925	1907	S	
921	1903	S		926	1908	R	
922	1904	R		927	1909	R	
923	1905	R^2		928	1910	S	

Note. Rarities as marked only apply to coins in EF condition—'fair' specimens are not uncommon, apart from 1905, but uncirculated pieces are probably rarer than indicated.

GEORGE V

Type A

Type C

Type **A**   *O*. GEORGIVS V D . G . BRITT : OMN : REX F . D . IND : IMP : , head l.,
B.M. on truncation. R. ONE FLORIN, cruciform shields, star of
Garter in centre, sceptre in each angle, date below.

B   Similar, but only 50% silver and 50% alloy.

C   *O*. Modified effigy as other denominations. R. New type. FID .
DEF IND . IMP — date . ONE FLORIN, cruciform sceptres crowned, G in
centre, shield in each angle.

No.	Type	Date	R	Varieties, Remarks, etc.
929	**A. .925 silver**............................	**1911**	*N*	
930	—..................................	—	*S*	*Proof*
931	—..................................	**1912**	*S*	
932	—..................................	**1913**	*S*	
933	—..................................	**1914**	*N*	
934	—..................................	**1915**	*S*	
935	—..................................	**1916**	*N*	
936	—..................................	**1917**	*S*	
937	—..................................	**1918**	*C*	
938	—..................................	**1919**	*N*	
939	**B. 'Debased' .500**....................	**1920**	*S*	
940	—..................................	**1921**	*C*	
941	—..................................	**1922**	*N*	

No.	Type	Date	R	Varieties, Remarks, etc.
941A	—	—	R^6	*Proof in gold,*
942	—	1923	*N*	
943	—	1924	*S*	
944	—	1925	*S*	
945	—	1926	*S*	
947	**C. New design**..........................	1927	*N*	*Proof*
948	—	1928	*N*	
949	—	1929	*N*	
950	—	1930	*N*	
951	—	1931	*S*	
952	—	1932	*R*	
953	—	1933	*S*	
954	—	1935	*N*	
955	—	1936	*N*	

Note. V.I.P. proofs exist for most of these dates from 1927.
As with other denominations of 1927, matt proofs exist but are exceedingly rare.

EDWARD VIII

955A

955A *O.* As the other coins. **R.** As the florin of George VI, but E R below the thistle and shamrock R^6 *Note*[1]

---

[1] The uniface trial piece referred to in the introduction appears on p. 12, plate C of Graham Dyer's monograph, and has the E R above the emblems.

GEORGE VI

A   C

Type **A** *O.* As halfcrown. R. : FID : DEF : : IND : IMP : – TWO SHILLINGS and
date, crowned rose between thistle and shamrock with **G** and **R**
below; engraver's initials K G on either side of stem of rose (.500
silver).
B Similar, but struck in cupro-nickel, closer milling on edge.
C New type, without IND : IMP : , K.G. omitted.

No.	TYPE	DATE	R	Remarks, etc.	No.	TYPE	DATE	R	Remarks, etc.
956	A. Æ	1937	N		966	—	1946	C²	
957	—	—	S	*Proof*	966A	B. Cu. ni.	1946	R⁶	*Proof or*
957A	—	—	R⁷	*Matt proof*					*pattern, see note¹ on page 91*
958	—	1938	S						
959	—	1939	C		967	—	1947	N	
960	—	1940	C		968	—	1948	N	
961	—	1941	C		968A	C. — New type	1949	N	
962	—	1942	C		968B	—	1950	N	
963	—	1943	C		968C	—	—	S	*Proof*
964	—	1944	C		968D	—	1951	N	
965	—	1945	C²		968E	—	—	R	*Proof*

Sand blasted dies exist for 968C and 968E.
V.I.P. proofs exist for most dates from 1938 onwards

ELIZABETH II

A   B

Type **A**   *O*. As halfcrown. **R**. A double rose in the centre within a circlet of radiating thistles, shamrocks and leeks, EF and CT beside lowest leek; above, FID : DEF : ; below, TWO SHILLINGS 1953.

   B   *O*. Similar but new legend ending DEI GRATIA REGINA. **R**. As last.

No.	Type	Date	R	Remarks, etc.	No.	Type	Date	R	Remarks, etc.
968F	**A. Cu.-ni.**	1953	*N*		968O	—	1961	*C²*	
968G	—	—	*S*	*Proof*	968P		1962	*C³*	
968H	**B.** —	1954	*C*		968Q	—	1963	*C³*	
968I	—	1955	*C*		968R	—	1964	*C³*	
968J	—	1956	*C*		968S	—	1965	*C³*	
968K	—	1957	*C*		968T	—	1966	*C³*	
968L	—	1958	*C*		968U	—	1967	*C³*	
968M	—	1959	*C²*		968V	—	1970	*S*	*Proof*
968N	—	1960	*C²*						

Note. V.I.P. proofs exist for all dates, 1954–1963 inclusive
Sand blasted dies exist for 1953.

EIGHTEEN PENCE

A   B

GEORGE III, BANK OF ENGLAND TOKENS

Type A   GEORGIUS III DEI GRATIA REX, laur. bust dr. and cuir. r. R. BANK /
           TOKEN / 1S. 6D. / date; all in oak-wreath. *Edge*, plain.
     B   GEORGIUS III DEI GRATIA REX, laur. head r. R. Similar, but wreath of
           oak and olive.

No.	TYPE OBVERSE	DAVIS No.	DATE	R	VARIETIES, Remarks, etc.
969	**A. Bust**......................	*D.* 61	**1811**	C	
970	—......................			S	*Proof*
971	—......................	*D.* 63	**1812**	C	
972	**B. Head**......................	*D.* 64	—	C	
973	—......................		—	S	*Proof*
974	—......................		—	R^7	*Proof in platinum. Montagu coll.*
975	—......................		—	R^7	Small lettering on *rev. Proof*
976	—......................	*D.* 65	**1813**	C	
976A	—......................	—	—	R^7	*Proof in platinum. (Ex. Cokayne Sale)*
977	—......................	*D.* 67	**1814**	C	
978	—......................	*D.* 68	**1815**	C	
979	—......................	*D.* 69	**1816**	C	

SHILLINGS

THE COMMONWEALTH

A

Type **A** As crown with *mm.* sun, but mark of value · XII ·
    B Similar, but *mm.* anchor.

No.	Type	Date	R	Varieties, Remarks, etc.
982	**A. Mm. sun**......................	**1649**	R	
982A	—.............................	—	R	No stops at value
982B	—.............................	—	R	No stop after OF or ENGLAND
983	—.............................	**1651**	N	
983A	—.............................	—	R^2	51 of date over 49
983B	—.............................	—	S	No stops on *obv.*
984	—.............................	—	R	No stop after THE
984A	—.............................	—	R^2	Only stops on *obv.* are at *mm.*
984B	—.............................	—	R	No stop after ENGLAND
984C	—.............................	—	R^3	Reads COMONWEALTH in error
984D	—.............................	—	R^7	Struck from a halfcrown reverse die (see 428)
984E	—.............................	—	R^2	No stops at mint mark
985	—.............................	**1652**	N	
985A	—.............................	—	R	2 of date over 1
985B	—.............................	—	R^2	— No stops on *rev.*
985C	—.............................	—	R^3	2 of date over 2 on its side
986	—.............................	—	N	No stop after THE
986A	—.............................	—	R	No stop after date
986B	—.............................	—	R	No stop after ENGLAND
986C	—.............................	—	R^3	Reads THE . COMMON . WEALTH . in error
986D	—.............................	—	R	No stops on *obv.*
986E	—.............................	—	R^2	V of VS over O
986F	—.............................	—	R^2	No stops at mint mark

No.	Type	Date	R	Varieties, Remarks, etc.[1]
986G	—	—	R^3	Reads COMMON . WEALTH ; no stop after ENGLAND
987	—	1653	N	
987A	—	—	R^3	Last D of ENGLAND struck over a P
988	—	—	R	No stop after ENGLAND
988A	—	—	R	No stop after THE
988B	—	—	R^4	— reads COMMONWEALH
989	—	—	R^4	Reads COMMONWEATH, error
989A	—	—	R^5	Reads COMMONWEAALTH, error
989B	—	—	R	No stops at mint-mark
989C	—	—	R^2	3 of date over 2
989D	—	—	R	Only stop on *rev.* is after date
990	—	1654	S	
990A	—	—	R	No stop after ENGLAND.
990B	—	—	R^4	Reads COMMMONWEALTH
991	—	—	R	4 of date over 3
992	—	—	R^4	Reads ENGLND, error
992A	—	—	R^2	No stop after OF
993	—	1655	R^2	
993A	—	—	R^2	No stop after ENGLAND
994	—	—	R^2	5 of date over 4
994A	—	—	R^3	5 of date over 4 over 3
995	—	1656	N	
995A	—	—	R	No stop after ENGLAND
995B	—	—	R	No stops at *mm.*
995C	—	—	R^3	Reads O . F . ENGLAND
996	—	1657	R^5	
996A	—	—	R^5	No stop after OF (B.M.)
997	—	—	R^5	No stops on *obv.*
998	B. *Mm.* anchor ...	1658	R^2	
998A	—	—	R^3	No stop after ENGLAND
999	—	—	R^2	8 of date over 7
999A	—	—	R^3	8 of date over 7, no stop after ENGLAND
999B	—	—	R^3	First O of COMMONWEALTH over M; second M over O; no stop after ENGLAND
1000	—	1659	R^7	
1001	—	1660	R^3	
1001A	—	—	R^3	No stops at mm.

1 Several new readings and other varieties, especially stop varieities, have been noted since the last edition; no doubt many remain unpublished.

1002

Patterns

1002 By Blondeau, 1651. Type as the ordinary shilling, but of much neater
workmanship and struck in a mill. *Edge*, milled R^3

1003 Similar. *Edge*, plain (B.M.) R^6

CROMWELL

1005

1005 By Simon, 1658. As illustration; there is almost always a flaw below
the P in front of the laurel-wreath S

1006 *Dutch copy (usually called 'Tanner's)*. Similar, but slightly different
features, no flaw, N of ANG reversed and &c omitted. *Edge*, plain. Thin
flan[1] R^6

1006A Similar. On thick flan R^6

1006B Similar. *Edge*, grained R^6

1007 Similar. *In bronze*

---

[1] Flan thickness of the Dutch copies varies as they were not struck to standard weights.

CHARLES II

A

Hammered Coinage

Type **A**   or first hammered coinage. As illustration, *mm*. on obv. only, and
with no inner circles and without mark of value.

    B   or second hammered coinage. Similar, but with mark of value XII
behind head; abbreviations of legends vary.

C

    C   or third hammered coinage. Similar, but with mark of value, *mm*.
both sides and also inner circles; abbreviations of legends vary.

Milled Coinage

    D   *O*. CAROLVS . II . . DEI . GRATIA, his first bust, laur. and dr. r. R. MAG .
BR . FRA . ET . HIB . REX and date, cruciform shields, etc., as crown.
Edge, upright milling.

    E   Similar, but first bust variety. This bust is very similar in size and
general style, but has a varied arrangement of the hair, which is particularly noticeable below the tie at the back of the head, and the top
two leaves of the laurel wreath (see illustration **F**, same bust without
elephant).

D   F

G   H   I

F Elephant below first bust variety.

G Elephant below quite a different head (not bust) *without any drapery*. The *obverse* die of the guinea was used to strike this coin[1]. See illustration above.

H As type **D**, but second bust. This bust is rather similar to the first bust, but very slightly larger, and has a different tie and one leaf at top of laurel-wreath instead of two. *Edge*, milled.[2]

K   N   M

I Plume below second bust and also in centre of the *reverse* in place of the star.

J Second bust, no plume below, but plume on reverse, as last.

K Third bust, a very large bust.

L Plume below second bust.

M Elephant and castle below second bust.

N Fourth bust, another large bust, not quite such fine work as the third bust, ties straight.

No.	Type	Date	R	Varieties, Remarks, etc.
	Hammered			
1009	**A. No value or circles**	none	*R*	
1010	—	—	*R*	No stop at top of *rev.*
1011	**B. Value, no circles**	—	R^2	BRI FR ET HIB
1012	—	—	R^3	BRI FR ET HI

[1] It has been suggested that the normal dies were lost in the Great Fire and a guinea die had to be used.

[2] Prior to 1669 upright milling was used; in 1669 this was changed to oblique milling which was retained until the recoinage of 1816 when upright milling was again used.

No.	Type	Date	R	Varieties, Remarks, etc.
1013	—	—	R^2	BR FR ET HIB
1014	—	—	R^2	BR FR ET HI
1015	C. Value and circles........	—	R	BRIT FRA ET HIB
1016	—	—	S	BRIT FR ET HIB
1017	—	—	S	R. Large letters, no stops at *mm*.
1018	—	—	R	BRI FR ET HIB
1019	—	—	R	BRI FRA ET HIB. Large mark of value
1019A	—	—	R^2	Small mark of value
1020	—	—	R	BR FR ET HIB
1021	—	—	R	BR FR ET HI
1021A	—	—	R	BRI : FR : ET HI :
	Milled			
1022	D. First bust	1663	C	
1022A	—	—	R^6	*Proof* in copper, plain edge
1023	—	—	R^4	Reads GARTIA, error
1024	—	—	R^3	Shields of Sco. and Ire. transposed
1025	E. First bust variety	—	C	
1025A	—	1666	R^5	
1026	F. — Elephant below	—	R^2	
1027	G. Guinea head, Elephant	—	R^4	
1028	H. Second bust	—	R^6	
1029	E. First bust variety	1668	R^4	
1030	H. Second bust	—	C	
1030A	—	—	R^2	8 of date over 7, (or, more likely 3)
1031	E. First bust variety	1669	R^6	9 of date over 6 or a die flaw
1032	H. Second bust	—	R^7	
1033	—	1670	R^2	
1034	—	1671	R^3	
1035	I. — plume both sides ...	—	R^2	
1036	H. —	1672	R	
1037	—	1673	R^2	
1037A	—	—	R^3	3 of date over 2
1038	I. — plume both sides ...	—	R^3	
1039	H. —	1674	R^2	
1039A	—	—	R^2	4 of date over 3
1040	I. — plume both sides ...	—	R^2	
1041	J. — plume *rev.* only......	—	R^4	Probably a mule of H/I
1042	K. Third bust	—	R^4	
1043	—	1675	R^3	
1043A	—	—	R^3	5 of date over 3
1044	H. Second bust	—	R^4	
1045	—	—	R^4	5 of date over 4
1046	I. — plume both sides ...	—	R^3	

No.	Type	Date	R	Varieties, Remarks, etc.
1047	**H.** —	**1676**	*S*	
1048	—	—	*R*	6 of date over 5
1049	**I.** — **plume both sides** ...	—	*R²*	
1050	**H.** —	**1677**	*R*	
1051	**L.** — **plume** *obv.* **only**	—	*R⁴*	Probably a mule of I/H
1052	**H. Second bust**	**1678**	*R²*	
1053	—	—	*R²*	8 of date over 7
1054	—	**1679**	*S*	
1055	—	—	*R²*	9 of date over 7
1056	**I.** — **plume both sides** ...	—	*R³*	
1057	**L.** — **plume** *obv.* **only**	—	*R³*	Probably a mule of I/H
1058	**H.** —	**1680**	*R⁶*	
1059	**I.** — **plume both sides** ...	—	*R⁵*	
1060	—	—	*R⁵*	80 of date over 79
1061	**H.** —	**1681**	*R³*	
1061A	—	—	*R³*	1 of date over 0
1062	**M.** — **Elephant and castle**	—	*R⁵*	1 of date over 0
1063	**H.** —	**1682**	*R⁴*	2 of date over 1
1064	—	**1683**	*R⁶*	
1065	**N. Fourth bust**	—	*R²*	
1066	—	**1684**	*S*	

Pattern

1067   By Blondeau, 1663. *O.* As type E. R. As usual type, but crowned rose,
         thistle, harp and lis in place of the shields, the legend is re-arranged so
         that the date is between two crowns.   *R⁶*

1067A — *In copper*   *R⁶*

1067A

JAMES II

Type A

Type **A**   As illustration.
    B   Similar, but with plume in place of star in centre of *reverse.*

1068	**A. Plain**..........................	**1685**	*S*	
1069	—	—	*R³*	No stops on *reverse*
1069A	**B. Plume on** *rev.*	—	*R⁶*	
1070	**A. Plain**..........................	**1686**	*S*	
1070A	—	—	*R²*	V of IACOBVS over S
1071	—	**1687**	*R²*	
1072	—	—	*S*	7 of date over 6
1072A	—	—	*R*	— G of MAG over A
1073	—	**1688**	*R*	
1074	—	—	*R²*	Second 8 of date over 7

WILLIAM AND MARY

Only one type, as illustration.

1075	**1692**	*S*	See note[1]
1075A	—	*R*	Inverted 1 in date
1076	**1693**	*N*	
1076A	—	*R⁴*	9 of date struck over 0

[1] The average condition of shillings of this reign is poor, and really first class examples are scarcer than the rarity indicated.

WILLIAM III

Type **i**   *O.* GVLIELMVS . III . DEI . GRA, first bust laur. dr. and cuir. r.; this bust
is distinctive in having the hair turned outwards above and below
the crown of the head. R. As the crown.

        B *(for Bristol)* below bust ⎫
        C *(for Chester)* below bust ⎪
        E *(for Exeter)* below bust ⎬ Combined with type i, iii or iv.
        N *(for Norwich)* below bust ⎪
        y or **Y** (for York) below bust ⎭

  ii   Second bust with hair across the breast (See note[1] on p. 115).
 iii   Third bust; this is rather like the first bust but the hair at the back all
turns downwards and inwards.

     i   ii   iii   C below third bust

           iv   vi   vii

  iv   Third bust variety. Very similar to last, but tie thicker, more hair
below bust, more aquiline profile and coarser features.
   v   Similar, but with plume in each angle of the reverse.
  vi   Fourth bust, known as the 'flaming hair' type on account of the
appearance of the hair at the top of the head.

Plain   Plumes   Roses

vii Fifth bust, known as the 'hair high' type. A narrower bust and with hair at top somewhat between that on the earlier busts and the fourth bust.

viii Similar, but with plumes in the angles on the reverse.

ix Similar, but with roses in the angles of the reverse.

x Plume below the fifth bust

No.	Type	Date	R	Varieties, Remarks, etc.
1077	**i. First bust**	**1695**	*N*	
1078	—	**1696**	*C*	
1078A	—	—	*R*	No stops on *rev.*
1078B	—	—	*R⁵*	Reads MAB for MAG
1079	—	—	*R⁵*	Proof on heavy flan
1080	—	—	*R⁴*	Reads GVLIEMVS in error
1080A	—	—	*R⁴*	Reads GVLIELMVS
1080B	—	—	*R⁴*	Colon after GVLIELMVS
1080C	—	—	*R⁴*	Second L of GVLIELMVS over M
1080D	—	**1669**	*R⁶*	Dated 1669 in error
1081	— **B below**	**1696**	*R*	See note²
1082	— **C below**	—	*S*	
1082A	— **C below**	—	*R⁴*	R of GRA struck over V. See note³
1083	— **C below**	—	*R⁵*	*Proof* on heavy flan
1084	— **E below**	—	*S*	
1085	— **N below**	—	*S*	
1086	— **y below**	—	*S*	
1087	— **Y below**	—	*R*	
1088	— **Y below**	—	*R⁴*	Y over Y upside down
1088A	**ii. Second bust**	—	*R⁷*	See note¹

¹ This bust, although known for other denominations, was not believed to exist on the shilling, and, in fact, did not appear in the first edition of this work. Seaby purchased a specimen in 1949 and this unique coin was sold by Spink & Son at the Lord Hamilton of Dalziel auction.
² A shilling of James I and also of Charles I are known overstruck with 1696B dies. These must have been trials made at the time the old hammered coin was called in.
³ Two specimens were noted in March 1990 both from the same obverse die and in mint condition.

No.		Type	Date	R	Varieties, Remarks, etc.
1089	iii.	Third bust, C below	—	R^3	Probably a mule
1089A		— E below	—	R^7	Probably a mule
1090		— y below	—	R^6	Probably a mule
1091	1.	First bust	1697	C	
1091A		—	—	R^4	Arms of Sco. and Ire. transposed
1091B		—	—	R^4	Irish shield at date
1092		—	—	R	No stops on rev.
1093		—	—	R^5	Reads GVLELMVS in error
1094		—	—	R^5	Reads GRI in error
1094A		—	—	R^3	E of DEI struck over A
1095		— B below	—	S	
1096		— C below	—	S	
1097		— C below	—	R^4	Shields of Sco. and Ire. transposed
1098		— E below	—	S	
1099		— N below	—	S	
1100		— y below	—	S	
1100A		— y below	—	R^7	Shields of Fra. and Ire. transposed
1100B		— y below	—	R^7	Shields of Sco. and Ire. transposed
1101		— Y below	—	R	
1102	iii.	Third bust	—	N	These are found with large and
1103		— B below	—	R	small lettering
1104		— C below	—	S	
1104A		— C below	—	R^2	No stops on reverse
1104B		— C below	—	R^4	Shield of Scotland at date
1104C		— C below	—	R^2	Reads FR . A . ET in error
1105		— E below	—	R	
1106		— N below	—	R	
1107		— y below	—	R	
1108	iv.	Third bust variety	—	N	
1108A		—	—	R^4	Reads GVLIELMVS in error
1108B		—	—	R^4	Reads GVLIELMVS in error
1109		— B below	—	R	
1110		— C below	—	R^3	
1111		— C below	—	R^5	On a thick flan, wt. 157.5 grs i.e. from fillet for halfcrown blank
1112		—	1698	S	
1113		—	—	R^5	Proof with plain edge
1114	v.	— plumes on rev.	—	R^4	
1115	vi.	Fourth bust	—	R	
1115A		—	—	R^6	Proof with plain edge
1116		—	1699	R	
1116A		—	—	R^7	Edge grained, struck on thick flan wt. 128.8 grs
1117	vii.	Fifth bust	—	R	

No.	Type	Date	R	Varieties, Remarks, etc.
1118	—	—	R^5	*Proof* with plain edge
1119	**viii.** — **plumes on** *rev.*	—	R^2	
1120	**ix.** — **roses on** *rev.*	—	R^3	
1121	**vii. Fifth bust**	**1700**	C	
1121A	—	—	S	Circular (smaller) 0's in date[1]
1122	—	—	R	No stops on *rev.*, taller O's in date[1]
1123	**x. plume below bust**	—	R^5	
1124	**vii.** —	**1701**	R	
1125	**viii.** — **plumes on** *rev.*	—	R^2	

1127 1699. In the British Museum there is a shilling of this date as those of the fourth bust, but the hair is more wiry and the bust is broader; hair on top is more like that on the early busts. It is in high relief. R^7

---

[1] There seems to be at least three differing types of 0 used in the date 1700. Type 1 has slightly ovoid figures and is the normal variety, type 2 has smaller, almost circular figures, and type 3 very elongated 0's. This exists both with and without stops on *rev.*

ANNE

Before Union with Scotland

Type **A** As crown. First bust.
    B Similar, but plumes in angles of reverse.
    C VIGO below first bust.

First bust   Second bust

Before Union reverses

  D Second bust, VIGO below. This bust is very like the first bust but the curls around the fillet vary slightly.
  E Second bust, plain below and on reverse.
  F Second bust, plumes in angles of reverse.
  G Second bust, roses and plumes alternately in angles.

After Union with Scotland

  H Second bust, E for *Edinburgh* below. R. The 'After Union' type with the top and bottom shields having the arms of England and Scotland impaled.

Third bust E   Edinburgh bust with E★

After Union reverses

I Similar, but E* below second bust.

I *var.* Similar, but top curls larger and coarser, with tie and back hair as the 'Edinburgh bust'. This is probably a locally-made copy of a 2nd bust London die.

J Third bust; very similar to the others but the curls to r. of the fillet hardly rise above the top of the head, i.e., they are very flat; plain reverse.

K Third bust, plumes in angles of the reverse.

L Third bust, E below; plain reverse.

M Second bust, roses and plumes alternately in angles of the reverse. This is different from type G in having the 'After Union' rev.

N Third bust, roses and plumes in the angles of the reverse.

O 'Edinburgh' bust with E* below. This is quite different from any of the English busts, the two curls rising to right of the fillet being quite long and both curl to r. instead of one to r. and the other to l.

P 'Edinburgh' bust with E below.

Q Fourth bust. This is also a distinctive bust, the whole of the hair more deeply engraved into thick curls and waves; not of such good style as the earlier busts. R. Roses and plumes in the angles.

R Similar, but plain in the angles of the reverse.

No.	Type	Date	R	Varieties, Remarks, etc.
	Before Union Reverse			
1128	**A. First bust**........................	1702	*S*	
1129	**B. — plumes on** *rev.*	—	*R*	
1130	**C. —** VIGO **below**................	—	*S*	
1130A	—	—	*R²*	Two stops before ANNA; no stop after GRATIA
1131	**D. Second bust,** VIGO **below**	1703	*N*	
1132	**E. —**	1704	*R⁵*	
1133	**F. — plumes on** *rev.*	—	*R²*	
1134	**E. —**	1705	*R²*	
1135	**F. — plumes on** *rev.*	—	*S*	
1136	**G. — roses and plumes**.......	—	*S*	
1137	—	1707	*R*	

No.	Type	Date	R	Varieties, Remarks, etc.
	After Union Reverse			
1138	**H. Second bust, E below**	—	S	
1138A	—	—	R^4	No stops on reverse
1139	—	—	R^6	Proof with plain edge
1140	**I.** — **E* below**	—	R^2	
1140A	**I.** *var.* —	—	R^3	Local dies
1141	**J. Third bust**	—	N	
1142	**K.** — **plumes on** *rev.*	—	S	
1143	**L.** — **E** *below*	—	N	
1143A	**O.** *'Edinburgh'* **bust, E***			
	below	—	R^5	See note[1]
1144	**H. Second bust, E below**	1708	R^2	
1145	**I.** — **E* below**	—	N	
1145A	—	—	R^4	8 of date over 7
1145B	— **E below**	—	R^3	Local dies
1145C	—	—	R^5	No rays to Garter Star on reverse
1146	**M.** — **roses and plumes**	—	R^3	
1147	**J. Third bust**	—	C^2	
1148	**K.** — **plumes on** *rev.*	—	N	
1149	**N.** — **roses and plumes**	—	R^2	
1150	**L.** — **E below**	—	R^2	
1150A	—	—	R^3	8 of date over 7
1151	**O.** *'Edinburgh'* **bust, E***			
	below	—	R	
1152	—	1709	R^2	
1153	**P.** — **E below**	—	R^4	See note[2]
1154	**J. Third bust**	—	C^2	
1155	**N.** — **roses and plumes**	1710	N	
1155A	**R. Fourth bust**	—	R^7	*Pattern* or *Proof* with plain edge
1156	**Q.** — **roses and plumes**	—	R^2	
1156A	—	—	R^6	*Proof* with plain edge
1157	**J. Third bust**	1711	R^4	Probably a mule
1158	**R. Fourth bust**	—	C^3	
1159	**Q.** — **roses and plumes**	1712	N	
1160	—	1713	S	3 of date over 2
1161	—	1714	N	

Note. We are inclined to believe that coins of this period showing un-barred letters, e.g., IIIB for HIB, are not true varieties but are due to the 'filling in' of dies.

[1] This differs from the normal 'Edinburgh' bust made in 1708/9 in that the general style, apart from the curls, is more like the third bust.
[2] These pieces are actually from the same die as 1709 E*, with the star either intentionally or accidentally filled in on the die.

GEORGE I

A   B   C

Type A   General type as the halfcrowns. First bust, two ends to tie of wreath.
        R. Roses and plumes in the angles.
     B   Similar, but plain in angles on reverse.
     C   As before, but SS C (for *South Sea Company*) alternately in the
        angles on the reverse.
     D   Second bust, similar, but bow and one end to tie, as illustration
        below. R. SS C alternately in angles.
     E   Second bust. R. Roses and plumes in the angles.

F

     F   W. C. C. (for *Welsh Copper Company*) below second bust. R. Two
        interlinked C's and a plume alternately in the angles.

No.	Type	Date	R	Varieties, Remarks, etc.
1162	**A. First bust, roses and plumes**............................	**1715**	*S*	
1163	—	**1716**	*R*³	
1164	—	**1717**	*S*	
1165	—	**1718**	*N*	
1166	—	**1719**	*R*²	
1167	—	**1720**	*S*	See note[1]
1167A	—	—	*R*⁴	20 of date over 18
1168	**B. — plain**	—	*N*	
1169	—	—	*N*	With 0 of date and lettering on *rev.* larger

[1] The so-called 'plain edge' variety is really a coin struck without going through the edging machine. It is very rare. No circulation coins were struck in collars until later in the eighteenth century.

1170	—	**1721**	R^4	
1171	**A. — roses and plumes**.......	—	R	
1171A	—	—	R^4	Roses and plumes in wrong angles
1172	—	—	S	1 of date over 0
1173	—	—	R	21 of date over 19 or 18
1174	—	**1722**	S	
1175	—	**1723**	S	
1176	**C. —** ss c	—	C^2	
1176A	—	—	R^5	c over ss between second and third quarter
1177	—	—	R^2	Arms of France at date[1]
1178	**D. Second bust,** ss c...........	—	N	
1179	**E. — roses and plumes**.......	—	S	
1180	**F. —** w.c.c. **below**...............	—	R^2	
1181	**E. — roses and plumes**.......	**1724**	S	
1182	**F. —** w.c.c. **below**...............	—	R^2	
1183	**E. — roses and plumes**.......	**1725**	S	
1184	—	—	R	No stops on *obv.*
1185	**F. —** w.c.c. **below**...............	—	R^3	
1186	**E. — roses and plumes**.......	**1726**	R^5	
1187	**F. —** w.c.c. **below**...............	—	R^2	
1188	**E. — roses and plumes**.......	**1727**	R^5	
1188A	—	—	R^5	No stops on *obv.*

[1] These pieces mostly turn up in very worn state; the rarity of a really fine specimen is perhaps R^4.

GEORGE II

Young head   Old head

A   B   F and G   D and E

Type **A**   Type as the early crowns and halfcrowns with the young head. ℞. Plumes in the angles.

B   Young head. ℞. Roses and plumes in the angles.

C   Young head. ℞. Plain in the angles.

D   Young head. ℞. Roses in the angles.

E   As last, but with broader bust with much older features, old head. ℞. Roses in the angles.

F   LIMA below old head. ℞. Plain in the angles.

G   Old head, nothing below bust or in the angles on reverse.

No.	Type	Date	R	Varieties, Remarks, etc.
1189	**A. Young head, plumes**	**1727**	S	
1190	**B. — roses and plumes**.......	—	N	
1191	**C. —**	**1728**	R^2	
1192	**B. — roses and plumes**.......	—	R	
1193	—	**1729**	R	
1194	—	**1731**	S	
1195	**A. — plumes**........................	—	R^2	
1196	**B. — roses and plumes**.......	**1732**	R	
1197	—	**1734**	N	A change to larger lettering
1198	—	**1735**	N	
1199	—	**1736**	N	
1199A	—	—	R^2	6 of date over 5
1200	—	**1737**	N	
1201	**D. — roses**	**1739**	C	
1201A	—	—	R^5	9 of date over 7
1201B	—	—	R^4	Very small Garter Star on reverse
1202	—	**1741**	C	
1202A	—	—	R^5	41 of date over 39
1203	**E. Old head, roses**...............	**1743**	C	
1203A	—	—	R^3	3 of date over 1
1204	—	**1745**	N	
1204A	—	—	R	5 of date over 3
1205	**F. — LIMA below**	—	C^2	
1206	—	**1746**	R^2	See note[1]
1207	—	—	R^2	6 of date over 5. See note[3]
1208	**G. —**......................................	—	R	*Proof only*
1209	**E. — roses**	**1747**	N	
1210	**G. —**	**1750**	N	Thin o in date
1210A	—	—	S	— o of date over 6
1211	—	—	S	Wide o in date, always (?) with 5 over 4
1212	—	**1751**	R^3	
1213	—	**1758**	C^3	Apparently struck for some years

NB. As in the case of other denominations dated 1743 and 1745, read IUS for IVS in GEORGIVS.

---

[1] I feel that the 1746 unaltered date LIMA is not really quite worth R^3, and have reduced it to R^2: the 6 over 5 coin is definitely less rare than the plain date, but scarcer than a reduction to R would indicate, and I have therefore let R^2 stand.

GEORGE III

Type A

Type A As illustration. This is known as the 'Northumberland' shilling. See note[1].

Type B[1]   No hearts   With hearts

B[1] As illustration.
B[2] Similar, but with semée of hearts in the Hanoverian shield.

No.	Type	Date	R	Varieties, Remarks, etc.
1214	**A. Young head**	**1763**	*S*	Called the 'Northumberland' shilling (see note[1])
1215	**B[1] Second type, without hearts**	**1786**	*R*[6]	No stops at date or over head. *Pattern only.*
1216	—	**1787**	*C*[3]	
1217	—	—	*R*[4]	*Proof* with plain edge on thick flan
1218	—	—	*N*	No stop over head
1219	—	—	*R*[2]	*— proof,*
1220	—	—	*R*[3]	*— proof,* plain edge
1221	—	—	*R*[4]	— Heavy flan
1222	—	—	*S*	No stops at date[2]
1223	—	—	*R*[4]	No stops on *obv.*
1224	—	—	*R*[4]	*— proof,* plain edge, stop after GRATIA

[1] So-called as £100 worth of these coins were distributed in Dublin by the Earl of Northumberland on his appointment as Lord Lieutenant. Many more than 2,000 pieces must have been struck, as the coins though scarce are not particularly rare.
[2] It is possible that on this variety the last 7 of 1787 is over a 6.

No.	Type	Date	R	Varieties, Remarks, etc.
1225	B² — with hearts................	—	C³	
1225A	—	—	R²	1 of date over 1 retrograde
1226	—	—	R⁴	Proof, plain edge. Heavy flan, struck without collar
1227	B² variety with hearts	1798	R⁵	No stop over head, large lettering, slightly different bust, known as the 'Dorrien and Magens' shilling. See note[1]

Type C   1232A

Type **C**   Last or new coinage. As illustration.

No.	Type	Date	R	Varieties, Remarks, etc.
1228	C. Laur. head only..............	1816	C²	
1229	—	—	R³	Proof
1230	—	—	R⁷	Proof in gold
1231	—	—	R³	Proof, plain edge
1232	—	1817	C	
1232A	—	—	R³	Reads GEOE:, the E struck over R
1233	—	—	R²	Proof, plain edge
1234	—	1818	S	
1234A	—	—	R	Date recut and second 8 higher
1235	—	1819	N	
1235A	—	—	R	9 of date over 8.
1236	—	1820	N	
1236A	—	—	R³	I of HONI over S
1237	—	—	R²	Proof

[1] 'In 1798 Mr. M. Dorrien Magens and nine other banking firms sent [to the Mint] silver bullion for coinage to the amount of upwards of £30,000. This was partly coined into Shillings, but their issue was prohibited by order of the Lords of the Committee of Council. The name given above is so rendered in the Mint book, but in Lowndes *London Directory* for 1798, the firm is described as Dorrien, Magens, Mello, Martin and Harrison, 22 Finch Lane, Cornhill. Dorrien Magens expressed his sentiments in an anonymous publication of the same year entitled, *'Thoughts upon a new Coinage of Silver.' Royal Mint Museum Catalogue*, Vol. I, p. 158.

1238   1240

Patterns

1238 By Yeo or Tanner, 1764. Very similar to type A above, but with rather finer portrait and with three curls instead of two on the shoulders. *Edge*, plain R^2

1239 — 1775. Similar R^4

1240 — 1778. Similar, but older bust R^3

1241 By Pingo, 1787. As the type B^2 shillings of this date, but with a border of dots each side. *Edge*, plain R

1242A

1242 By Droz, 1787. GEORGIUS . III . D . G . MA . BR . F . ET . H . REX, a tall laureate head of the king r., with long hair and pointed truncation, 1787 below. R. No legend, the royal cypher *GR* crowned within branches. *Edge*, milled R^3

1242A Similar. In Brass (B.M.) R^5

1243 By Milton, 1798. GEORGIVS . III . DEI . GRATIA . REX., very large head with short hair, laur., r., 1798 below. R. M. B . F. ET . H . REX . F . D . B . ET . L . D . S . R . I . A . T . ET . E., large plain shield crowned, with the British and Hanoverian arms in six divisions. *Edge*, plain R^5

1244 Similar. *In copper* R^5

1245

1245 By W. Wyon, undated (1816). GEORGIUS III DEI GRATIA, very much like
the head on the shillings of the final issue but smaller. R. BRITAN-
NIARUM REX FIDEI DEFENSOR, square shield, garnished and crowned, the
colours of the arms are not indicated. *Edge*, milled R^6

GEORGE IV

Type A   *O*. Laur. head, as crown. R. Garnished shield crowned, thistle on l.,
shamrock on r., WWP in centre of the leaves; rose, ANNO and date
below. Initials J.B.M. in border.
   B   *O*. Similar. R. Square-topped shield in Garter, crowned; ANNO and
date below.

A   B

C

C   *O*. GEORGIUS IV DEI GRATIA, bare head l., date below. R. BRITAN-
NIARUM REX FIDEI DEFENSOR, lion on crown, ornament below.
Known as the 'lion' shilling.

No.	Type	Date	R	Varieties, Remarks, etc.
1246	**A. First head, first** *rev.*	**1820**	R^5	*Pattern.* No JBM in border
1247	—	**1821**	N	See note[1]
1248	—	—	R^3	*Proof*
1249	**B. — second** *rev.*	**1823**	R	
1250	—	—	R^4	*Proof*
1251	—	**1824**	N	
1252	—	—	R^4	*Proof*
1253	—	**1825**	N	
1253A	—	—	R^4	*Proof*
1253B	—	—	R^3	5 of date struck over a 3
1254	**C. Second head, lion** *rev.*	—	C	
1254A	—	—	R^7	Roman I in date
1255	—	—	R	*Proof*
1256	—	—	R^5	*Proof*, plain edge. In Barton's metal
1257	—	**1826**	C^2	
1257A	—	—	R^3	6 of date struck over a 2
1258	—	—	S	*Proof*, issued in the sets
1259	—	**1827**	R	
1260	—	**1829**	S	
1261	—	—	R^3	*Proof*

1247
Enlarged to show JBM on border

1262

[1] Considerably scarcer in mint condition.

1262 By W. Wyon and J. B. Merlen, 1824. As type C, but with inner circle. R. BRITANNIARUM REX FID : DEF : and spray, inner circle, square-topped shield, crowned, motto on scroll below. *Edge*, milled R^6

1263 Similar. *Edge*, plain R^6

1263

1264 Similar. 1825. As type C, but reading FID : DEF : , the lion is smaller, and the crown narrower and deeper. *Edge*, milled R^5

1265 Similar. In Barton's metal R^6

WILLIAM IV

Only one type, as illustration.

N.B.—Unless stated, the 3 of date has a straight top.

1266	**1831**	N	*Proof only*, with plain edge, issued in the sets
1267	—	R^4	— milled edge
1268	**1834**	C	
1269	—	R^2	*Proof*
1270	—	R^2	— round top to 3 in date
1271	**1835**	S	
1272	—	R^4	*Proof*, round top to 3 in date
1273	**1836**	N	
1274	—	R^4	*Proof*, round top to 3 in date
1275	—	R^6	— plain edge. *In copper*
1276	**1837**	R	
1277	—	R^4	*Proof*

VICTORIA

A¹   A²

A⁵   A³   A⁷

Type **A¹**   Young head. *O*. VICTORIA DEI GRATIA BRITANNIAR : REG : F : D : , young head, bound with fillet, l., w.w. on truncation. R. As William IV.

A²   Second young head; similar, but slightly larger head and curl at back longer.

A³   As last, but without w.w. (Some of the early dates show traces of the w.w. having been removed from the die).

A⁴   As last, but with die number above the date.

A⁵   Third young head. Another slight change of head; it is in lower relief, slightly larger and hair at the back is varied; also the nose is more pronounced, the mouth fuller and the angle of truncation slightly altered. Very pronounced border beads and rim.

A⁶   As last, but with die number above the date.

A⁷   Fourth young head; older features. From 1880, larger lettering on *rev.*, longer line below SHILLING. From 1885, the line is again shorter, but with a thicker, more 'dumpy' centre than on the earlier coins of this type.

B¹   B²

B¹   Jubilee type. *O*. VICTORIA DEI GRATIA BRITT : REGINA : F : D : , tall bust l., dr. and veiled, with small crown. R. No legend, square-topped shield within Garter, crowned, date below.

B² Similar, but much larger bust and slight changes to reverse type.

Type C   1296 Reverse

C Old head. VICTORIA . DEI . GRA . BRITT . REGINA . FID . DEF . IND .
IMP ., her coronetted old head l., veiled and dr. R. Three shields in
form of trefoil within the Garter; ONE SHILLING above, date below.

D As last, but the rose on the reverse is significantly larger.

N.B.—In the following table the column headed DIE NO. indicates in the first
place whether there is a die number on the coin. The number, where shown, is
the highest die number we have noted for that particular date; there may, however, be higher.

No.	TYPE	DIE No.	DATE	R	VARIETIES, Remarks, etc.
1278	**A¹ Young head**, w.w.	none	**1838**	*S*	
1278A	—	—	—	*R⁴*	Mule **A³/A¹**
1279	—	—	—	*R⁴*	*Proof*
1280	—	—	**1839**	*R*	
1281	—	—	—	*R²*	*Proof*, plain edge
1282	**A² Second young head**, w.w	—	—	*S*	*Proof*, plain edge, from the set
1283	**A³ Second young head, no** w.w.	—	—	*N*	
1284	—	—	—	*R*	*Proof*, plain edge
1284A	—	—	—	*R⁶*	*Proof*, edge milled
1285	—	—	**1840**	*R²*	
1286	—	—	—	*R⁵*	*Proof*
1287	—	—	**1841**	*R*	
1288	—	—	**1842**	*S*	
1289	—	—	—	*R⁵*	*Proof*
1290	—	—	**1843**	*R*	
1291	—	—	**1844**	*S*	
1292	—	—	**1845**	*R*	
1293	—	—	**1846**	*S*	
1294	—	—	**1848**	*R²*	8 of date over 6
1295	—	—	**1849**	*S*	
1296	—	—	**1850**	*R³*	
1297	—	—	—	*R⁴*	50 of date over 49
1298	—	—	**1851**	*R²*	

No.	Type	Die No.	Date	R	Varieties, Remarks, etc.
1299	—	—	**1852**	*S*	
1300	—	—	**1853**	*S*	
1301	—	—	—	*R²*	*Proof*, issued in the sets
1302	—	—	**1854**	*R²*	1302A 1854/1 *R⁴*
1303	—	—	**1855**	*S*	
1304	—	—	**1856**	*S*	
1305	—	—	**1857**	*S*	
1305A	—	—	—	*R⁴*	Reads REG F : Ɔ :
1306	—	—	**1858**	*S*	
1307	—	—	**1859**	*S*	
1307A	—	—	—	*R³*	damaged 8
1308	—	—	**1860**	*R*	
1309	—	—	**1861**	*R*	
1309A	—	—	—	*R³*	D in F : D : over B
1310	—	—	**1862**	*R²*	
1311	—	—	**1863**	*R²*	1311A 1863/1 *R⁴*
1312	**A⁴** —	80	**1864**	*N*	
1313	—	130	**1865**	*N*	
1314	—	70	**1866**	*N*	
1314A	—	63	—	*R³*	Reads BBITANNIAR
1315	—	37	**1867**	*S*	
1316	**A⁵ Third young head**	none	—		Does this exist?
1317	—	—	—	*R⁴*	*Proof*
1317A	—	—	—	*R⁵*	*Proof*, with plain edge
1317B	**A⁶** —	25	—	*R³*	
1318	—	54	**1868**	*N*	
1319	—	15	**1869**	*R*	
1320	—	20	**1870**	*R*	
1321	—	} 56 {	**1871**	*N*	
1322	—		—	*R⁵*	*Proof*
1323	—	19	—	*R⁶*	*Proof*, with plain edge
1324	—	155	**1872**	*C*	
1325	—	141	**1873**	*C*	
1326	—	76	**1874**	*N*	
1327	—	74	**1875**	*N*	
1328	—	36	**1876**	*S*	
1329	—	70	**1877**	*N*	
1330	—	} 76 {	**1878**	*N*	
1331	—		—	*R⁶*	*Proof*
1332	—	} 26 {	**1879**	*R²*	See note on page 135
1333	—		—	*R⁴*	*Proof*
1334	**A⁷ Fourth young head**	none	—	*N*	
1335	—	—	**1880**	*N*	

No.	Type	Die No.	Date	R	Varieties, Remarks, etc.
1336	—	—	—	R^3	*Proof*
1337	—	—	—	R^5	*Proof,* with plain edge
1338	—	—	1881	N	
1338A	—	—	—	N	Shorter line below shilling
1339	—	—	1881	R^4	*Proof*
1340	—	—	—	R^6	*Proof,* with plain edge
1341	—	—	1882	S	
1342	—	—	1883	N	
1343	—	—	1884	N	
1344	—	—	—	R^5	*Proof*
1345	—	—	1885	N	
1346	—	—	—	R^5	*Proof*
1347	—	—	1886	N	
1348	—	—	—	R^7	*Proof*
1349	—	—	1887	S	
1350	—	—	—	R^5	*Proof*
1351	B¹ Jubilee head	—	—	C^3	
1352	—	—	—	S	*Proof,* issued in the sets
1353	—	—	1888	S	
1354	—	—	1889	R^2	
1355	B² — large	—	—	N	
1356	—	—	—	R^3	*Proof*
1357	—	—	1890	N	
1358	—	—	1891	N	
1359	—	—	—	R^5	*Proof*
1360	—	—	1892	N	
1361	C Old head	—	1893	C	
1361A	—	—	—	N	Smaller lettering on *obv*
1362	—	—	—	N	*Proof,* issued in the sets
1363	—	—	1894	N	
1364	—	—	1895	R^2	
1364A	D Old head	—	—	N	
1365	—	—	1896	N	
1365A	C —	—	—	R^3	
1366	D —	—	1897	N	
1367	—	—	1898	N	
1368	—	—	1899	N	
1369	—	—	1900	N	
1370	—	—	1901	N	

1317B
Pellet over die no.
peculiar to third Young Head

1326

Patterns

1371   By W. Wyon, 1839. As the current coin but reverse is ruled with fine
       horizontal lines R^5

1372   By Ch. W. Wiener and Wyon, 1863. *O.* VICTORIA DEI GRATIA BRITAN-
       NIAR : REG : F : D :, head of Queen l. wearing wreath composed of
       roses, shamrocks and thistles, two tie ends on neck. R. As current coin.
       Edge, plain R^3

1373   Similar, but different features and without the tie ends, also with C.H.W.
       on neck in raised letters R^3

1374

1374   Similar, but with coronetted head, back hair looped with pearls, C.H.W.
       incuse on neck R^3

1375   Similar, VICTORIA DEI GRATIA, as last but C.H.W. raised R^3

1376   By Wiener and Taylor, 1863. *O.* VICTORIA DEI GRATIA 1863, small
       crowned bust dr. l., ornamental border. R. . HALF . . FLO . . RIN . .
       1863 ., square-topped shield, crowned, in tressure over cross. *Edge*,
       plain R

1377   Similar, *O.* VICTORIA REGINA, coronetted head l., C.W. on neck. R. As
       last. *Edge*, plain R

1377A Similar. Edge milled R^2

1378   Similar. *In copper* R

1378A Similar. *Edge*, milled R^4

1379   Similar. In copper R

1380   Similar, but VICTORIA DEI GRATIA. *Edge*, plain R

1380A Similar. *Edge*, milled R^3

---

[1] Tower Hill shillings, up to No. 1332, were struck on Boulton presses using hand finished dies.
Each die was worked over by a die improver who sharpened up on details of engraving, over-
punched indistinct letters and added the last two figures of the date. This explains various errors.

1381

1381	Similar. *In copper*	R
1382	As last, but wreathed head. *Edge*, plain	R
1383	Similar. *In copper*	R
1384	— 1865. *O.* VICTORIA DEI GRATIA, coronetted head, C.W. on neck. R. HALF FLORIN divided by two ornaments, MDCC CLXV, design as before. *Edge*, plain	R
1385	Similar. *In copper*	R
1385A	Similar. *Edge*, milled	R^4
1386	Similar, but wreathed head. *Edge*, plain	R
1387	Similar. *In copper*	R
1388	As 1384, but VICTORIA REGINA. *Edge*, plain	R
1389	Similar. *In copper*	R
1390	Similar. *Edge*, milled. *In copper*	R
1391	By Wiener and Taylor, undated. As 1384. R. Shield in Garter crowned. *Edge*, plain	R
1392	Similar. *In copper*	R
1393	Similar, but wreathed head. *Edge*, plain	R
1394	Similar. *In copper*	R
1395	As 1391, but VICTORIA REGINA. *Edge*, plain	R
1396	Similar. *In copper*	R
1397	Undated. *O.* As 1384. R. No legend, garnished shield of arms, crowned within Garter. *Edge*, plain	R
1397A	Similar. *Edge*, milled	R^2

1398   1401

1398	*O.* As 1386. In imitation of engraving, small shield of arms within Garter, crowned, motto on riband beneath, scroll ornament in field, the whole on groundwork of horizontal lines. *Edge*, plain	R^4
1399	*O.* As 1388. R. ONE SHILLING stamped incusely on a broad engine-turned and raised border, large figure 1 also engine-turned in centre, W.J.T. beneath. *Edge*, plain	R^4

1400   *O.* Similar, but VICTORIA DEI GRATIA, and the initials CH.W. incuse. **R.** As last. *Edge*, plain R^4

1401   By W. Wyon and Pistrucci, 1875. *O.* As the current young head shillings. **R.** Pistrucci's St. George, date in exergue. *Edge*, plain R^6

1402   Similar. *Edge*, milled R^6

1403   Similar, but without date or beaded border on *rev.* R^5

1403A   Similar. In aluminium R^6

1404   By L. C. Wyon, 1875. *O.* VICTORIA DEI GRATIA BRITANNIAR : REG : F : D :, coronetted head left. **R.** As 1401. *Edge*, milled R^6

1404A   Similar but edge plain R^6

1405   By W. Wyon and W. J. Taylor, 1880. *O.* As the current young head shillings. **R.** No legend, crowned shield in Garter, as the Geo. III last issue shilling, but without the Hanoverian arms in centre. *Edge*, plain R^6

1406   By L. C. Wyon, 1887. As the usual Jubilee shillings but date is above the crown, and ONE SHILLING is at the bottom; the Garter is not quite the same. *Edge*, milled R^7

1407   1888. *O.* As last. **R.** Square shield, crowned, within the Garter. ONE SHILLING above in larger lettering than last, date below. *Edge*, milled R^7

1408   *O.* As last. **R.** ONE SHILLING above a plain square shield, crowned, scroll with motto and date below R^7

1409   *O.* As the large head Jubilee shillings. **R.** As 1406, but ONE SHILLING in smaller letters R^7

EDWARD VII

Only one type, as illustration.

1410	**1902**	N		1415	**1906**	N	
1411	—	N	*Proof*, matt surface	1416	**1907**	S	
1412	**1903**	R		1417	**1908**	R	
1413	**1904**	R		1418	**1909**	S	
1414	**1905**	R^2		1419	**1910**	N	

Note: Rarities indicated for coins of Edward VII only apply to EF specimens. Worn pieces are fairly easy to obtain apart 1904 and 1905, which are probably R even in low grade, and R^3 in EF or better condition. Mint state examples of all dates other than 1902 or 1910 are becoming increasingly difficult to find.

GEORGE V

A   C and D   D

Type **A** *O*. GEORGIVS V DEI GRA : BRITT : OMN : REX, head l., B.M. on truncation. R. As last, but beaded border.

     B Similar, but only 50% silver and 50% alloy.

     C *O*. Modified effigy, slightly smaller, BM nearer to back of neck,
more pronounced beading. R. Similar, but beading more pronounced.

     D *O*. Similar. R. New type. As before but without inner circle, larger
lion and crown and single stops in legend.

No.	TYPE	DATE	R	VARIETY, Remarks, etc.
1420	**A. .925 silver**........................	**1911**	*C*	
1421	—	—	*S*	*Proof*
1422	—	**1912**	*N*	
1423	—	**1913**	*N*	
1424	—	**1914**	*N*	
1425	—	**1915**	*N*	
1426	—	**1916**	*N*	
1427	—	**1917**	*N*	
1428	—	**1918**	*N*	
1429	—	**1919**	*N*	
1430	**B. 'debased' .500**...............	**1920**	*N*	* See Appendix II
1431	—	**1921**	*S*	* See Appendix II
1432	—	**1922**	*S*	
1433	—	**1923**	*N*	
1433A	—	—	R^4	Nickel[1]
1434	—	**1924**	*R*	
1434A	—	—	R^4	Nickel[1]
1435	—	**1925**	*R*	
1436	—	**1926**	*S*	
1437	**C. Modified effigy**...............	—	*S*	
1438	—	**1927**	*S*	

[1] Nickel shillings of 1923 and 1924 are trial pieces, struck when the introduction of nickel coinage
was being considered. See also 2149A.

1439	**D. New type**	1927	*S*	
1440	—	—	*N*	*Proof*
1440A	—	—	*R⁷*	*Matt proof*
1441	—	1928	*N*	
1442	—	1929	*N*	
1443	—	1930	*R*	
1444	—	1931	*S*	
1445	—	1932	*N*	
1446	—	1933	*N*	
1447	—	1934	*N*	
1448	—	1935	*N*	
1449	—	1936	*C*	**Edw. VIII**

1449A *Pattern*, 1925. As the fourth coinage, current coin. In nickel but lion's
tail slightly different style. R

The rarities given for first and second coinage pieces apply only to coins in
Good EF condition; strictly mint state (BU) coins are becoming difficult to
obtain, and are somewhat scarcer than the rarities given here.

EDWARD VIII

1449B *O*. As the other coins. **R**. As the 'Scottish' shillings of George VI[1] R^6

---

[1] No 'English' shilling of Edward VIII was struck. A pattern 'Scottish' shilling was offered in
May 1992 for £20,000.

GEORGE VI

Type A   Type B

Type E   Type F

Type A *O*. As the other denominations. R. Somewhat similar to the last
issue of George V but date in field divided by crown and two roses
in the legend. Known as the English shilling.

B *O*. Similar. R. FID : DEF . IND : IMP ONE . SHILLING, crowned lion,
holding sword and sceptre, seated facing on crown between date
and two small Scottish shields, one bearing cross of St. Andrew and
the other a thistle. Known as the Scottish shilling.

C and D As A and B, but struck in cupro-nickel, closer milling on edge.

E and F As last, but new types without IND : IMP

1450	**A. .500 Æ**	1937	*N*	Note[1]	1464	**A.** —		1943	*C*	
1451	—	—	*S*	*Proof*	1465	**B.** —		—	*C*	
1452	**B. .500 Æ**	1937	*N*		1466	**A.** —		1944	*C*	
1453	—	—	*S*	*Proof*	1467	**B.** —		—	*C*	
1454	**A.** —	1938	*S*	Note[4]	1468	**A.** —		1945	*C*[2]	
1455	**B.** —	—	*S*		1469	**B.** —			*C*[2]	
1456	**A.** —	1939	*S*		1470	**A.** —		1946	*C*[2]	
1457	**B.** —	—	*S*		1470A	—		—	*R*[6]	Note[2]
1458	**A.** —	1940	*C*		1471	**B.** —			*C*[2]	
1459	**B.** —	—	*C*		1472	**C. Cu.-Ni.**		1947	*N*	Note[3]
1460	**A.** —	1941	*C*		1473	**D.** —		1947	*N*	
1461	**B.** —	—	*C*		1474	**C.** —		1948	*N*	
1462	**A.** —	1942	*C*		1475	**D.** —		—	*N*	
1463	**B.** —	—	*C*							

[1] Coins of George VI are only as rare as marked in uncirculated condition.

[2] *Pattern or proof*, in Cu.-Ni. See note[1] on p. 91.

[3] A small number of these shillings were struck in .500 Æ. See B.M. collection. They are
extremely rare.

[4] See page 91 Note 3.

Note: Matt proofs of 1937 English and Scottish shillings exist and are extremely rare.

1475A	E. — **New type**	1949	N		1475F	—	—	S	Proof
1475B	F. —	—	N		1475G	E. —	1951	N	
1475C	E. —	1950	N		1475H	—	—	R	Proof
1475D	—	—	S	Proof	1475I	F. —	—	N	
1475E	F. —	—	N		1475*	E. —	1952	R⁷	Proof

Note. Proofs from sandblasted dies known, 1950–1951.

ELIZABETH II

Type A   Type B   Type C

Type A   *O.* As halfcrown. R. Crowned shield bearing the three leopards of England dividing date. Known as the English shilling.

     B   As last, but the shield bears the Scottish lion rampant. Known as the Scottish shilling.

     C   As A, but the *obv.* legend ends DEI . GRATIA . REGINA

     D   *O.* As last. R. As B.

1475K	A. Cu-ni.	1953	N		1475z	D. —	—	R		
1475L	—	—	N	Proof	1475AA	C. —	1960	C²		
1475L	**Bis**	—	R⁶	See note¹	1475BB	D. —	—	C²		
1475M	B. —	—	N		1475CC	C. —	1961	C³		
1475N	—	—	N	Proof	1475DD	D. —	—	S		
1475o	C. —	1954	C		1475EE	C. —	1962	C³		
					1475FF	D. —		C³		
1475P	D. —	—	C		1475GG	C. —	1963	C³		
1475Q	C. —	1955	C		1475HH	D. —	—	C³		
1475R	D. —	—	C		1475II	C. —	1964	C³		
1475s	C. —	1956	C		1475JJ	D. —	—	C³		
1475T	D. —	—	C		1475KK	C. —	1965	C³		
1475U	C. —	1957	C²		1475LL	D. —	—	C³		
1475V	D. —	—	C²		1475MM	C. —	1966	C³		
1475W	C. —	1958	C²		1475NN	D. —	—	C³	Note²
1475X	D. —	—	C²		1475oo	C. —	1970	R	Proof
1475Y	C. —	1959	C²		1475PP	D. —	—	R	Proof

¹ Shillings from sand-blasted dies with matt finish exist.

² These coins are found with an inverted reverse. Since they were the last coins to be struck at Tower Hill it is most likely that they were struck unofficially as mementos.

142

TENPENCE
VICTORIA

Pattern
1476   By L. C. Wyon, 1867. *O.* VICTORIA D : G : BRITANNIAR : REG : F : D : ,
       bust of the Queen in coronet to left, 1867 below. **R.** ONE FRANC TEN
       PENCE, square shield, crowned, in wreath. *Edge*, plain   *R*³

NINEPENCE¹
GEORGE III

Pattern Bank Tokens
1478   By T. Wyon Junior, 1812. GEORGIUS III DEI GRATIA REX, his laur. head r.
       R. BANK TOKEN 9D. 1812 in wreath of oak and olive. *Edge*, plain.
       Davis 71   *R*³
1479   Similar. *In copper. D.* 72   *R*⁴
1480   Similar, but 9 PENCE. *D.*—   *R*⁶

EIGHTPENCE
GEORGE V

1481   1482

Patterns
1481   By Huth, 1913. GEORGIVS V DEI GRATIA, draped bust l. **R.** BRI 1913 REX
       OCTORINO, cruciform shields, etc.²   *R*³
1481A Similar. *In copper*   *R*⁴
1482   EIGHT PENCE instead of OCTORINO   *R*³
1482A Similar. *In copper*   *R*⁴

---

¹ I have left out the Cromwell 'ninepences' intentionally as we consider them to be 'Tanner' sixpences on thick flans. (See note² on p. 144).
² These coins exist in gold, platinum and nickel on flans of varying thickness; all are *R*⁴.

SIXPENCES

THE COMMONWEALTH

Type B

Type **A**   As the larger coins with *mm.* sun, but mark of value . VI .
   B   Similar, but *mm.* anchor.

No.	Type	Date	R	Varieties, Remarks, etc.
1483	**A.** *Mm.* **sun**	**1649**	*S*	
1484	—	**1651**	*N*	
1484A	—	—	*R*	No stops at *mm.*
1485	—	—	*R*	51 of date over 49[1]
1485A	—	—	*R*	No stop after COMMONWEALTH
1486	—	**1652**	*N*	
1486A	—	—	*R*	No stops on reverse
1487	—	—	*R*	52 of date over 49
1487A	—	—	*R*	2 of date over 1
1487B	—	—	*R*⁵	Reads COMMMONWEALTH[2]
1488	—	**1653**	*S*	
1488A	—	—	*R*	No stop after THE
1489	—	**1654**	*R*	
1490	—	—	*R*²	4 of date over 3
1491	—	**1655**	*R*³	
1492	—	**1656**	*S*	
1492A	—	—	*R*	Only stops on obv. are at *mm.*
1493	—	**1657**	*R*⁵	7 of date over 6
1493A	—	—	*R*⁵	— NGLAN over GLAND
1494	**B.** *Mm.* **anchor**	**1658**	*R*³	
1494A	—	—	*R*³	Colon after ENGLAND
1495	—	—	*R*³	8 of date over 7
1495A	—	—	*R*⁴	D of ENGLAND over D inverted
1496	—	**1659**	*R*⁶	
1497	—	**1660**	*R*³	
1497A	—	—	*R*⁴	No stop after THE

[1] This obverse die occurs paired with reverse dies dated 52 over 49, and what appears to be 52 over 51 over 49.

[2] We have seen two examples of this '3M' spelling error. Each is from a different reverse die, one clearly reading 1652/1/49, the other 1652/49 but it is unclear if also over a 1. The obverse die was also used for a half unite in gold (ex Lockett Collection).

1498

Patterns

1498   By Blondeau, 1651. Type as the ordinary sixpence, but of much neater
      workmanship and struck in a press. *Edge*, milled R^2
1498A Similar. On thinner flan. *Edge*, plain R^4

1499

1499   By Ramage, 1651. As illustration. *Edge*, * TRVTH * AND * PEACE *
      1651 between two rows of beading R^5
1500   Similar. *In gold* R^7
1501   Similar. *Edge*, plain. *In copper* R^6
1502   Similar. *Edge*, * * * * * * etc., between two rows of beading[1] R^7
1503   Similar. *In copper, plated* R^7

CROMWELL

Patterns

1504   By Simon, 1658. *O.* OLIVAR . D . G . R P . ANG . SCO . HIB &C PRO, his
      laur. bust dr. l., laurel leaf points to first limb of A., four berries in
      wreath. *R.* As other denominations. *Edge*, milled R^6
1504A Similar. *Edge*, plain. *In pewter* R^7
1505   *Dutch copy (usually called Tanner's).* Similar, but HIB . PRO, no &C,
      laurel leaf points to P., no berries in wreath. *Edge*, milled[2] R^5
1506   Similar. *Edge*, plain R^4

---

[1] No. 1502 is probably not in silver, but silver-plated copper i.e. 1502 and 1503 are the same coin.
   They are in the B.M. and only a specific gravity test could determine their metal content.
[2] These are on flans varying greatly in weight and thickness. The heavier pieces were at one time
   regarded as ninepences.

CHARLES II

Type A   Type B   Type C

Hammered Coinage
Type **A** or first hammered coinage. As illustration, without mark of value or
    inner circles.
B or second hammered coinage. As illustration, with mark of value but
    still no inner circles.
C or third hammered coinage. As illustration, with mark of value and
    inner circles.

Milled Coinage

Type D

D   One type only, as illustration. *Edge*, milled.

No.	Type	Date	R	Varieties, Remarks, etc.
1507	**A. No value or inner circles**	none	R	
1508	**B. Value, no circles**.............	—	R^5	Reads HIB
1509	—....................................	—	R^5	Reads HI
1510	**C. Value and circles**...........	—	S	
1511	—....................................	—	R^6	On thicker flan (B.M.)
				Possibly from fillet for
				shilling blank
1512	**D. Milled coinage**...............	**1674**	N	
1513	—....................	**1675**	N	
1514	—....................................	—	R	5 of date over 4
1515	—....................................	**1676**	R	
1515A	—....................................	—	R	6 of date over 5
1516	—....................................	**1677**	N	
1517	—....................................	**1678**	R	8 of date over 7
1518	—....................................	**1679**	R	
1519	—....................................	**1680**	R^2	

No.	Type	Date	R	Varieties, Remarks, etc.
1520	**D. Milled coinage**...............	**1681**	N	
1521	—..................................	**1682**	R^2	
1522	—..................................	—	R	2 of date over 1
1523	—..................................	**1683**	N	
1524	—..................................	**1684**	S	See note[1]

JAMES II

Type A   A   B

Type **A**   *O*. As illustration. R. As illustration, shields of early shape.
     B   *O*. As last. R. Later shape of shields.

No.	Type	Date	R	Varieties, Remarks, etc.
1525	**A. Early shields**..................	**1686**	S	
1526	—..................................	**1687**	R	
1526A	—..................................	—	R	7 of date over 6
1526B	**B. Later shields**..................	—	S	
1526C	—..................................	—	R^2	Later shields, altered from early shields
1527	—..................................	—	R	— 7 of date over 6
1528	—..................................	**1688**	R^2	Later shields, altered from early shields. See note[1]

[1] Sixpences of Charles II, James II and William and Mary are not uncommon in average condition. In EF or better grades they are much rarer than indicated here.

WILLIAM AND MARY

Only one type. As illustration.

No.	Date	R	Varieties, Remarks, etc.
1529	**1693**	N	
1530	—	R^3	3 of date upside down
1531	**1694**	R^2	See note[1]

---

[1] Sixpences of Charles II, James II and William and Mary are not uncommon in average condition. In EF or better grades they are much rarer than indicated here.

WILLIAM III

Type i　　　　　　Type iv　　　　　　Type vi

Type **i**　First bust, the back hair curls outwards above and below the crown of the head at back. **R.** Usual type with cruciform shields, the Irish shield has the 'early' harp with the female bust very high and the right hand corner of harp low; the crowns are large, being as wide as the shield.

　ii　Similar, but with 'later' harp. On this variety both top corners of the harp are more in line.

　iii　As last, but with small crowns, not as wide as the shield.

　iv　Second bust. This has a larger head and two locks of hair spread right across the breast, and is in very low relief.[1]

　v　Third bust, large crowns. This bust has the hair at back turning downwards and inwards; it also has a longer tie.

　vi　Third bust, small crowns.

　　　B (*for Bristol*) below bust
　　　C (*for Chester*) below bust
　　　E (*for Exeter*) below bust
　　　N (*for Norwich*) below bust
　　　y or **Y** (*for York*) below bust

　　　　　　Combined with type i, ii, iii, v or vi

Type vii　　　　　　Type viii

　vii　As v, but with plumes in angles of reverse.
　viii　As v, but with roses in angles of reverse.
　ix　Small plume below third bust; large crowns.

---

[1] There is a second bust sixpence of much finer style in the National Collection. This is undoubtedly a pattern together with the crown and halfcrown (E.S.C. 93 and 540) of similar style. (See 'The Second Bust Coinage of William III', by P. Alan Rayner, *SCMB*, 1954).

No.		Type	Crowns	Date	R	Varieties, Remarks, etc.
1532	i.	Early harp, first bust..	Large	1695	R	
1533		—	—	1696	C^2	
1533A		—	—	—	R	No stops on *obverse*
1534		—	—	—	R^2	Second 6 of date over 5
1534A		—	—	—	R^5	On heavy flan
1534B		—	—	—	R^4	Shield of Scotland at date
1534C		—	—	—	R^7	Shield of France at date
1534D		—	—	—	R^4	Reads DFI[1]
1535		— B below................	—	—	N	
1535A		—	—	—	S	B altered from E
1536		— C —	—	—	S	
1537		— E —	—	—	R	
1538		— N —	—	—	S	
1539		— y —	—	—	C	
1540		— Y —	—	—	R	
1541		—	—	—	R^2	No stops on *obverse*
1542	v/i.	— third bust, Y below	Large	—	R^7	A mule
1542A		— E below................	—	—	R^7	A mule
1543	ii.	Later harp, first bust..	—	—	R^2	
1544		—	—	—	R^3	No stops on *rev.*
1545	iii.	—	Small	—	R^3	
1546	ii.	— B below................	Large	—	R^3	
1546A		—	—	—	R^3	No stops on *obv.*
1547	iii.	—	Small	—	R^2	
1548		—	—	—	R^3	No stops on *obv.*
1548A		— C below	—	—	R^4	
1548B		— E below................	—	—	R^3	E is very small
1549		— N below	—	—	R^3	
1550	iv.	— Second bust............	—	—	R^4	
1551		—	—	—	R^5	Reads GVLELMVS
1552	iii.	— First bust................	—	1697	C	
1552A		—	—	—	R^6	Struck on a shilling blank
1552B		—	—	—	R^5	Arms of France and Ireland transposed
1553		—	—	—	R^3	Reads GVLIELMVS
1554	ii.	— B below................	Large	—	R	
1555	iii.	—	Small	—	N	
1555A		—	—	—	N	B altered from E

[1] From an F. punch with both serifs, not a broken E punch or from a clogged die.

No.		Type	Crowns	Date	R	Varieties, Remarks, etc.
1556	**ii.**	**— C below**	Large	—	R^2	
1557	**iii.**	**—**	Small	—	N	
1558		**—**	—	—	R^5	Irish shield at date
1559	**ii.**	**— E below**	Large	—	R	
1560	**iii.**	**—**	Small	—	S	
1560A		**—**	—	—	R^4	E over B below bust
1561		**— N below**	—	—	N	
1561A		**—**	—	—	R^5	Reads GVLIEMVS
1562		**— y below**	—	—	R	
1563		**—**	—	—	R^5	Irish shield at date
1564	**iv.**	**Later harp, second bust**	Small	1697	R^2	See note[1]
1564A		**—**	—	—	R^4	GR in GRA struck over DE
1565		**—**	—	—	R^4	Reads GVLIEMVS
1565A		**—**	—	—	R^4	Reads GVLIELMVS
1565B		**—**	—	—	R^4	G of GRA over I and reads GVLIELMVS
1566	**v.**	**— Third bust**	Large	—	C^2	
1566B		**—**	—	—	R^4	Reads GVLIELMVS
1566C		**—**	—	—	R^3	Reads GVLIEIMVS
1567	**vi.**	**—**	Small	—	R	
1567A		**—**	—	—	R^3	G of GRA over D
1568	**v.**	**— B below**	Large	—	R	
1568A		**—**	—	—	R^4	Reads IRA for FRA
1569		**— C below**	—	—	R^3	
1570	**vi.**	**—**	Small	—	R^3	
1571	**v.**	**— E below**	Large	—	R^3	
1572	**vi.**	**—**	Small	—	R	
1573		**— Y below**	—	—	R^2	
1574	**v.**	**—**	Large	1698	N	
1575	**vii.**	**— plumes on** *rev.*	—	—	R	
1576	**v.**	**—**	—	1699	R^3	
1577	**vii.**	**— plumes on** *rev.*	—	—	S	
1578	**viii.**	**— roses on** *rev.*	—	—	R^2	
1578A		**—**	—	—	R^4	Reads GVLIELMVS
1579	**v.**	**—**	—	1700	N	
1580	**ix.**	**— plume below**	—	—	R^6	
1581	**v.**	**—**	—	1701	S	

Note. There are a great number of error readings on sixpences of this reign.

[1] I have increased the rarity to R^2. This coin is quite scarce even in poor state, and notoriously difficult to find in VF or better, when the rarity would perhaps be R^4.

ANNE

Type A

Before Union with Scotland

Type **A** As illustration, VIGO below bust and plain in angles of reverse; top centre of each shield indented.

B Similar, but plain below bust.

C¹ As last, but with a plume in each angle of the reverse.

C² Similar, but top centre of each shield turns up.

Type C¹   Type D   Early Shield   Late Shield

D Similar, but roses and plumes alternately in the angles.

After Union with Scotland

Type F   Type I   Type J   Type E

E As type B, but with 'After Union' reverse, with the top and bottom shields bearing the arms of England and Scotland impaled.

F Similar, but **E** for *Edinburgh* below bust.

G Similar, but **E★** for *Edinburgh* below bust

H As last with **E★**, but '*Edinburgh*' bust, cruder style, more pointed nose, two top curls thicker and taller.

I As type E, but with a plume in each angle of reverse.

J Similar, but roses and plumes alternately in the angles.

No.	Type	Date	R	Varieties, Remarks, etc.
	Before Union Reverse			
1582	A. VIGO **below bust**	**1703**	*C*	
1583	B. **Plain below bust**	**1705**	*R*²	
1584	C¹ — **plumes on** *rev.*	—	*N*	Shields shaped as last two
1584A	C² —	—	*R*	Shields shaped as next two
1585	D. — **roses and plumes**	—	*S*	
1586	—	**1707**	*S*	
	After Union Reverse			
1587	E. **Plain**	—	*N*	
1587A	—	—	*R*²	Reads BR . FRA as on 'Before Union' coins
1588	F. E **below bust**	—	*S*	
1589	—	—	*R*⁴	*Proof*, with plain edge
1590	I. **Plumes on** *rev.*	—	*S*	
1591	E. **Plain**	**1708**	*S*	
1592	F. E **below bust**	—	*R*	
1592A	—	—	*R*³	8 of date over 7
1593	G. E* **below bust**	—	*R*	
1593A	—	—	*R*²	8 of date over 7
1593B	H. E* **below 'Edinburgh' bust**	—	*R*	
1594	I. — **Plumes on** *rev.*	—	*R*	
1595	J. **Roses and plumes**	**1710**	*R*	See note[1]
1596	E. **Plain**	**1711**	*C*²	Lis 2.2 mm. high
1596A	—	—	*C*²	Larger lis in arms (2.6 mm. high)

Note: Coins of 1705 occur mainly weakly struck. It is difficult to find well struck coins in better than fine condition.

There are a large number of local reverse dies made at Edinburgh, occurring mainly on 1593 and 1593B.

---

[1] This coin is notoriously difficult to obtain in good condition and is usually weakly struck: a piece better than 'VF' would be at least *R*².

GEORGE I

| Type A | Type B | Type C |

Type A General type as the larger denominations; roses and plumes on reverse.

    B Similar, but SS C in angles of reverse.

    C As type A, but smaller roses and plumes.

1597	**A. Roses and plumes**...........	**1717**	*R*	
1598	—	—	*R*⁴	See note[1]
1599	—	**1720**	*R*	20 of date altered from 17
1600	**B. SS C on** *rev.*	**1723**	*C*	Small lettering on *obv.*
1601	—	—	*R*	Large lettering both sides
1602	**C. Small roses and plumes**	**1726**	*R*	

GEORGE II

| Type A | Type B | Type C |

Type A As the other early coins with 'young head' bust; plain in angles of reverse.

    B Young head. R. Plumes in the angles.

    C Young head. R. Roses and plumes in the angles.

    D Young head. R. Roses in the angles.

---

[1] Sixpences of 1717 with a plain edge are currency coins which were not put through the edging machine. See Dyer and Gaspar, *Plain-Edged Sixpence* of 1717, SNC 1983, pp. 6–7.

Type E   Type F   Type G

E   Old head; a broader bust with much older features. R. Roses in the angles.

F   LIMA below old head. R. Plain in the angles.

G   Old head. R. Plain in the angles.

1603	**A. Young head**	**1728**	R^2	
1604	—	—	R^4	*Proof*, with plain edge
1605	**B.** — **plumes on** *rev.*	—	S	
1606	**C. Roses and plumes**...........	—	N	
1607	—	**1731**	N	
1608	—	**1732**	N	
1609	—	**1734**	R^2	
1610	—	**1735**	R^2	
1610A	—	—	R^3	5 of date over 4
1611	—	**1736**	R	
1612	**D.** — **Roses on** *rev.*	**1739**	N	
1612A	—	—	R^3	O in GEORGIVS over R
1613	—	**1741**	N	
1614	**E.** — **Old head, roses**.........	**1743**	N	
1615	—	**1745**	S	
1616	—	—	R^2	5 of date over 3
1617	**F.** LIMA **below old head**.......	—	S	
1618	—	**1746**	C^2	
1618A	—	—	R^2	6 of date over 5
1619	**G.** — **Old head, plain**.........	—	R^2	*Proof only*
1620	—	**1750**	S	
1621	—	**1751**	R^2	
1622	—	**1757**	C^3	
1623	—	**1758**	C^3	
1624	—	—	R	8 of date over 7
1624A	—	—	R^3	Stop in centre of D in DEI

NB. As with the coins of other denominations dated 1743 and 1745 read IUS for IVS in GEORGIVS.

GEORGE III

Type A   Type B

Type **A**[1] As type B shilling, cruciform shields with crown in each angle.
   A[2] Similar, but with semée of hearts in the Hanoverian shield.
   B Last or new coinage. *O.* GEOR : III D : G : BRITT : REX F : D :, laur.
head r., date below. R. Garnished shield, crowned, within Garter.

1625	A[1] **First type, without hearts**	**1786**	R^6	*Pattern only*
1626	—	**1787**	C^3	
1627	—	—	R^2	*Proof*, with plain edge
1628	—	—	R^4	*Proof*, with plain edge on heavy flan
1629	A[2] **— with hearts**.................	—	C^3	
1630	**B. Last or new coinage**.......	**1816**	C^2	
1631	—	—	R^7	*Proof in gold*
1631A	—	—	R^5	*Proof*
1632	—	**1817**	C	
1633	—	—	R^2	*Proof*, with plain edge
1633A	—	—	R^4	*Proof*, milled edge
1634	—	**1818**	S	
1635	—	—	R^3	*Proof*
1636	—	**1819**	S	
1636A	—	—	R	8 of date very small
1636B	—	—	R	9 of date over 8, *proof*
1637	—	—	R^2	*Proof*
1638	—	**1820**	S	
1639	—	—	R^2	*Proof*
1639A	—	—	R^4	1 of date inverted

1640

Patterns

1640   By Pingo, 1787. As the current sixpence of this date with hearts, but
       with border of dots each side. *Edge*, plain   S
1640A As last, but without hearts   R²
1641   By ? 1787. *O*. GEO : III . D . G . REX., laur. bust cuir. r., dot below. R. No
       legend, star of the Garter. *Edge*, plain   R³
1642   By Droz, 1788. *O*. No legend, the royal cypher, *G R* crowned, within
       laurel branches. R. BRITANNIA, Britannia seated, date in ex. *Edge*,
       milled   S
1643   Similar. *In gold*   R⁶
1644   Similar. *In copper*   R⁴
1645   1790. Similar, but rather smaller, and date in legend instead of in ex-
       ergue. *Edge*, plain   N
1646   Similar. *Edge*, milled   N
1647   1791. Similar to last, but date in ex. *Edge*, plain   R
1648   Similar. *In gold*   R⁶
1649   Similar. *In copper*   R²
1650   Similar. Undated. As no. 1645 but composed of two obverses.   R⁵
1651   By T. Wyon, 1816. GEORGIVS III DEI GRATIA, laur. head r., rather as the
       current coin but a little smaller. R. BRITT . REX FID . DEF., shield in
       Garter crowned, date above the Garter divided by the crown. *Edge*,
       milled   R⁵
1652   Similar. *Edge*, plain   R⁵

GEORGE IV

Type A   Type B   Type C

Type A   *O*. GEORGIUS IIII D : G : BRITANNIAR : REX F : D : , his laur. head l., B.P.
below. R. Ornately garnished shield, crowned, between rose, thistle
and shamrock, ANNO and date below.
     B   *O*. Similar. R. Square-topped shield, crowned, in Garter, ANNO and
date below.
     C   *O*. GEORGIUS IV DEI GRATIA, bare head left, date below. R. As the last
issue shillings, lion on a crown.

No.	TYPE	DATE	R	VARIETIES, Remarks, etc
1653	**A. First head, first** *rev.*	**1820**	R^6	*Pattern or proof only*
1654	—	**1821**	*C*	
1655	—	—	R^2	*Proof*
1656	—	—	R^3	Reads BBITANNIAR[1]
1657	**B. — second** *rev.*	**1824**	*N*	
1658	—	—	R^3	*Proof*
1659	—	**1825**	*C*	
1659A	—	—	R^4	*Proof.* See note[2]
1660	—	**1826**	R^2	
1661	—	—	R^3	*Proof*
1662	**C. Second head, third** *rev.*...	—	*C*	See note[1] on page 158
1663	—	—	*S*	*Proof*, issued in the sets
1663A	—	—	R^5	*Proof in pewter*, on thick flan
1664	—	**1827**	R^2	
1665	—	**1828**	*S*	
1666	—	**1829**	*N*	
1667	—	—	R^4	*Proof*

Patterns
1668   By W. Wyon, 1825. As type C, but reads FID : DEF : (instead of FIDEI
DEFENSOR) and the lion and crown are rather narrower R^7
1669   Similar. 1826. As type B, but the bust is smaller R^6

---

[1] The first B was struck from a broken punch and when an attempt was made to strengthen it a
new B was mistakenly struck over the second letter, giving the appearance of BBITANNIAR,
although the original R shows through (below on the die, above on the coin).
[2] A proof in Barton's metal might turn up some day as all other denominations of this date are
known.

WILLIAM IV

Type as illustration. All 3s of date have straight tops except where noted.

1670	1831	N	
1671	—	R²	Proof
1672	—	S	Proof, with plain edge, issued in the sets
1672A	—	R⁷	Proof on very thin flan. 30 grs
1673	—	R⁷	Proof, with plain edge, In palladium
1674	1834	C	
1674A	—	R	Date in large numerals
1674B	—	R³	Proof
1675	—	R⁴	Proof, round-topped 3 in date
1676	1835	S	
1677	—	R⁶	Proof, round-topped 3 in date
1678	1836	R²	
1679	—	R⁶	Proof, round-topped 3 in date
1680	1837	S	
1681	—	R⁶	Proof

---

[1] There are two varieties of bust on the third coinage sixpences of George IV's reign.

VICTORIA

Type A¹   Type A³   Type A⁵

Type **A¹**   Young head l. R. SIX / PENCE in wreath, crown above, date below.
A²   Similar, but with die number between wreath and date.
A³   Second young head; similar, but head in lower relief, with die number.
A⁴   At last, but without die number.
A⁵   Third young head, the Queen's hair is thinner and in longer waves, no lock on cheek. Larger lettering on reverse.

Type B   Type D

B   Withdrawn Jubilee type. *O*. As the Jubilee shillings, veiled bust with small crown. R. As the Jubilee type shillings; shield in Garter.
C   Second Jubilee type. *O*. Similar. R. with SIX PENCE as type A, but crown of different design.
D   Old head type. *O*. As other denominations. R. As last.

N.B.—The column headed DIE NO. indicates that the pieces have a die number on them above the date; the figure shown is the highest die number noted, but there may be higher ones.

No.	TYPE	DIE No.	DATE	R	VARIETIES, Remarks, etc.
1682	A¹ **First young head**...........	none	**1838**	*N*	
1683	—	—	—	*R³*	*Proof*
1684	—	—	**1839**	*S*	
1685	—	—	—	*S*	*Proof*, with plain edge, issued in sets
1686	—	—	**1840**	*R*	
1687	—	—	**1841**	*R*	
1688	—	—	**1842**	*R*	
1689	—	—	**1843**	*R*	
1690	—	—	**1844**	*S*	
1690A	—	—	—	*R²*	Large 44 in date
1691	—	—	**1845**	*R*	
1692	—	—	**1846**	*S*	
					(See note¹)
1693	—	—	**1848**	*R³*	
1693A	—	—	—	*R³*	8 of date altered from 6
1693B	—	—	—	*R³*	8 of date struck over 7.²
1695	—	—	**1850**	*R*	
1695A	—	—	—	*R²*	5 of date over 3.³
1696	—	—	**1851**	*R*	
1697	—	—	**1852**	*R*	
1698	—	—	**1853**	*S*	
1699	—	—	—	*R²*	*Proof*, issued in the sets
1700	—	—	**1854**	*R³*	
1701	—	—	**1855**	*S*	
1701A	—	—	—	*R²*	5 of date over 3
1701B	—	—	—	*R³*	*Proof*
1702	—	—	**1856**	*S*	
1703	—	—	—	*S*	Longer line below PENCE
1704	—	—	**1857**	*R*	
1705	—	—	—	*R*	Longer line below PENCE

¹ A sixpence dated 1847 was reported as having been found in Norfolk. It was apparently sent to both the Royal Mint and British Museum who said they could find nothing wrong with it but were not prepared to say it was authentic (*Eastern Daily Press*, 17 July 1973).
² Although mentioned by some authors, I have still not traced a coin dated 1849: probably those referred to in Mint records are dated 1848, but struck in 1849.
³ Ron Stafford says that the overstruck figure is not typical of the period and might be struck from a broken punch.

No.	Type	Die No.	Date	R	Varieties, Remarks, etc.
1706	—	—	1858	R^2	
1707	—	—	—	R^5	*Proof*
1708	—	—	1859	S	
1708A	—	—	—	R	9 of date over 8
1709	—	—	1860	R	
1711	—	—	1862	R^3	
1712	A^1 —	none	1863	R^2	
1713	A^2 —	41	1864	S	
1714	—	32	1865	R	
1715	—	58	1866	N	
1716	A^1 —	none	—	R^3	
1717	A^3 Second young head	} 18 {	1867	R^2	
1718	—		—	R^5	*Proof*
1718A	A^3 —	—	—	R^2	
1719	—	15	1868	R^2	
1720	—	} 17 {	1869	R^2	
1720A	—		—	R^5	*Proof*
1721	—	} 10 {	1870	R^2	
1722	—		—	R^5	*Proof,* with plain edge
1723	—	} 52 {	1871	R	
1723A	—		—	R^5	*Proof,* with plain edge
1724	A^4 —	none	—	R^2	
1725	—	—	—	R^6	*Proof*
1726	A^3 —	62	1872	R	
1727	—	124	1873	S	
1727A	—	—	—	R^4	
1728	—	53	1874	S	
1729	—	74	1875	S	
1730	—	29	1876	R^2	
1731	—	33	1877	S	
1732	A^4 —	none	—	S	
1733	A^3 —	} 65 {	1878	S	
1734	—		—	R^5	*Proof*
1734A	—	30	—	R^4	Last 8 of date over 7
1735	—	6	—	R^3	Reads DRITANNIAR, D punched over B in error
1736	—	24	1879	S	
1737	A^4 —	none	—	R	122 teeth on reverse
1737A	—	—	—	R^5	*Proof*
1737B	—	—	—	R^5	*Proof* with plain edge

1737c	A⁵	**Third young head**	—	**1880**	R	
1738		—	—	—	R⁵	*Proof*, milled edge, from Rev. die of 1839
1739		—	—	—	R⁴	*Proof*
1740		—	—	**1881**	S	
1741		—	—	—	R⁴	*Proof*
1742		—	—	—	R⁵	*Proof*, with plain edge
1743		—	—	**1882**	R²	
1744		—	—	**1883**	S	
1745		—	—	**1884**	S	
1746		—	—	**1885**	S	
1747		—	—	—	R⁶	*Proof*
1748		—	—	**1886**	N	
1749		—	—	—	R⁶	*Proof*
1750		—	—	**1887**	C	
1751		—	—	—	R⁵	*Proof*
1752	**B.**	**Jubilee, withdrawn type**	—	**1887**	C³	
1752a		—	—	—	R²	R of VICTORIA over V
1752b		—	—	—	R³	J.E.B. on truncation half sovereign obv. die?
1753		—	—	—	S	*Proof*, issued in the sets
1754	**C.**	— **reverse**	—	—	C²	
1755		—	—	—	R³	*Proof*
1756		—	—	**1888**	N	
1756a		—	—	—	R⁶	*Proof*
1757		—	—	**1889**	N	
1758		—	—	**1890**	S	
1758a		—	—	—	R⁴	*Proof*
1759		—	—	**1891**	S	
1760		—	—	**1892**	S	
1761		—	—	**1893**	R³	
1762	**D.**	**Old head**	—	—	N	
1763		—	—	—	N	*Proof*, issued in the sets
1764		—	—	**1894**	S	
1765		—	—	**1895**	S	
1766		—	—	**1896**	S	
1767		—	—	**1897**	N	
1768		—	—	**1898**	N	
1769		—	—	**1899**	N	
1770		—	—	**1900**	N	
1771		—	—	**1901**	C	

1772 By W. Wyon, 1840. As the current coin, but the reverse ruled with fine horizontal lines R^4

1773 1841. *O.* From the die of the half-sovereigns. VICTORIA DEI GRATIA, head l. R. As the current sixpence. *In gold* R^7

1774

1774 By W. Wyon and L. C. Wyon, 1856. *O.* As the current coin. R. HALF / SHILLING in wreath, date below. *Edge*, plain R^4

1775 Similar, but $\frac{1}{2}$ / SHILLING. *Edge*, plain R^7

1776 By ?, 1884. *O.* ? legend; veiled bust, crowned. R. Cruciform crowned shields with national emblems in the angles R^6

1777

1777 By L. C. Wyon, 1887. As the ordinary withdrawn Jubilee sixpence, but with date above divided by the crown, and SIX PENCE below. *Edge*, milled R^7

1778 By Spink and Son, 1887. As their crown, but without the ornate border. *Edge*, plain[1] R^2

1779 Similar. *In gold* R^4

1780 Similar. *In copper* (10 struck) R^5

1781 Similar. *In aluminium* (20 struck) R^4

1782 Similar. *In tin* (9 struck) R^5

1783 Similar. *Edge*, milled R^2

1783A Similar. *In copper* R^4

1784 Similar. *In gold* R^4

1784A Similar. *In brass or nickel-bronze* R^5

---

[1] Some of these coins have MADE IN BAVARIA lightly incuse on the edge. There are also two reverse dies, with and without SPINK & SON.

EDWARD VII

1787

O. As the florin. Ŗ. As the late Victorian pieces with SIX PENCE.

1785	**1902**	*N*		1790	**1906**	*S*
1786	—	*N*	*Proof*, matt surface	1791	**1907**	*S*
1787	**1903**	*S*		1792	**1908**	*R*
1788	**1904**	*R*		1793	**1909**	*S*
1789	**1905**	*S*		1794	**1910**	*N*

Note. Rarities of this and the following reign only apply to 'EF or better' specimens. Apart from 1902 and 1910, sixpences of this reign are very hard to get in strictly mint condition.

GEORGE V

Type A

Type E

Type A *O*. As other denominations. R. As Edward VII shilling, FID : DEF :
  IND : IMP : — SIXPENCE, lion on crown dividing date.
  B Similar, but only 50% silver and 50% alloy.
  C Similar, but new beading and broader rim on obverse.
  D *O*. Modified effigy, slightly smaller bust, BM nearer the back of
  neck. R. As before.
  E *O*. Similar. R. SIX PENCE · — · A · — · D · and date around three oak
  sprigs with six acorns, KG in centre. *Edge* with 104 serrations.
  F Similar, but closer milling, 140 serrations.

1795	A. .925	1911	C	
1796	—	—	S	*Proof*
1797	—	1912	N	
1798	—	1913	S	
1799	—	1914	N	
1800	—	1915	N	
1801	—	1916	N	
1802	—	1917	R	
1803	—	1918	N	
1804	—	1919	N	
1805	—	1920	N	
1806	B. 'Debased' .500	—	S	
1807	—	1921	N	
1808	—	1922	N	
1809	—	1923	R	
1810	—	1924	N	
1811	—	1925	N	
1812	C. New rim	—	S	
1813	—	1926	S	
1814	D. Modified effigy	—	S	
1815	—	1927	S	
1815A	—	1927	R^6	*Proof* in nickel

N.B. First, second and third issue coins are becoming increasingly difficult to get in
mint condition and are probably rarer than marked.
V.I.P. proofs exist of most dates from 1928 onwards. All are rare

1816	**E. New** *rev.*	—	*N*	*Proof*
1816A	—	—	*R*⁶	Matt Proof
1817	—	**1928**	*N*	
1818	—	**1929**	*N*	
1819	—	**1930**	*N*	
1820	**F.** — **Closer milling**............	**1931**	*N*	
1821	—	**1932**	*S*	
1822	—	**1933**	*N*	
1823	—	**1934**	*S*	
1824	—	**1935**	*N*	
1825	—	**1936**	*C*	

1825A *Pattern*, 1925, in Nickel. As the fourth coinage coins of 1928   *R*⁷

EDWARD VIII

1825B

1825B *O*. As the other coins. ℞. FID . DEF . IND . IMP . 1937 SIXPENCE. Six rings
of St. Edmund intertwined, KG below R^6

GEORGE VI

Type A   Type C

Type A   *O*. As other denominations. ℞. FID . DEF . IND . IMP . above GRI
crowned dividing date, KG / SIXPENCE below (.500 Æ).
B   Similar, but struck in cupro-nickel, closer milling on edge.
C   New type. As type B, but without IND IMP and with G^{VI}R as central
device; no K.G.

1826	A.Æ	1937	N		1836A	B. Cu. Ni.		1946	R^6	Pattern or
1827	—	—	S	Proof						proof. See
1828	—	1938	S							note[1] on
1829	—	1939	S							page 91
1830	—	1940	N		1837	—		1947	S	
1831	—	1941	C		1838	—		1948	S	
1832	—	1942	C		1838A	C. — New type		1949	N	
1833	—	1943	C		1838B	—		1950	N	
1834	—	1944	C		1838C	—		—	S	Proof
1835	—	1945	C^2		1838D	—		1951	N	
1836	—	1946	C^2		1838E	—		—	S	Proof
					1838F	—		1952	R	

Note. Sand blasted proofs exist for 1950 and 1951. The proofs of 1952 are from polished dies.
V.I.P. proofs exist for most dates. Matt proofs exist for 1937 and are extremely rare.

ELIZABETH II

Type A   Type B

Type A *O.* As halfcrown. R. A garland of interlaced rose, thistle, shamrock
and leek, the rose is at the top between two leaves, the leek on l., the
thistle on the r., the shamrock is at the bottom between small shamrock and leaf, EF and CT in lower field; FID . DEF . above, SIX PENCE .
1953 below.

B   As before, but *obv.* legend ends DEI . GRATIA . REGINA.

1838G	A. cu.-Ni.	1953	*N*	*Proof*	1838P	B. —	1961	*C²*
1838H	—	—	*S*		1838Q	—	1962	*C²*
1838I	B.	1954	*C*		1838R	—	1963	*C²*
1838J	—	1955	*C*		1838S	—	1964	*C³*
1838K	—	1956	*C*		1838T	—	1965	*C³*
1838L	—	1957	*C*		1838U	—	1966	*C³*
1838M	—	1958	*C²*		1838V	—	1967	*C³*
1838N	—	1959	*C²*		1838W	—	1970	*S Proof*
1838O	—	1960	*C²*					

N. B. So called V.I.P. proofs exist for most dates. All are rare.
Proofs from sandblasted dies were struck in 1953.

GROATS OR FOURPENCES

CHARLES II

Type A

Hammered Coinage
1839 Type **A** As illustration. Known as 'third hammered coinage'   *N*

Milled Coinage
1840 Type **B** As illustration. Known as the 'undated Maundy'   *N*

Type B   Type C

C   Dated issue. As illustration. Listed below.

No.	Date	R	Remarks, etc.	No.	Date	R	Remarks, etc.
1841	**1670**	R^2		1849	**1678**	*N*	
1842	**1671**	*R*		1850	—	*S*	8 of date over 7
1843	**1672**	*S*	2 of date over 1	1850A	—	*R*	8 of date over 6
1844	**1673**	*S*		1851	**1679**	C^2	
1845	**1674**	*S*		1852	**1680**	*C*	
1845A	—	R^3	4 over 4 on its side	1853	**1681**	*C*	
1845B	—	*R*	7 of date over 6	1853A	—	R^3	B of HIB over R
1846	**1675**	*S*		1854	—	*S*	1 of date over 0
1846A	—	R^3	5 of date over 4	1855	**1682**	*N*	
1847	**1676**	*S*		1856	—	*S*	2 of date over 1
1847A	—	*S*	7 of date over 6	1857	**1683**	*C*	
1847B	—	*S*	Second 6 of date over 5	1858	**1684**	*R*	
1848	**1677**	*N*		1859	—	*N*	4 of date over 3

JAMES II

Only one type. As illustration.

1860	**1686**	S	
1861	—	R	Date over crown
1862	**1687**	N	7 of date over 6
1862A	—	R	8 of date over 7
1863	**1688**	S	
1863A	—	R^3	1 of date over 8
1864	—	S	8 of date over 7

These pieces are not scarce in 'fair' or 'fine' condition.

WILLIAM AND MARY

Type A   Type B

Type **A**   As illustration; no tie to the wreath. Large letters, *rev.* small crown, tapered serifs on the 4.

     B   Similar, but different bust, with a tie to the wreath. Small letters, *rev.* broad crown, untapered serifs on the 4.

1865		**1689**	C	GV below bust, threepence *obv.* die used in error
1866	**A**	—	C	G below bust
1867	—	—	R	— stop before G
1868	—	—	R	— with berries in wreath
1868A	—	—	R^3	GVLEELMVS
1869	—	**1690**	N	
1869A	—	—	R	6 of date over 5
1870	—	**1691**	R	
1871	—	—	S	1 of date over 0
1872	**B**	**1692**	S	Small lettering both sides
1873	—	—	R	— 2 of date over 1

1873A	—	—	R^3	— stop between R and I of MARIA
1874	—	—	S	Small lettering on *obv.* only
1875	—	—	R	Large lettering both sides
1876	—	1693	R^2	
1877	—	—	R	3 of date over 2
1878	A	1694	R	
1878A	—	—	R	Smaller lettering both sides
1879	B	—	R^2	

Note. On the small denominations from 4d to 1d of William and Mary and William III there are a large number of small inscription errors, particularly where the use of V or A is concerned. There is also a large variation in the placing of the legends.

WILLIAM III

Only one type. As illustration.

1880	1697	R^7		1883	1700	S	
1881	1698	R		1884	1701	R	
1882	1699	S		1885	1702	N	See note[1]

[1] This date, 1702, does not occur upon any other coins of this reign and should not correctly occur upon this. At this period the New Year commenced on the 25 March, whilst the king died on 8 March.

ANNE

          Type A   Type B

Type **A**   Bust 1, small face, curls at back of head point downwards. R. 1, small crown above the figure 4.

Type **B**   Bust 2, larger face, curls at back of head point upwards. R. 1.

Type **C**   Bust 2. R. 2, large crown with pearls on arch, larger serifs on the figure 4.

Type **D**   As type **C** but with re-engraved hair.

1886	**A**	**1703**	*R*	MAG. BR. FR.
1887	—	**1704**	*N*	—
1888	**B**	**1705**	*R*	—
1889	—	**1706**	*N*	MAG. BR. FRA.
1890	—	**1708**	*N*	MAG. BRI. FR.
1891	—	**1709**	*N*	—
1892	—	**1710**	*N*	— larger crown
1892A	**C**	—	*N*	
1892B	**D**	—	*N*	
1893	**C**	**1713**	*N*	
1893A	**D**	—	*N*	

GEORGE I

Only one type. As illustration.

1894	**1717**	*S*		1896	**1723**	*S*	
1895	**1721**	*S*		1897	**1727**	*R*	Smaller letters and date on *rev*.

GEORGE II

Type B

Type A, rev. 1, small dome-shaped crown with no pearls on arch.
Type B, rev. 2, double domed crown with pearls, large figure 4.

1898	A	1729	S		1904		1740	S	Threepence *obv.*
1899	—	1731	S						die used in
1900	B	1732	S						error
1901	—	1735	S		1905	B	1743	S	
1902	—	1737	S		1905A	—	1743	R³	3 of date over 0
1903	B	1739	S		1906	—	1746	N	
					1907	—	1760	S	

GEORGE III

Type A   *O*. GEORGIVS . III . DEI . GRATIA, youngish laur. bust draped r. R. As
before.

1908	1763	N	
1908A	—	R⁷	*Proof*
1909	1765	R⁵	
1910	1766	S	
1911	1770	S	
1912	1772	S	
1913	—	S	2 of date over 0
1914	1776	N	See note¹
1915	1780	N	
1916	1784	S	
1917	1786	R	

N.B.—For types **B, C** and **D** of George III, for George IV and for 'figure 4' type fourpences of William IV see under Maundy Money sets.

¹ Dr G. H. Bullmore has kindly pointed out that this coin turns up with a defective 6, appearing very much like a 5. A genuine groat of 1775 has not yet been discovered. Collectors are warned.

WILLIAM IV

O. GULIELMUS IIII D : G : BRITANNIAR : REX F : D : , head r. R. FOUR PENCE, Britannia seated r., date in exergue. *Edge*, milled.

N.B.—For fourpences of the other type (i.e. with figure 4 on reverse) see Maundy Money sets.

1918	**1836**	C^2	
1919	—	R^2	*Proof*
1920	—	S	*Proof*, with plain edge
1921	—	R^5	*— In gold*
1921A	—	R^6	— on flan of half-thickness (wt. 1.323 gm.)
1922	**1837**	C	See note[1]
1923	—	R^4	*Proof*
1923A	—	R^4	*Proof*, with plain edge

1924   1926

Patterns

1924 By W. Wyon, 1836. As current coin, but FOUR PENCE continuous, not broken by the figure of Britannia. *Edge*, milled R^3

1925 Similar. *Edge*, plain R^3

1926 *O.* Similar. R. Similar, but 4 P either side of Britannia in place of legend. *Edge*, milled R^2

1927 Similar. *Edge*, plain R^2

1928 Similar. *In gold* R^5

---

[1] On the later strikings, the obverse die appears to have been re-cut; the hair is finer, and the eyes more prominent.

VICTORIA

Type **A** As illustration. Edge, milled.
    B Similar, but with Jubilee head.

N.B.—For fourpences of the other type (i.e. with figure 4 on reverse) see Maundy Money sets.

1929	A	1837	R^6	*Proof*, obverse die is that of an early threepence with plain edge
1929A	—	—	R^6	*Proof*, edge milled, reverse is inverted
1930	—	1838	C	
1931	—	—	R^4	*Proof*, with plain edge
1931A	—	—	R	Second 8 of date over 8 on side
1932	—	1839	N	
1933	—	—	S	*Proof*, with plain edge, issued in the sets
1933A	—	—	R^2	*Proof*, with plain edge, reverse inverted
1934	—	1840	C	
1934A	—	—	S	Round 0 in date
1935	—	1841	R	
1936	—	1842	N	
1937	—	—	R^3	*Proof*, with plain edge
1937A	—	—	R	2 of date over 1
1938	—	1843	N	
1938A	—	—	R^2	4 of date over 5
1939	—	1844	S	
1940	—	1845	N	
1941	—	1846	N	
1942	—	1847	R^4	7 of date over 6
1943	—	1848	N	
1944	—	—	R	Second 8 of date over 6
1944A	—	—	R	Second 8 of date over 7
1945	—	1849	S	
1946	—	—	R	9 of date over 8
1947	—	1851	R	
1948	—	1852	R^3	2 of date slightly slanted
1949	—	1853	R^5	
1950	—	—	R	*Proof*, issued in the sets
1951	—	—	R^4	*Proof*, with plain edge
1951A	—	—	R3	As 1853 *proof*, edge milled.

1952	—	1854	*C*	
1953	—	1855	*N*	
1954	—	1857	R^6	*Proof only*
1955	—	—	R^3	As 1857 proof, obv. die of threepence with late obv. R. similar. *Edge* milled
1955A	—	1862	R^3	*Proof only*, with plain edge
1955B	—	—	R^3	As 1862 proof, obv. die of threepence with late obv. R. similar. *Edge* plain
1955C	—	—	R^4	*Proof* with milled edge
1956	B	1888	*N*	*Only issued for colonial use*
1956A	—	—	R^4	*Proof*

1929   1954   1955B

THREEPENCES

CHARLES II

Type A

Hammered

1957 Type **A**   As illustration. Usually known as the third hammered
coinage   *N*

Milled

1958 Type **B**   As illustration on left below. Usually known as the 'undated
Maundy'.   *N*

Type B   Type C

Type **C**   Dated issue. As illustration on right above. Listed below.

No.	Date	R	Varieties, Remarks, etc.
1959	**1670**	*S*	
1960	**1671**	*N*	
1961	—	*R*	Reads GRⱯTIA
1961A	—	*R*	Reads GRATIA
1962	**1672**	*N*	2 of date over 1
1963	**1673**	*N*	
1964	**1674**	*N*	
1965	**1675**	*S*	
1966	**1676**	*N*	
1966A	—	*R*	6 of date over 5
1967	—	*S*	Reads ERA instead of FRA
1968	**1677**	*S*	
1969	**1678**	*N*	
1970	**1679**	*C*	
1971	—	*R*	O of CAROLVS over A
1972	**1680**	*N*	
1973	**1681**	*N*	

1974	—	S	1 of date over 0
1975	**1682**	N	
1976	—	S	2 of date over 1
1977	**1683**	N	
1978	**1684**	N	
1979	—	S	4 of date over 3

JAMES II

Only one type, as illustration.

1980	**1685**	S	
1980A	—	R⁵	On flan for the groat
1981	**1686**	S	
1981A	—	R	Mule with fourpence *obv*. die
1982	**1687**	S	
1983	—	S	7 of date over 6
1984	**1688**	S	
1985	—	S	8 of date over 7

These pieces are only scarce in very fine condition or better.

WILLIAM AND MARY

Type **A**   As illustration. Hardly any tie to wreath.
   B   Busts of better style, with a tie to the wreath. R. As last.

1986	**A**	**1689**	*C*	See note[1]
1987	—	—	*C*	Hyphen stops on *rev.*
1987A	—	—	*S*	LMV in GVLIELMVS over MVS
1988	—	—	*S*	No stops on *rev.*
1989	—	**1690**	*N*	
1989A	—	—	*R*	Small letters, 6 of date over 5
1989B	—	—	*R*	Small letters, 9 of date over 6
1989C	—	—	*N*	Large letters
1990	—	**1691**	*R³*	
1990A	**B**	—	*R*	
1991	—	**1692**	*R*	G below bust
1992	—	—	*R*	GV below bust
1993	—	—	*R*	GVL below bust
1994	—	**1693**	*R*	G below bust
1994A	—	—	*S*	— 3 of date over 2
1995	—	—	*R*	GV below bust
1996	—	**1694**	*S*	G below bust
1997	—	—	*S*	— reads MARIA
1998	—	—	*S*	GV below the bust
1999	—	—	*S*	GVL below the bust

[1] These pieces occur with either Roman I or Arabic 1.

WILLIAM III

Only one type, as illustration.

2000	**1698**	*N*	
2001	**1699**	*S*	
2002	**1700**	*N*	
2003	**1701**	*N*	1s of date like z, small lettering
2003A	—	*S*	GBA for GRA
2004	—	*N*	1s of date like j, large lettering

ANNE

Type A   Type C

Type **A**   Bust 1, broad bust, tie riband pointing outwards.
Type **B**   Bust 2, taller and narrow bust, tie riband pointing inwards.
Type **C**   Bust 3, similar to bust 1 but larger and hair more finely engraved.

2005	**A**	**1703**	*R*	MAG. BR. FR., 7 of date above crown
2006	—	—	*R*	— 7 of date not above crown
2007	**B**	**1704**	*S*	—
2008	—	**1705**	*S*	—
2009	—	**1706**	*N*	MAG. BR. FRA.
2010	**C**	**1707**	*N*	MAG. BR. FR.
2011	—	**1708**	*N*	MAG. BRI. FR.
2011A	—	—	*R*	— 8 of date over 7
2012	—	**1709**	*N*	—
2013	—	**1710**	*N*	—
2014	—	**1713**	*N*	—
2014A		—	*N*	— Mule with fourpence *obv* die

GEORGE I

Only one type, as illustration.

2015	1717	N	
2016	1721	S	
2017	1723	S	
2018	1727	S	Smaller letters and date

GEORGE II

Type C

Type **A** R. 1, pearls on arch.
Type **B** R. 2, ornate arch.
Type **C** R. 3, double-domed crown with pearls.

2019	A	1729	S	
2020	B	1731	S	
2021	—	—	S	Small lettering on *obv*.
2022	C	1732	S	
2023	—	—	S	Stop over head
2024	—	1735	S	
2025	—	1737	N	
2026	—	1739	N	
2027	—	1740	N	
2028	—	1743	N	
2029	—	—	N	Large lettering both sides
2030	—	—	N	Stop over head, small lettering
2031	—	1746	N	
2031A	—	—	R	6 of date over 3
2032	—	1760	N	

GEORGE III

Type **A**   As groat. **R**. As last.

2033	**1762**	C^3	Over 30 different dies used
2034	**1763**	C^2	
2034A	—	R^7	*Proof*
2035	**1765**	R^5	
2036	**1766**	S	
2037	**1770**	S	
2038	**1772**	N	Small lettering on *obv.*
2039	—	N	Large lettering on *obv.*, with very large III
2040	—	N	— small III
2041	**1780**	N	
2042	**1784**	S	
2043	**1786**	N	

N.B.—For threepences of George III type B, C and D, George IV and other dates of William IV see the Maundy Money sets.

WILLIAM IV

As the Maundy threepence. Issued for use in the West Indies only, not for use in Britain.

2044	**1834**	S		2046	**1836**	S	
2045	**1835**	N		2047	**1837**	R	

THREEPENCES OF VICTORIA

1   2   3   4

Type **A**	Young head
Obverse 1	First bust, young head, high relief, ear fully visible.
Obverse 2	First bust variety, slightly older portrait with acquiline nose, top of ear covered by hair strands.
Obverse 3	Second bust, slightly larger, lower relief, mouth fuller, nose more pronounced, rounded truncation.
Obverse 4	Third bust, older features, mouth closed, hair strands leading from 'bun' vary.
Reverse A	Tie ribbon closer to tooth border, cross on crown further from tooth border.
Reverse B	Tie ribbon further from tooth border, cross on crown nearer to tooth border.

A1	obverse 1	reverse A
A2	obverse 2	reverse A
A3	obverse 3	reverse A
A4	obverse 3	reverse B
A5	obverse 4	reverse B

Type **B**   Jubilee type; the same as Maundy threepence. See note 1 on page 184 and 185

    C   Old head; the same as the Maundy threepence. See note 1 on page 184

2065   2071   2079

2091   Reverse A   Reverse B

No.	Type	Date	R	Remarks, etc.	No.	Type	Date	R	Remarks, etc.
2048	A^1	1838	S	For Colonial use only.	2067A	A^1	1860	S	
					2068	—	1861	N	
2048A	—	—	R^4	Reads BRITANNIAB. For Colonial use only.	2068A	A^2	—	N	
					2069	—	1862	N	
					2070	—	1863	S	
					2071	—	1864	N	
2049	—	1839	R	⎫	2072	—	1865	S	
2050	—	1840	S	⎬	2073	—	1866	N	
2051	—	1841	S	⎬ For Colonial	2074	—	1867	N	
2052	—	1842	S	⎬ use only.	2074A	A^3	—	R	
2053	—	1843	N	⎬	2074B	A^4	—	S	
2054	—	1844	S	⎭	2075	A^2	1868	N	
2055	—	1845	C		2075A	—	—	R^3	Reads RRITAN-
2056	—	1846	R^2						NIAR.
2056A	—	1848	R^4	For Colonial use only.	2075B	A^4	—	R	
					2075C	—	1869	R	
2057	—	1849	R	See Note²	2076	—	1870	N	
2058	—	1850	N		2077	—	1871	S	
2059	—	1851	N		2078	—	1872	S	
2059A	—	—	R^2	5 over 8	2079	—	1873	C	
2059B	—	1852	R^4	See Note²	2080	—	1874	C	
2060	—	1853	R^2		2081	—	1875	C	
2061	—	1854	N		2082	—	1876	C	
2062	—	1855	R		2083	—	1877	N	
2063	—	1856	N		2084	—	1878	N	
2064	—	1857	S		2085	—	1879	N	
2065	—	1858	N		2086	—	—	R^4	Proof
2065A	—	—	R^2	Reads BRITANNIAB	2087	A^5	1880	N	
					2088	—	1881	C	
2065B	—	—	R^2	Second 8 over 6	2089	—	1882	S	
					2090	—	1883	C	
2065C	—	—	R	Second 8 over 5	2091	A^4	1884	C	
					2092	A^5	1885	C	
2066	—	1859	N		2092A	—	—	R^5	Proof
2066A	A^2	—	N		2093	—	1886	C	
2067	—	1860	N		2094	—	1887	N	

[1] The ordinary threepences of this and subsequent reigns can be distinguished from the Maundy coins as they have a somewhat dull surface whereas the Maundy threepences look more like proofs with a highly polished field. The latter tone much more easily, and are often bluish or quite dark. The young head threepences are rather scarcer than marked in really first class condition.

[2] It is possible that threepences were struck for Colonial use in 1847; a piece dated 1852 and undoubtedly a Colonial issue was shown to me by Mr. P. Mitchell in February 1990.

2095	—	—	R^4	*Proof*	2105	C	**1893**	N	*Proof*
2096	**B**	**1887**	C^2	See note[1]	2106	—	**1894**	C
2097	—	—	S	*Proof*	2107	—	**1895**	C
2098	—	**1888**	S	See note[1]	2108	—	**1896**	C
2099	—	**1889**	C		2109	—	**1897**	C
2100	—	**1890**	C		2110	—	**1898**	C
2101	—	**1891**	C		2111	—	**1899**	C
2102	—	**1892**	S		2112	—	**1900**	C
2103	—	**1893**	R^2	See note[1]	2113	—	**1901**	C
2104	**C**	—	C					

Pattern

2113A By L. C. Wyon, 1868. As type A, but the head of the Queen is laureate
as on the Maltese third-farthing R^6

---

[1] The Jubilee type threepence was struck in 1887 for currency, but not until 1888 for inclusion in
the Maundy sets. The rare Jubilee type threepence of 1893 differs from the Maundy threepence
of that year as the coinage changed to the 'Old head' before Easter.

EDWARD VII

O. As the florins. R. As usual. As the threepence in the Maundy set.

2114	**1902**	*N*			2119	**1906**	*S*
2115	—	*N*	*Proof*		2120	**1907**	*S*
2116	**1903**	*S*			2121	**1908**	*N*
2117	**1904**	*S*			2122	**1909**	*S*
2118	**1905**	*S*			2123	**1910**	*S*

Note: These coins are commoner than marked in worn state, but apart from 1902 and 1910, they are probably at least *R* in mint state.

There is a slight change in the style of the figure 3 on the reverse from 1904 onwards.

GEORGE V

Type **A** As the other early coins. R. As usual. As the threepences in the Maundy sets.

B Similar, but metal changed to 50% silver and 50% alloy. As the threepence in the Maundy sets except 1920.

C Modified effigy, as the sixpence. R. As last. Differs from the Maundy threepence.

Type D

D *O.* As last. R. THREE . . PENCE ., date, three oak-sprigs with three acorns, G in centre. Different type from the threepence in the Maundy sets.

2124	**A. .925 silver**................	**1911**	*N*	
2125	—................	—	*S*	*Proof*
2126	—................	**1912**	*N*	
2127	—................	**1913**	*N*	
2128	—................	**1914**	*N*	
2129	—................	**1915**	*N*	
2130	—................	**1916**	*C*	
2131	—................	**1917**	*C*	
2132	—................	**1918**	*C*	
2133	—................	**1919**	*C*	
2134	—................	**1920**	*C*	
2135	**B. 'Debased' .500**................	—	*N*	
2136	—................	**1921**	*N*	
2137	—................	**1922**	*S*	
2138	—................	**1925**	*S*	
2139	—................	**1926**	*R*	
2140	**C. Modified effigy**................	—	*S*	
2141	**D. New** *rev.*................	**1927**	*S*	*Proof only*
2141A	—................	—	*R⁶*	*Matt proof*
2142	—................	**1928**	*R*	
2143	—................	**1930**	*R*	
2144	—................	**1931**	*C*	
2145	—................	**1932**	*C*	
2146	—................	**1933**	*C*	
2147	—................	**1934**	*C*	
2148	—................	**1935**	*C*	
2149	—................	**1936**	*C*	**Edw. VIII**

Note: These coins are very common in low grade and are of no commercial value.

Patterns

2149A	1923. As normal type. *Pure nickel*	*R⁶*
2149B	1925. As 4th coinage. *In nickel*	*R⁶*
2149c	1925. As 4th coinage. Matt *proof in nickel*	

EDWARD VIII

Pattern

2149D *O.* As the other coins. R. FID . DEF . IND . IMP . 1937 THREE . PENCE. Three rings of St. Edward intertwined, KG below.   *R*[6]

GEORGE VI

O. As the sixpence. R. FID : DEF : IND : IMP — THREE·PENCE, shield of St. George on Tudor rose dividing date, K.G. below.

2150	**1937**	*N*			2155	**1941**	*N*	
2151	—	*S*	*Proof*		2156	**1942**	*R*	Only struck in small
2151A	—	*R*[6]	*Matt proof*		2157	**1943**	*R*	quantities, and solely for
2152	**1938**	*N*			2158	**1944**	*R*[2]	use in the West Indies.
2153	**1939**	*R*			2159	**1945**	*R*[6]	See note[1]
2154	**1940**	*N*						

Starting with 1937 a twelve-sided aluminium-bronze threepence was struck and issued in large quantities at the same time as the silver threepence; these have been omitted here as they seem to be more applicable to a review of the copper and bronze coinage.

V.I.P. proofs exist for most dates. All are rare.

---

[1] At one time it was thought that this coin did not exist and that all specimens had been melted down. I have seen a genuine coin therefore one or two coins must have escaped destruction.

HALFGROATS OR TWOPENCES

THE COMMONWEALTH

2160 As illustration. No legend or date. Those from very crude dies are contemporary forgeries.   *C*

2160A Similar, but shields transposed.   *R*³

CHARLES II

Type A

Type **A** (Hammered). No inner circle, but without the mark of value, mintmark on obverse only. Known as 'first hammered coinage' (*M.S.C.*,
type II).

B (Hammered). Similar, but with mark of value added. Known as
'second hammered coinage' (*M.S.C.*, type III).

Type C   Type E

C (Machine made). As illustration; with mark of value and mintmark
on both sides. (*M.S.C.*, type V).[1]

D (Machine made). Still with no inner circle, but with legends at
bottom l. and with bust to edge of coin. Has the first bust with
single-arched crown as before. (*M.S.C.*, type VI).[1]

E (Hammered). With inner circles and mark of value, as illustration.
Known as 'third hammered coinage'. (*M.S.C.*, type IV).

---

[1] These are usually catalogued as second hammered coinage and Simon probably made the dies
for a hammered coinage, but they were undoubtedly struck in a machine. They are not, however,
quite as well made as the 'undated Maundy'.

Milled Coinage

F   As type D, but rather better struck and with second bust which has a
crown with double-arch. Known as 'undated Maundy' or fourth
issue.

Type G

G   Dated issue. As groat, but with two interlinked CS. Illustrated above.

	Hammered			
2161	**A. No value or inner circle**	no date	*S*	MAG BRIT FR ET HIB REX
2162	—	—	*R*	MAG BRIT FR FT H REX
2163	—	—	*R*	MAG B FR ET H REX
2164	**B. Value, no inner circle**	—	*R⁵*	MAG B FR ET H
2165	**E. Value, inner circles**	—	*N*	MAG BRI FRA ET HIB
2166	—	—	*R*	MAG BR FR ET HIB
	Machine made			
2167	**C. Value, no inner circle**	—	*R*	M B F ET H
2168	**D. — bust to edge**	—	*N*	M B F & H
	Milled			
2169	**F. — Second bust to edge**	—	*C*	M B F & H
2170	**G. Dated issue**	1668	*S*	
2171	—	1670	*N*	
2172	—	1671	*N*	
2173	—	—	*N*	2 of date over 1
2174	—	1673	*S*	
2175	—	1674	*N*	
2176	—	1675	*S*	
2177	—	1676	*N*	
2178	—	1677	*S*	
2179	—	1678	*N*	
2180	—	—	*S*	8 of date over 6
2181	—	1679	*C*	
2181A	—	—	*R*	HIB over FRA in legend
2182	—	1680	*N*	
2183	—	—	*R*	80 of date over 79
2184	—	1681	*N*	
2185	—	1682	*N*	
2186	—	1682	*S*	2 of date over 1
2187	—	—	*S*	— reads ERA for FRA
2188	—	1683	*N*	
2189	—	—	*S*	3 of date over 2
2190	—	1684	*S*	

JAMES II

O. As the other coins. ℞. II crowned.

2191	**1686**	*N*	
2192	—	*R*	Reads IACOBVS
2193	**1687**	*N*	
2193A	—	*R²*	Reads ERA for FRA
2194	**1688**	*S*	
2195	—	*S*	last 8 of date over 7

WILLIAM AND MARY

O. As type A groat and threepence. ℞. As before, but 2 crowned.

2196	**1689**	*C*	Legend continuous above bust
2197	**1691**	*C*	See note[1]
2198	**1692**	*N*	
2199	**1693**	*N*	
2200	—	*S*	GV under the bust
2200A	—	*S*	3 of date over 2
2201	**1694**	*S*	
2201A	—	*R*	4 of date over 3
2201B	—	*R*	— no stop after G of DG
2202	—	*S*	GVLI under bust
2203	—	*S*	— HI for HIB
2204	—	*S*	GVL under bust
2205	—	*S*	— reads MARLA

Note. On the small denominations of William and Mary there are a large number of inscription errors, particularly where the use of O or A is concerned. There is also a large variation in the placing of the legends.

[1] From 1691 to 1694 all these have small letters both sides; see illustration.

WILLIAM III

Type B

O. As groat and threepence. *R.* As last.

Type **A**　R 1, crown to edge of coin, large figure 2.
Type **B**　R 2, crown within inner circle of legend, smaller figure 2.

2206	**Type A**	**1698**	*R*
2207	**Type B**	**1699**	*S*
2208	—	**1700**	*S*
2209	—	**1701**	*N*

ANNE

Type A

O. As groat and threepence. *R.* As last.

Type **A**　R 1, crown to edge of coin, small figure 2.
Type **B**　R 2, crown within inner circle of legend, large figure 2.

2210	A	1703	*R*	MAG. BR. FRA.
2211	—	1704	*N*	—
2212	—	—	*R*	— All date well above crown
2213	—	—	*R*	— No stops on obv.
2214	—	1705	*N*	—
2215	—	1706	*S*	—
2216	—	1707	*S*	—
2217	B	1708	*N*	MAG. BRI. FR.
2218	—	1709	*R*	—
2219	—	1710	*N*	—
2220	—	1713	*N*	—

GEORGE I

O. As groat and threepence. **R.** As last.

2221	**1717**	*N*		2224	**1726**	*C*	
2222	**1721**	*C*		2225	**1727**	*S*	Smaller letters.
2223	**1723**	*R*					

GEORGE II

Type B

Type **A**   Rev. 1, small crown and figure 2.
Type **B**   Rev 2, large crown and figure 2.

2226	**A**	**1729**	*N*		2233	**B**	**1743**	*N*
2227	—	**1731**	*N*		2233A	—	—	*S*	3 of date
2228	**B**	**1732**	*N*						over 0
2229	—	**1735**	*N*		2234	—	**1746**	*N*
2230	—	**1737**	*N*		2235	—	**1756**	*N*
2231	—	**1739**	*S*		2236	—	**1759**	*N*
2232	—	**1740**	*R*		2237	—	**1760**	*N*

GEORGE III

Type **A**   *O*. As groat. **R**. As last.

2238	**1763**	*S*	
2238A	—	*R⁶*	Proof
2239	**1765**	*R⁴*	
2240	**1766**	*N*	
2241	**1772**	*N*	
2242	—	*N*	Second 7 of date over 6
2243	**1776**	*N*	
2244	**1780**	*N*	
2245	**1784**	*N*	
2246	**1786**	*C*	
2247	—	*C*	Large lettering on *obv*.

N.B.—For George III types **B**, **C** and **D** and all later twopences (except the next two coins) see under Maundy sets.

VICTORIA

O. Young head. **R**. As before.

2248	**1838**	*C²*	Struck for Colonial use
2249	**1848**	*C*	Struck for Colonial use

Perhaps these coins were also struck in one or two other early years for use in some of the Colonies.

THREE-HALFPENCE

These little coins were never issued for circulation in Britain and were never current here but were struck for use in some of the Colonies which used the ordinary Imperial currency.

WILLIAM IV

As the threepence, and the Maundy, but $1\frac{1}{2}$ crowned on the reverse.

2250	**1834**	*C*		2252	**1836**	*N*	
2251	**1835**	*R*		2253	**1837**	R^2	
2251A	—	*N*	5 of date over 4				

VICTORIA

O. Usual type with young head. R. As last.

2254	**1838**	*N*		2259B	—	R^2	1843 struck over 1834
2255	**1839**	*C*		2259C	—	R^5	*Proof*
2256	**1840**	R^2		2260	**1860**	*R*	
2257	**1841**	*S*		2261	**1862**	*R*	
2258	**1842**	*S*		2261A	—	R^5	*Proof*
2259	**1843**	C^2		2262	**1870**	R^5	*Proof or Pattern only*
2259A	—	R^5	*Proof*				

PENNIES

THE COMMONWEALTH

2263   As halfgroat, but · I · above shield. Illustrated above.

CHARLES II

Type **A**   (Hammered). As illustration on left below. Without mark of value or inner circles; mintmark, crown on obverse only. Known as 'first hammered coinage'. (*M.S.C.*, type II).

     B   (Hammered). As illustration on right above. Similar to last, but without mintmark. (*M.S.C.*, type I).

     C   (Machine made). Similar, but with mark of value behind bust and the mintmark both sides. (*M.S.C.*, type V).[1]
     D   (Machine made). Still with no inner circles and with the mark of value behind bust which goes to bottom of coin, legend starts at bottom l.; *mm.* crown, reverse only. First bust, as before, with single-arched crown. (*M.S.C.*, type VI).[1]
     E   (Hammered). As illustration, with mark of value and inner circles. Known as 'third hammered coinage'. (*M.S.C.*, type IV).

Milled Coinage
     F   As type D, but more carefully struck, and has the second bust with double-arched crown. Known as the 'undated Maundy'.
     G   Dated issue. As illustration on r. above.

---

[1] These are usually catalogued as second hammered coinage and Simon probably made the dies for a hammered coinage but they were undoubtedly struck in a machine. They are not quite so well made as the 'undated Maundy'.

No.	Type	Date	R	Varieties, Remarks, etc.
	Hammered			
2264	**A. No value or inner circle**.....	none	R^2	MAG BRIT FR ET HIB REX
2265	**B. — no** *mm.*	—	R^3	M BR F ET HI REX
2266	—	—	R	CPOLVS II D G M BP F FT HI PFX
2267	**E. Value and inner circles**	—	R^2	MAG BR FR RT HIB
2268	—	—	R^2	MAG B F ET HIB
2269	—	—	R	M BR FR ET HIB
2270	—	—	C	M B F ET HIB
	Machine made			
2271	**C. Value, no inner circle**	—	R^2	M B F ET H
2271A	—	—	R^4	Reads AVSPCE
2272	**D. — bust to edge**	—	S	M B F & H
	Milled			
2273	**F. — Second bust to edge**	—	N	M B F & H
2274	**G. Dated issue**........................	1670	S	
2275	—	1671	S	
2276	—	1672	S	2 of date over 1
2277	—	1673	S	
2278	—	1674	S	
2279	—	—	S	Reads ƆRATIA
2280	—	1675	S	
2280A	—	—	R	Reads ƆRATIA
2281	—	1676	R	
2281A	—	—	R	Reads ƆRATIA
2282	—	1677	S	
2283	—	—	R	Reads ƆRATIA
2284	—	1678	R	
2285	—	—	R	Reads ƆRATIA
2286	—	1679	R	
2287	—	1680	S	
2287A	—	—	R^5	On flan of 2d size and thinner[1]
2288	—	1681	R^2	
2289	—	1682	R	
2290	—	—	R	2 of date over 1
2290A	—	—	R^2	ERA for FRA
2291	—	1683	S	3 of date over 1
2292	—	1684	R	
2292A	—	—	R	4 of date over 3

[1] There are 2 specimens in existence, both from same dies, which clearly read MAC. In fact the C is probably from the font for 2ds, and is definitely a C and not a filled or broken G. Incidentally, the same coins show CAROLVS III, where a third numeral was punched in and then partially covered by a stop. There are other anomalies too.

JAMES II

As other small coins, but I crowned on reverse.

2293	**1685**	*S*	
2294	**1686**	*S*	
2295	**1687**	*S*	
2295A	—	*R*	7 of date over 6
2295B	—	*R²*	7 of date over 8
2296	**1688**	*S*	
2297	—	*S*	Last 8 of date over 7

WILLIAM AND MARY

Type **A**   As the halfgroat, but I under crown, legend continuous over the heads.

     B   Similar, but legend broken by the heads.

     C   Similar to *Obv.* **B**, but the date is split by the crown.

2298	**A**	**1689**	*R²*	See note[1]
2299	—	—	*R⁵*	Reads GVIELMVS
2299A	—	—	*R³*	Reads MARIA
2300	**B**	**1690**	*R*	
2301	—	**1691**	*S*	1 of date over 0
2302	—	**1692**	*R*	
2303	—	—	*R*	2 of date over 1
2304	—	**1693**	*S*	
2305	**C**	**1694**	*S*	
2306	—	—	*R*	No stops on *obv.*
2306A	—	—	*S*	HI for HIB
2306B	—	—	*S*	— 9 of date over 6

[1] This date is difficult to read as it has been very badly punched into the die, but all pieces with the legend continuous over the heads on *obverse* are of this date.

WILLIAM III

O. As groat. R. As last.

2307	**1698**	*S*		2311	**1698**	*S*	Reads HI. BREX
2308	—	*S*	6 of date above crown	2312	**1699**	*R*	
2309	—	*S*	9 of date above crown	2313	**1700**	*R*	
2310	—	*S*	Reads IRA for FRA	2314	**1701**	*S*	

ANNE

O. As groat. R. As last.

2315	**1703**	*R*	BR. FRA
2316	**1705**	*S*	BR. FR
2317	**1706**	*S*	—
2318	—	*S*	— 0 of date above crown
2319	**1708**	*R²*	BRI. FR
2320	**1709**	*S*	—
2321	**1710**	*R²*	—
2322	**1713**	*R*	— 3 of date over 0

GEORGE I

O. As groat. R. As last.

2323	**1716**	*C*		2327	**1723**	*S*	See note[1]
2324	**1718**	*C*		2328	**1725**	*C*	
2325	**1720**	*C*		2329	**1726**	*R*	
2326	—	*C*	Reads HIPEX	2330	**1727**	*R*	Reads BRI·FR

[1] Coins of 1727 have smaller lettering like the other denominations.

GEORGE II

Type **A** R 1, date over small crown.
    B R 2, large crown dividing date.

2331	A	1729	S			2342	—	1750	C	
2332	—	1731	N			2343	—	1752	C	
2333	B	1732	N			2344	—	—	S	2 of date over 0
2334	—	—	S	A slight variety of		2345	—	1753	C	
				bust		2345A	—	—	R	3 of date over 2
2335	—	1735	S			2346	—	1754	C	
2336	—	1737	S			2347	—	1755	C	
2337	—	1739	N			2348	—	1756	C	
2338	—	1740	N			2349	—	1757	C	
2339	—	1743	N			2349A	—	—	N	Colon after GRATIA
2340	—	1746	N			2350	—	1758	C	
2341	—	—	R	6 of date over 3 or		2351	—	1759	C	
				5 over 3?		2352	—	1760	S	

GEORGE III

Type **A** Youngish laur. bust dr. r. R. As before.

2353	A	1763	S			2357	—	1776	N
2353A	—	—	R⁷	*Proof*		2358	—	1779	N
2353B	—	1765	R⁷			2359	—	1780	S
2354	—	1766	N			2360	—	1781	C
2355	—	1770	C			2361	—	1784	C
2356	—	1772	N			2362	—	1786	C

Note: For type B, C and D of George III and all later pennies, see Maundy
Money sets.

Shape of crown on reverse varies for type **A**.

HALFPENNY

THE COMMONWEALTH

2363   As illustration. No legend and no mark of value.   N
            From 1672 halfpence were struck in copper.

SMALL SILVER AND MAUNDY MONEY

Small Silver Coins. Most numismatic works have erroneously classified as Maundy money all the small coins (i.e., 4d, 3d, 2d and 1d) struck after the Commonwealth except for early Charles II hammered coins, Britannia groats, modern threepences and one or two odd pieces. However, it is difficult to decide exactly when the ordinary issue of small pieces for currency stops and the issue of pieces specially for the Maundy begins. I gave this interesting subject much consideration and was inclined to agree with Dr. G. C. Brooke in drawing the line at the beginning of the reign of George II, but now feel that it should be sometime in the reign of George III.[1]

For centuries pennies were the only coins used for distribution as Maundy money and it would seem that they continued exclusively to be so used until late in the eighteenth century as pennies were the only small coin struck in certain years until 1781. Concurrently, however, other small coins were used for distribution as largesse and for other royal charities and some may have been struck solely for these purposes.

The average state of preservation to-day of these small pieces prior to the reign of George II is not good, especially the 4d, 3d and 2d, which implies that they were used for ordinary currency. Except for those coins that we know to have been issued for currency (i.e., threepences, Britannia groats, etc.) the small denominations from 1800 to the present day usually turn up in almost perfect condition, which indicates they were not used for currency. With regard to the small coins of the reign of George II, the average condition is certainly much above that of the earlier reigns, and the condition of the first type of George III is even more so, but it is still not so good as the condition of those after 1800. So some of them may have circulated.

In the foregoing lists of 4d, 3d, 2d and 1d I have included all coins up to the end of the first issue of George III (1786). To these I have added those pieces of later date that are known to have been struck for circulation in Britain or any part of the British Empire which used the Imperial Coinage.

In the following list I have included every year in which all four coins were issued, and in so doing have duplicated all those pieces struck before 1792, as well as the odd coins after that date. This has been done to help those collectors who collect sets only.

Maundy Money. These are coins struck specially for the Maundy celebration. They are legal tender. In early times and, perhaps, up to the reign of George II and/or some dates up to 1800, the penny was the only coin used.

---

[1] See *Numismatic Chronicle*, 1934, part 1, page 55.

202   ENGLISH SILVER COINAGE

Since then it has been usual to use fourpences, threepences, twopences and pennies in equal proportion or as nearly equal as possible.

The Maundy set, therefore, consists of these four coins which are usually collected in pieces of uniform date. Collectors sometimes wonder why Maundy Money of Victoria and Edward VII and, in fact, of many earlier reigns is more common than the modern issues. It was the practice of the Royal Mint to make very many more sets than were required for the ceremony and it was possible for collectors and others to purchase them each year through a bank. In 1909, following a complaint by the recipients of the bounty, a restriction in the amount of Maundy money coined was made on the express command of the king, Edward VII. Therefore, today the number struck is strictly limited i.e., the coins given to the recipients at the Maundy ceremony plus a certain number for officials taking part, and for certain official gifts, and some Mint employees—about 1,000 of each denomination. After decimalisation, Maundy coins were declared legal tender for 4, 3, 2 and 1 New Pence. It is not possible to differentiate between some issues of silver threepences struck for Maundy sets and those issued for currency. All silver threepences are legal tender for 3p.

Maundy Celebration. This takes place on Maundy Thursday (the day before Good Friday). Traditionally The Maundy Service was held at Westminster Abbey but since 1970 the distribution has taken place from a different Cathedral each year. The reigning monarch or his representative distributes the Maundy money and other gifts to a certain number of old men and women. The number of coins of each denomination distributed corresponds to the age of the Sovereign. Furthermore, Maundy money consists of as many pence as the monarch's age, hence when H.M. King George V was fifty, 50 men and 50 women each received 5 sets of coins (= 50d). The next year they received 5 sets with an additional penny. These coins are presented in a white bag. The Maundy ceremony is of great antiquity coming down to us from the early Christian church, and is derived from the day on which Christ washed his disciples' feet and gave a commandment for them to do likewise. In the middle ages it was a practice for many to perform this ceremony, and at the same time to provide selected persons with clothes, food and money. The first English monarch known to have done this was Edward II, who washed the feet of fifty poor men, although there is a written record as early as the reign of John that a definite sum was set aside for the distribution.[1] As time has gone on this practice of washing feet has ceased but the distribution of money and gifts continued. Within comparatively recent years gifts of clothes and food have been replaced by money. These are given in addition to the Maundy coins.

There is extensive literature on the subject, the latest being *Silver Pennies & Linen Towels* by B. Robinson, 1992.

---

[1] See *British Numismatic Journal*, Vol. XVI, p. 209.

SMALL SILVER and/or MAUNDY MONEY SETS

Each set consists of four coins: 4d, 3d, 2d and 1d.

All coins earlier than 1792 listed below, have also been included under their respective denominations in the preceding pages, where will also be found those odd pieces of the years in which the complete set was not issued. After 1792 the coins listed under their various denominations are the ones which were struck for currency as well as for the Maundy ceremony.

CHARLES II

2364   Type **A**   *Hammered*. With mark of value and inner circle   *N*

2365   Type **B**   *Milled*. Undated Maundy   *N*

Type **C**   *Milled*. Dated sets as below

No.	Date	R	Remarks, etc.	No.	Date	R	Remarks, etc.
2366	1670	R	See note[1]	2374	1678	R²	
2367	1671	S		2375	1679	R	
2368	1672	R		2376	1680	S	
2369	1673	S		2377	1681	R²	
2370	1674	S		2378	1682	R	
2371	1675	S		2379	1683	S	
2372	1676	S		2380	1684	R	
2373	1677	S					

[1] All pieces of this date we have seen have the 2 of date over 1

JAMES II

2381	**1686**	*S*
2382	**1687**	*S*
2383	**1688**	*S*

WILLIAM AND MARY

2384	**1689**	R^3		2387	**1693**	R^2
2385	**1691**	*R*		2388	**1694**	*R*
2386	**1692**	*R*				

WILLIAM III

2389	**1698**	*R*		2391	**1700**	R^2
2390	**1699**	R^2		2392	**1701**	*R*

ANNE

2393	**1703**	*R*		2397	**1709**	R^2
2394	**1705**	*R*		2398	**1710**	*R*
2395	**1706**	*S*		2399	**1713**	*R*
2396	**1708**	*R*				

GEORGE I

2400	**1723**	*R*
2401	**1727**	*R*

GEORGE II

2402	**1729**	*R*		2407	**1739**	*S*
2403	**1731**	*R*		2408	**1740**	*S*
2404	**1732**	*S*		2409	**1743**	*S*
2405	**1735**	*S*		2410	**1746**	*S*
2406	**1737**	*S*		2411	**1760**	*R*

GEORGE III

Type **A**¹   *O*. GEORGIVS III DEI GRATIA, youngish laur. bust dr.r. R. Normal type.
      A²   As **A**¹, but new reverse dies of similar type but flatter design.

Type **B**   *O*. Similar, but smaller head and much larger bust, also cuirassed and with older features. R. Similar, but the figures 4, 3 and 2 are in thin script. Hence this type, only issued in 1792, is known as "Wire money".

Type **C**   *O*. As last. R. Normal types.

D   *O*. As illustrations; laur. head only. R. Normal type.

2412	A¹	1763	S			2419	B	1792	R
2413	—	—	R⁶	*Proof set*		2420	C	1795	N
2414	—	1766	S			2421	—	1800	C
2415	—	1772	S			2422	D	1817	S
2416	—	1780	S			2423	—	1818	S
2417	A²	1784	S			2424	—	1820	S
2418	—	1786	S						

GEORGE IV

Small head

O. As on the larger coins of the first issue.   R.   Numeral and date in wreath.

2425	**1822**	*N*	See note[1]	2431	**1827**	*N*	
2426	—	*R⁴*	*Proof set*	2432	**1828**	*N*	
2427	**1823**	*N*		2433	—	*R⁵*	*Proof set*
2428	**1824**	*R*		2434	**1829**	*N*	
2429	**1825**	*N*		2435	**1830**	*N*	
2430	**1826**	*N*					

WILLIAM IV

2436	**1831**	*S*		2441	**1834**	*S*	
2437	—	*R*	*Proof set*	2442	**1835**	*S*	
2438	—	*R⁵*	*— In gold*	2443	**1836**	*S*	
2439	**1832**	*S*		2444	**1837**	*S*	
2440	**1833**	*S*					

[1] The head on the threepence of 1822 is smaller than on the threepences of the other dates. According to Hawkins the first punch broke and as there was no time to engrave another with the correct size head, a die was made up using the punch of the bust of the twopence.

Of the individual coins of this and the following reigns the threepence is the most scarce in good condition as some of them apparently found their way into circulation after 1845.

VICTORIA

Type **A**   *O*. Young head. **R**. Normal.

Type **B**   Similar, but Jubilee type bust.[1]

Type **C**   Similar, but 'old head' bust.

---

[1] The Jubilee bust was not used on the Maundy money of 1887 as the Maundy ceremony was some weeks prior to the Jubilee.

2445	A	1838	N		2482	A	1870	N	
2446	—	—	R^3	Proof set	2483	—	1871	N	
2447	—	—	R^5	— In gold	2484	—	—	R^4	Proof set, R s
2448	—	1839	N						inverted
2449	—	—	R	Proof set	2485	—	1872	N	
2450	—	1840	N		2486	—	1873	N	
2451	—	1841	S		2487	—	1874	N	
2452	—	1842	N		2488	—	1875	N	
2453	—	1843	N		2489	—	1876	N	
2454	—	1844	N		2490	—	1877	N	
2455	—	1845	N		2491	—	1878	N	
2456	—	1846	N		2492	—	—	R^3	Proof set
2457	—	1847	N		2493	—	1879	N	
2458	—	1848	N		2494	—	1880	N	
2459	—	1849	S		2495	—	1881	N	
2460	—	1850	N		2495A	—	—	R^3	Proof set
2461	—	1851	N		2496	—	1882	N	
2462	—	1852	N		2497	—	1883	N	
2463	—	1853	N		2498	—	1884	N	
2464	—	—	R^2	Proof set	2499	—	1885	N	
2465	—	1854	N		2500	—	1886	N	
2466	—	1855	S		2501	—	1887	S	
2467	—	1856	N		2502	B	1888	S	
2468	—	1857	N		2503	—	—	R^2	Proof set
2469	—	1858	N		2504	—	1889	S	
2470	—	1859	N		2505	—	1890	S	
2471	—	1860	N		2506	—	1891	S	
2472	—	1861	N		2507	—	1892	S	
2473	—	1862	N		2508	C	1893	C	
2474	—	1863	N		2509	—	1894	C	
2475	—	1864	N		2510	—	1895	C	
2476	—	1865	N		2511	—	1896	C	
2477	—	1866	N		2512	—	1897	C	
2478	—	1867	N		2513	—	1898	C	
2479	—	—	R^3	Proof set	2514	—	1899	C	
2480	—	1868	N		2515	—	1900	C	
2481	—	1869	N		2516	—	1901	C	

EDWARD VII

2517	**1902**	*C*		2522	**1906**	*C*	
2518	—	*N*	*Proof set*, matt	2523	**1907**	*C*	
2519	**1903**	*C*		2524	**1908**	*C*	
2520	**1904**	*C*		2525	**1909**	*S*	
2521	**1905**	*C*		2526	**1910**	*S*	

GEORGE V

Type **A**   *O*. As the other coins. R. Normal type. .925 silver.
     B   Similar, but metal changed to .500 silver.
     C   *O*. Modified effigy as other denominations.
     D   Similar. R. Re-engraved.

2527	**A**	**1911**	*S*		2541	—	**1924**	*S*	
2528	—	—	*S*	*Proof set*	2542	—	**1925**	*S*	
2529	—	**1912**	*S*		2543	—	**1926**	*S*	
2530	—	**1913**	*S*		2544	—	**1927**	*S*	Note[1]
2531	—	**1914**	*S*		2545	**C**	**1928**	*S*	
2532	—	**1915**	*S*		2546	—	**1929**	*S*	
2533	—	**1916**	*S*		2547	**D**	**1930**	*S*	
2534	—	**1917**	*S*		2548	—	**1931**	*S*	
2535	—	**1918**	*S*		2549	—	**1932**	*S*	Note[2]
2536	—	**1919**	*S*		2550	—	**1933**	*S*	
2537	—	**1920**	*S*		2551	—	**1934**	*S*	
2538	**B**	**1921**	*S*		2552	—	**1935**	*R*	Note[3]
2539	—	**1922**	*S*		2553	—	**1936**	*R*	**Edw. VIII**[2]
2540	—	**1923**	*S*						

[1] When the type change took place in 1927/8 the design of the current threepence was altered but the Maundy threepence remained as before; so for the first time the Maundy and current threepences were of different design.

[2] Personally distributed by the reigning monarch. In 1932 it was the first time that this had been done for about two hundred and fifty years. In 1936 it was distributed by King Edward VIII but the coins still bore the portrait of George V.

[3] The King's Jubilee Year when most of the bags of Maundy coins were bought up by American visitors.

GEORGE VI

Type **A** *O*. As other coins. ℞. Normal. .500 silver.
     B Similar, but good silver. .925 fineness.
     C As last, but without IND. IMP.

2554	**A**	**1937**	*S*	Note[1]	2562	**A**	**1945**	*R*	Note[2]
2555	—	**1938**	*R*		2563	—	**1946**	*R*	Note[2]
2556	—	**1939**	*R*		2564	**B**	**1947**	*R*	Note[3]
2557	—	**1940**	*R*	Note[2]	2565	—	**1948**	*R*	Note[2]
2558	—	**1941**	*R*		2566	**C**	**1949**	*R*	
2559	—	**1942**	*R*		2567	—	**1950**	*R*	Note[2]
2560	—	**1943**	*R*		2568	—	**1951**	*R*	Note[2,4]
2561	—	**1944**	*R*	Note[2]	2569	—	**1952**	*R*	Note[2,5]

---

[1] Proofs of the Maundy were included in the 1937 specimen sets, but these cannot be distinguished from the ordinary Maundy coins which are of proof quality.
In this reign also the Maundy threepence is of different design to the current silver threepences.

[2] Personally distributed by the reigning monarch. In 1952 it was distributed by Queen Elizabeth II, but the coins were of George VI.

[3] When the coinage was changed to cupro-nickel in 1947 it was decided that the Maundy pieces should not be struck in this metal, but should once again be made in good silver. The Queen's Maundy are now the only coins struck regularly in .925 silver.

[4] Proofs from Sand blasted dies exist for this date.

[5] Also struck *in copper*.

ELIZABETH II

Type A　*O.* ELIZABETH II DEI GRA : BRITT : OMN : REGINA F : D : , bust as other coins. R. Normal 925 : 1000 fineness.

Type B　As before but ELIZABETH II DEI GRATIA REGINA F : D :

No	Type	Date	R	Maundy Ceremony Venue
2570	A	1953	R^2	St. Paul's Cathedral, (see note [1], page 213)
2571	B	1954	R	Westminster Abbey
2572	—	1955	R	Southwark Cathedral
2573	—	1956	R	Westminster Abbey
2574	—	1957	R	St. Alban's Cathedral
2575	—	1958	R	Westminster Abbey
2576	—	1959	R	Windsor, St George's Chapel
2577	—	1960	R	Westminster Abbey
2578	—	1961	R	Rochester Cathedral
2579	—	1962	R	Westminster Abbey
2580	—	1963	R	Chelmsford Cathedral
2581	—	1964	R	Westminster Abbey
2582	—	1965	R	Canterbury Cathedral
2583	—	1966	R	Westminster Abbey
2584	—	1967	R	Durham Cathedral
2585	—	1968	R	Westminster Abbey
2586	—	1969	R	Selby Abbey
2587	—	1970	R	Westminster Abbey
2588	—	1971	R	Tewkesbury Abbey
2589	—	1972	R	York Minster
2590	—	1973	R	Westminster Abbey
2591	—	1974	R	Salisbury Cathedral
2592	—	1975	R	Peterborough Cathedral
2593	—	1976	R	Hereford Cathedral
2594	—	1977	R	Westminster Abbey
2595	—	1978	R	Carlisle Cathedral
2596	—	1979	R	Winchester Cathedral
2597	—	1980	R	Worcester Cathedral
2598	—	1981	R	Westminster Abbey
2599	—	1982	R	St Davids Cathedral
2600	—	1983	R	Exeter Cathedral
2601	—	1984	R	Southwell Minster

2602	—	1985	R	Ripon Cathedral
2603	—	1986	R	Chichester Cathedral
2604	—	1987	R	Ely Cathedral
2605	—	1988	R	Lichfield Cathedral
2606	—	1989	R	Birmingham Cathedral
2607	—	1990	R	Newcastle Cathedral
2608	—	1991	R	Westminster Abbey
2609	—	1992	R	Chester Cathedral

[1] Sand blasted proofs exist for this date; also a set in gold which is probably unique (ex Norweb Collection).

PART TWO

DECIMAL CURRENCY
1971–

DECIMAL CURRENCY

INTRODUCTION

On the 19 December 1961, the Chancellor of the Exchequer announced the appointment of a Committee of Enquiry, under the chairmanship of the Rt. Hon. the Earl of Halsbury, to advise on the most convenient and practical form which a decimal currency might take, including the major and minor units to be adopted. This decision to appoint a committee was doubtless influenced by the publication in the previous year of a joint report by the British Association for the Advancement of Science and the Association of the British Chambers of Commerce, entitled 'Decimal Coinage and the Metric System — Should Britain Change?' Plans for the decimalisation of the coinage of Australia and New Zealand and a desire that our coinage should harmonise with that of our Commonwealth partners was also a prime consideration. In the post-war years many former colonies had attained independence and had changed from the British £ s d system to a decimal based currency. Britain's currency was appearing to many to be somewhat antiquated.

Various decimal systems were considered by the Committee and some pattern and trial pieces date from this period. A decision to adopt a system based on the £ Sterling of 100 pence was made and details of the new denominations and designs adopted by the Royal Mint were made known to the public on 15 February 1968, exactly three years to the day before the new currency was introduced.

The new system allowed the florin, or two shilling piece, the shilling and the sixpence to fit into the new structure as the ten new pence, five new pence and two and a half new pence respectively. It was considered that the sixpence would not be maintained as an active denomination; it was finally withdrawn on 30 June 1980. As a measure to avoid hoarding by speculators all currency issues of £ s d. coins from 1 January 1967 onwards bore the date 1967, although a proof set was struck of coins dated 1970.

The only silver or cupro-nickel coin which would have no logical equivalent under the new system was the halfcrown. It was demonetized on 1 July 1970 although it continued to be used in Malta until 1972. A proclamation respecting the circulation of pre-decimal issues was signed on 28 July 1971 and came into force on 30 August 1971. It stated 'Cupro-nickel or silver coins issued by our Mint before the fifteenth day of February 1971, in accordance with the Coinage Acts of 1870 to 1946, being coins of the denominations: 5s; 4s; 2s; 1s and 6d shall . . . be treated as coins of the new currency and as being of the denominations respectively of 25p; 20p; 10p; 5p; and 2 1/2p.'

Although the change to decimalisation was not effected until 15 February 1971, the ten and five new pence coins were issued in 1968 and circulated alongside their equivalent two shilling and one shilling pieces. The bronze two, one and one half new pence were also issued in 1968, dated 1971, but not legalised for currency until 1971. They were released in a blue wallet which also contained the new five pence and ten pence coins. In October 1969, the fifty new pence coin was issued, circulating as a ten shilling piece at the same time as the ten shilling note.

The word 'new' was omitted in 1982, and all coins in cupro-nickel and bronze now show the value in words and figures. A portrait of the Queen by Arnold Machin appears on all decimal coins before 1985. In that year a new effigy by Raphael Maklouf was introduced for all coinage except the Maundy pieces which continue to bear the Gillick portrait.

Following decimalisation the Maundy coins retained their traditional numeric denominations and thus became new pence. At a stroke therefore the previous Maundy coinage had its face value re-valued upwards.

During 1972 the Queen and Prince Philip celebrated their Silver Wedding and the occasion was marked by the issue of a commemorative twenty-five pence coin. It is identical in size to the old crown piece although it bears no denomination. Both the obverse and reverse designs are by Arnold Machin.

A new reverse design by David Wynne for the fifty pence piece, showing nine clasped hands, was issued in 1973 to commemorate British entry into the E.E.C. on 1 January of that year. Proofs in cupro-nickel were issued in cases, and a very few piedforts were struck in fine silver for V.I.P.s'.

The tradition of marking historic and Royal events by striking a crown was continued in 1977, when a twenty five pence coin, showing a modern equestrian portrait of her Majesty with regalia on the reverse, was issued to commemorate the Silver Jubilee. Proofs of a very high standard of workmanship were issued in fine silver and displayed in blue leatherette cases.

Crowns of twenty five pence were again issued in 1980 in honour of the Queen Mother's 80th Birthday, and in 1981 on the occasion of the wedding of the Prince of Wales and Lady Diana Spencer. Fine silver proofs and nickel specimens were issued in both cases. The Queen Mother crown shows her small head in the centre of bows and lions, a punning reference to the Bowes-Lyon family. The wedding crown has conjoined busts of the Royal couple on the reverse.

These are likely to be the last of the traditional five shilling crowns as the increase in raw materials and production costs no longer make such issues an economic proposition. A commemorative crown was issued in 1990 for the 90th Birthday of Queen Elizabeth, the Queen Mother, with a face value of five pounds. This coin is listed in Part Three of this work.

During the early 1980's there was a feeling that due to inflation the value of the five pence and ten pence coins was decreasing. After all, the basic specification of the five pence had remained unchanged since 1816. It was also felt that the weight of small change was excessive because there was a large gap between a ten pence and a fifty pence piece. This led, in 1982, to the introduction of the twenty pence coin, bringing back memories of the last twenty pence or four shilling piece — the double florin of 1887–1890. This twenty pence piece, however, is set to survive for longer than its predecessor as it does not have to compete with a twenty-five pence piece in general use. The coin is the same shape as the fifty pence piece. The crowned Tudor rose reverse design surrounded by a raised border is very effective. Silver double-thickness (piedfort) proofs were struck in modest numbers. It has been very successful and over 1400 million twenty pence pieces have been issued. As a result no new ten pence (prior to the introduction of the smaller size in 1992) and very few five pence coins have been struck since 1982.

In December 1984 the smallest coin, the half penny, was demonetised as its value had been so reduced by inflation. Since then the ten pence and five pence coins have been reduced in size in 1992 and 1990 respectively. All pre-decimal one shilling coins plus the same size five pence coins ceased to be legal tender on 31 December, 1990. The pre-decimal two shilling coins plus the same size ten pence coins will cease to be legal tender during 1993.

No firm decisions for the future development of the Royal Mint coinage have been announced. Readers should refer to the statement from the Royal Mint on page 237. The fifty pence coin is now the largest and heaviest coin in circulation and any future changes may well involve that coin.

FIFTY PENCE

TYPE A

Type **A**   *O*. ELIZABETH II D . G . REG . F . D . (date). Coronetted bust r.
      R. Britannia and Lion r., NEW PENCE above, 50 in exergue.

No.	TYPE	DATE	R	VARIETIES, Remarks, etc.
3001	Cu-Ni..........................	**1969**	C^2	
3002	—..........................	**1970**	C^2	
3003	—..........................	**1971**	N	Proof from the set
3004	—..........................	**1972**	N	Proof from the set
3005	—..........................	**1974**	N	Proof from the set
3006	—..........................	**1975**	N	Proof from the set
3007	—..........................	**1976**	C^2	
3008	—..........................	—	N	Proof from the set
3009	—..........................	**1977**	C^2	
3010	—..........................	—	N	Proof from the set
3011	—..........................	**1978**	C^2	
3012	—..........................	—	N	Proof from the set
3013	—..........................	**1979**	C^2	
3014	—..........................	—	N	Proof from the set
3015	—..........................	**1980**	C^2	
3016	—..........................	—	N	Proof from the set
3017	—..........................	**1981**	C^2	
3018	—..........................	—	N	Proof from the set

TYPE B

Type **B**   *O*. As type A, but no date.
             R. Nine interlinked hands around 50, 1973 above, PENCE below.

No.	Type	Date	R	Varieties, Remarks, etc.
3019	Cu-Ni............................	**1973**	C^2	Commemorates Britain's entry into the EC.
3020	—............................	—	N	Proof in case
3021	.925 Æ............................	—	R^4	Proof Piedfort; a few issued for VIP's.

TYPE C

Type **C**   *O*. As type A.
             R. As type A, but legend reads FIFTY PENCE, 50 in exergue.

3022	Cu-Ni............................	**1982**	C^2	
3023	—............................	—	N	Proof from the set
3024	—............................	**1983**	C^2	
3025	—............................	—	N	Proof from the set
3026	—............................	**1984**	N	Uncirculated from the set
3027	—............................	—	N	Proof from the set

TYPE D

Type **D**   *O*. Legend begins at 7 o'clock. New crowned bust r. R. as type C.

No.	TYPE	DATE	R	VARIETIES, Remarks, etc.
3028	Cu-Ni..........................	**1985**	*N*	
3029	—..............................	—	*N*	Proof from the set
3030	—..............................	**1986**	*N*	Uncirculated from the set
3031	—..............................	—	*N*	Proof from the set
3032	—..............................	**1987**	*N*	Uncirculated from the set
3033	—..............................	—	*N*	Proof from the set
3034	—..............................	**1988**	*N*	Uncirculated from the set
3035	—..............................	—	*N*	Proof from the set
3036	—..............................	**1989**	*N*	Uncirculated from the set
3037	—..............................	—	*N*	Proof from the set
3038	—..............................	**1990**	*N*	Uncirculated from the set
3039	—..............................	—	*N*	Proof from the set
3040	—..............................	**1991**	*N*	Uncirculated from the set
3041	—..............................	—	*N*	Proof from the set
3042	—..............................	**1992**	*N*	Uncirculated from the set
3043	—..............................	—	*N*	Proof from the set
3044	—..............................	**1993**	*N*	Uncirculated from the set
3045	—..............................	—	*N*	Proof from the set

TYPE E

Type **E**   *O*. As type D, but legend ELIZABETH II DEI. GRA. REG. F . D. (no date).
R. A conference table seen from above, around which are twelve
chairs representing the member countries of the E.C., 1992, 1993,
50 PENCE.

No.	TYPE	DATE	R	VARIETIES, Remarks, etc.
3076	Cu-Ni............................	**1992/ 93**	*N*	Commemorates Britain's Presidency of the Council of Ministers, and the completion of the European Single Market.
3077	—............................	—	*N*	Proof from the set
3078	.925 Æ........................	—	*N*	Proof in case
3079	—............................	—	*N*	Proof Piedfort in case
3080	.916 A/........................	—	*N*	Proof in case

TWENTY FIVE PENCE

TYPE A

Type A· O. ELIZABETH II D. G. REG. F. D. Bust r. as illustration.
R. ELIZABETH AND PHILIP. 20 November 1947–1972, Crowned EP
and Cupid motif. *Undated.*

No.	TYPE	DATE	R	VARIETIES, Remarks, etc.
3101	Cu-Ni...........................	**1972**	C	Issued to commemorate the Royal Silver Wedding on 20 November 1972.
3102	—	—	N	Proof from the set
3103	.500 Æ.......................	—	S	Proof in case

TYPE B

Type **B**   *O*. ELIZABETH II D. G. REG. F. D. 1977. Queen on horse 1.
         R. Coronation regalia crowned in floral border.

No.	Type	Date	R	Varieties, Remarks, etc.
3104	Cu-Ni............................	**1977**	C^2	Issued to commemorate the Silver Jubilee.
3105	—	—	*C*	Specimen issued in folder
3106	—	—	*N*	Proof from the set
3107	.925 Æ	—	*N*	Proof in case

TYPE C

Type **C** *O*. As type A.

R. QUEEN ELIZABETH THE QUEEN MOTHER AUGUST 4th 1980. Her small bust in centre, surrounded by bows and lions.

No.	TYPE	DATE	R	VARIETIES, Remarks, etc.
3108	Cu-Ni..........................	**1980**	C	Issued to commemorate the 80th Birthday of Her Majesty Queen Elizabeth, the Queen Mother.
3109	—.............................	—	C	Specimen issued in folder
3110	.925 Æ.......................	—	S	Proof in case

T<small>YPE</small> D

Type **D**   *O*. As type A.

R. H R H THE PRINCE OF WALES AND LADY DIANA SPENCER 1981. Their conjoined heads 1.

No.	T<small>YPE</small>	D<small>ATE</small>	R	V<small>ARIETIES</small>, Remarks, etc.
3111	Cu-Ni............................	**1981**	*C*	Issued to commemorate the wedding of HRH Prince Charles and Lady Diana Spencer.
3112	—	—	*C*	Specimen issued in folder
3113	.925 Æ.........................	—	*S*	Proof in case

TWENTY PENCE

Type A

Type **A**   *O*. ELIZABETH II D. G. REG. F. D. Coronetted bust r.
              R. TWENTY PENCE. Crowned Tudor Rose dividing date; 20 below.

No.	Type	Date	R	Varieties, Remarks, etc.
3126	Cu-Ni	**1982**	C^3	
3127	—	—	N	Proof from the set
3128	.925 Æ	—	S	Proof Piedfort
3129	Cu-Ni	**1983**	C^2	
3130	—	—	N	Proof from the set
3131	—	**1984**	C^2	
3132	—	—	N	Proof from the set

Type B

Type **B**   *O*. New crowned bust r. R. as type A.

No.	Type	Date	R	Varieties, Remarks, etc.
3133	Cu-Ni	**1985**	C^2	
3134	—	—	N	Proof from the set
3135	—	**1986**	N	Uncirculated from the set
3136	—	—	N	Proof from the set
3137	—	**1987**	C^2	
3138	—	—	N	Proof from the set
3139	—	**1988**	C	
3140	—	—	N	Proof from the set
3141	—	**1989**	C^2	
3142	—	—	N	Proof from the set
3143	—	**1990**	C^2	
3144	—	—	N	Proof from the set
3145	—	**1991**	N	
3146	—	—	N	Proof from the set
3147	—	**1992**	N	
3148	—	—	N	Proof from the set
3149	—	**1993**	N	
3150	—	—	N	Proof from the set

TEN PENCE

TYPE A   TYPE B

Type **A**   *O*. ELIZABETH II D. G. REG. F. D. (date). Coronetted bust r.
             R. Crowned lion passant guardant, NEW PENCE above, 10 below.

No.	TYPE	DATE	R	VARIETIES, Remarks, etc.
3201	Cu-Ni............................	**1968**	C^3	
3202	—	**1969**	C^3	
3203	—	**1970**	C^2	
3204	—	**1971**	C	
3205	—	—	N	Proof from the set
3206	—	**1972**	N	Proof from the set
3207	—	**1973**	C^3	
3208	—	—	N	Proof from the set
3209	—	**1974**	C^2	
3210	—	—	N	Proof from the set
3211	—	**1975**	C^3	
3212	—	—	N	Proof from the set
3213	—	**1976**	C^3	
3214	—	—	N	Proof from the set
3215	—	**1977**	C^2	
3216	—	—	N	Proof from the set
3217	—	**1978**	N	Proof from the set
3218	—	**1979**	C^3	
3219	—	—	S	Proof from the set
3220	—	**1980**	C^2	
3221	—	—	N	Proof from the set
3222	—	**1981**	C	
3223	—	—	N	Proof from the set

Type **B**   *O*. As type A. **R**. As type A, but legend reads TEN PENCE

No.	Type	Date	R	Varieties, Remarks, etc.
3224	Cu-Ni............................	**1982**	*N*	Uncirculated from the set
3225	—	—	*N*	Proof from the set
3226	—	**1983**	*N*	Uncirculated from the set
3227	—	—	*N*	Proof from the set
3228	—	**1984**	*N*	Uncirculated from the set
3229	—	—	*N*	Proof from the set

TYPE C

Type **C**   *O*. New portrait. Legend starts at 7 o'clock. **R**. As type B.

3230	Cu-Ni............................	**1985**	*N*	Uncirculated from the set
3231	—	—	*N*	Proof from the set
3232	—	**1986**	*N*	Uncirculated from the set
3233	—	—	*N*	Proof from the set
3234	—	**1987**	*N*	Uncirculated from the set
3235	—	—	*N*	Proof from the set
3236	—	**1988**	*N*	Uncirculated from the set
3237	—	—	*N*	Proof from the set
3238	—	**1989**	*N*	Uncirculated from the set
3239	—	—	*N*	Proof from the set
3240	—	**1990**	*N*	Uncirculated from the set
3241	—	—	*N*	Proof from the set
3242	—	**1991**	*N*	Uncirculated from the set
3243	—	—	*N*	Proof from the set
3244	—	**1992**	*N*	Uncirculated from the set
3245	—	—	*N*	Proof from the set
3246	.925 Æ..........................	—	*N*	Proof

TYPE D

Type **D** as type C but with reduced diameter 24.5mm.

No.	TYPE	DATE	R	VARIETIES, Remarks, etc.
3247	Cu-Ni............................	**1992**	C^3	
3248	—	—	N	Proof from the set
3249	.925 Æ.........................	—	N	Proof
3250	—	—	S	Proof Piedfort
3251	Cu-Ni............................	**1993**	C^2	
3252	—	—	N	Proof from the set

FIVE PENCE

TYPE A

Type **A**   *O*. ELIZABETH II. D. G. REG. F. D. (date). Coronetted bust r.
         R. Crowned thistle, NEW PENCE above, 5 below.

3301	Cu-Ni............................	**1968**	C^2	
3302	—	**1969**	C^2	
3303	—	**1970**	C^3	
3304	—	**1971**	C^2	
3305	—	—	N	Proof from the set
3306	—	**1972**	N	Proof from the set
3307	—	**1973**	N	Proof from the set

No.	Type	Date	R	Varieties, Remarks, etc.
3308	—	**1974**	*N*	Proof from the set
3309	—	**1975**	*C³*	
3310	—	—	*N*	Proof from the set
3311	—	**1976**	*N*	Proof from the set
3312	—	**1977**	*C*	
3313	—	—	*N*	Proof from the set
3314	—	**1978**	*C²*	
3315	—	—	*N*	Proof from the set
3316	—	**1979**	*C³*	
3317	—	—	*N*	Proof from the set
3318	—	**1980**	*C³*	
3319	—	—	*N*	Proof from the set
3320	—	**1981**	*N*	Proof from the set

Type B

Type **B**   *O*. As type A. **R**. As type A, but legend reads FIVE PENCE

No.	Type	Date	R	Varieties, Remarks, etc.
3321	—	**1982**	*N*	Uncirculated from the set
3322	—	—	*N*	Proof from the set
3323	—	**1983**	*N*	Uncirculated from the set
3324	—	—	*N*	Proof from the set
3325	—	**1984**	*N*	Uncirculated from the set
3326	—	—	*N*	Proof from the set

TYPE C

Type **C** *O*. New portrait. Legend starts at 7 o'clock. R. As type B.

No.	TYPE	DATE	R	VARIETIES, Remarks, etc.
3327	Cu-Ni............................	**1985**	*N*	Uncirculated from the set
3328	—...............................	—	*N*	Proof from the set
3329	—...............................	**1986**	*N*	Uncirculated from the set
3330	—...............................	—	*N*	Proof from the set
3331	—...............................	**1987**	*C*	
3332	—...............................	—	*N*	Proof from the set
3333	—...............................	**1988**	*C²*	
3334	—...............................	—	*N*	Proof from the set
3335	—...............................	**1989**	*C²*	
3336	—...............................	—	*N*	Proof from the set
3337	—...............................	**1990**	*N*	Uncirculated from the set
3338	—...............................	—	*N*	Proof from the set
3339	.925 Æ.......................	—	*N*	Proof

TYPE D

Type **D** As type C but smaller diameter 18mm.

No.	TYPE	DATE	R	VARIETIES, Remarks, etc.
3340	Cu-Ni............................	**1990**	C^3	
3341	—............................	—	N	Proof from the set
3342	.925 Æ............................	—	N	Proof
3343	—............................	—	S	Proof Piedfort
3344	Cu-Ni............................	**1991**	C^3	
3345	—............................	—	N	Proof from the set
3346	—............................	**1992**	C^2	
3347	—............................	—	N	Proof from the set
3348	—............................	**1993**	C^2	
3349	—............................	—	N	Proof from the set

MAUNDY MONEY SETS

After decimalization, in 1971, Maundy Money continued to be issued in
.925 Æ and in the old denominations of four pence, three pence, two pence
and penny. The complete issues for the reign of Elizabeth II are listed on
pages 212–13.

PART THREE

HIGH VALUE COINS

HIGH-VALUE COINS

INTRODUCTION

Through the 1970s there was inflation and this led to the need for higher denomination coins than the fifty pence piece. The paper one pound note was beginning to have a short life since its condition deteriorated rapidly through constant use. The first pound coin since 1642 (apart from gold issues) was introduced in 1983 and the pound note was gradually phased out. This coin was struck in nickel-brass, reminiscent of the old twelve sided threepence. The coin is of chunky format with the Royal Arms and the words 'One Pound' on the reverse design. Specimens in nickel-brass, silver proofs and piedforts were issued and it has been the practice to alter the reverse design every year from 1984–88. Since 1989 the reverse design of previous years (the so-called regional variants, 1984–87) has been repeated in rotation. The design for 1993 repeats the first design from 1983 prior to the introduction of a new series of four regional variants.

The Arnold Machin portrait of the Queen appears on the 1983 and 1984 one pound coins but all other coins in this section bear the crowned effigy of the Queen by Raphael Maklouf, introduced in 1985.

Two pound coins were issued in 1986 to commemorate the Edinburgh Commonwealth Games. These were struck in gold, Sterling silver proof, .500 silver and nickel-brass uncirculated standard. Two further two pound coins were issued in 1989 for the tercentenary of the Bill of Rights (England & Wales), and for the Claim of Right (Scotland). Sterling silver and nickel-brass versions were struck with some of the former also being piedforts. These two pound coins are strictly commemorative and although legal tender were not intended as such. They were distributed by the Post Office rather than the banks, which is unusual.

As with the 'English' and 'Scottish' versions of the pre-decimal Elizabeth one shilling pieces, the regional variants of the one pound and two pound coins are legal tender throughout the United Kingdom.

It could be argued that as the two and one pound coins are struck in nickel-brass they are not strictly speaking part of the ESC series. Most collectors, however, include them in their collections of modern coins as our highest non-precious metal denominations. They also form an interesting series with all their proof and piedfort variants and are therefore included in this book. It is possible that inflation will lead to the eventual introduction of even higher denominations both as commemoratives and for every day use.

A further crown-sized coin with a face value of £5 was issued in 1990 for the 90th Birthday of Queen Elizabeth, the Queen Mother. The face value of a cupro-nickel crown had been five shillings or twenty-five pence since 1951, although the equivalent of five shillings in 1951 was £3.27 in 1990. Thus it is hoped that this new £5 face value will stand for many years. Versions have been struck in gold, sterling silver and cupro-nickel.

A second five pound crown is planned for 1993 to commemorate the 40th Anniversary of the Coronation, but no design details were available at press date.

What of the future? Will there continue to be a separate UK coinage? There is a movement within the EEC towards a unified coinage possibly based on the ECU (European Currency Unit) although again no decisions have yet been made. A number of EC countries have issued coins denominated in ECU's (or dual denominated) or have authorised the issue of patterns. Quite a number of other 'unofficial' patterns exist. To date the British Royal Mint has neither issued nor authorised any such pieces for the United Kingdom, and it seems very likely that individual UK coinage will at least see out the Twentieth century.

The Royal Mint has contributed the following statement on the future of English silver coinage.

'The introduction of the new, smaller 10 pence coin in September 1992 completed the process of decimalisation of coinage in the United Kingdom. It brought an end to the circulation of the florin, itself an early attempt at decimalisation, which had been a feature of our coinage for well over a hundred years.

There are no plans for further changes in the size, weight or composition of the coinage except for the introduction, in September 1992, of copper-plated steel one and two pence coins. These will circulate alongside the bronze coinage and there will be no noticeable difference between them.

In the longer term lies the possibility of a single European Currency though the United Kingdom has not yet decided to participate. Under the Treaty of Maastricht on European Monetary Union, coins will still be issued by member states, though the treaty provides for the harmonisation of denominations and technical specifications of coins to the extent necessary to permit their smooth circulation throughout the Community. Member states, however, would retain responsibility for the design and manufacture of coins.

The prospect of a single European coinage is many years away and very substantial issues would be involved in planning for such an eventuality.

The size of the problem is perhaps illustrated by the fact that in the twelve Community States there are upwards of 175,000 million coins presently in circulation, including 15,000 million in the United Kingdom alone. To replace them would be an immense and costly task.'

FIVE POUNDS

Type **A**   *O*. ELIZABETH. II. DEI. GRATIA. REGINA. F. D. FIVE POUNDS.
R. A Cypher in the form of a letter 'E' (for Elizabeth) in duplicate
and interlaced, flanked by a rose and a thistle. 1900. QUEEN ELIZA-
BETH THE QUEEN MOTHER. 1990.

No.	TYPE	DATE	R	VARIETIES, Remarks, etc.
3501	Cu-Ni............................	**1990**	*C*	Issued to commemorate the 90th Birthday of Her Majesty Queen Elizabeth, the Queen Mother.
3502	—	—	*N*	Specimen in presentation folder
3503	.925 Æ	—	*N*	Proof in case
3504	.916 A/	—	*S*	Proof in case

Type **B**   *O*. Design to be announced
R.

No.	TYPE	DATE	R	VARIETIES, Remarks, etc.
3505	Cu-Ni............................	**1993**	*C*	Issued to commemorate the 40th Anniversary of the Coronation.
3506	—	—	*N*	Specimen in presentation folder
3507	.925 Æ	—	*N*	Proof in case
3508	.916 A/	—	*S*	Proof in case

TWO POUNDS

Type **A**   *O.* ELIZABETH II. DEI. GRATIA. REGINA. F. D. TWO POUNDS
  R. Scottish thistle over cross of St Andrew, 1986 above.
  Edge: Grained. (and, except for the *N*) XIII COMMONWEALTH GAMES.
  SCOTLAND. 1986.

No.	TYPE	DATE	R	VARIETIES, Remarks, etc.
3601	Ni-Br............................	**1986**	*C*	
3602	—	—	*N*	Specimen in presentation folder
3603	—	—	*N*	Proof from the set
3604	.500 Æ..........................	—	*N*	
3605	.925 Æ..........................	—	*N*	Proof in case
3606	.916 *N*..........................	—	*S*	Proof in case

TYPE B   TYPE C

Type **B**   *O*. As type A.

       R. TERCENTENARY OF THE BILL OF RIGHTS. Crown above WM mono-
gram superimposed on transverse sceptre, 1689/1989 in two lines in
the field below.
Edge: Grained.

No.	TYPE	DATE	R	VARIETIES, Remarks, etc.
3607	Ni-Br............................	**1989**	C	Issued to commemorate the tercentenary of the Bill of Rights.
3608	—	—	N	Specimen in presentation folder
3609	—	—	N	Proof from the set
3610	.925 Æ.........................	—	S	Proof in case
3611	—	—	R	Proof Piedfort in case

Type **C**   *O*. As type A.

       R. TERCENTENARY OF THE CLAIM OF RIGHT. Scottish crown over
design as type B.

3612	Ni-Br............................	**1989**	N	Issued to commemorate the tercentenary of the Claim of Right in Scotland.
3613	—	—	N	Specimen in presentation folder
3614	—	—	N	Proof from the set
3615	.925 Æ.........................	—	S	Proof in case
3616	—	—	R	Proof piedfort in case

ONE POUND

TYPE A   TYPE B

Type **A** *O*. ELIZABETH II. D. G. REG. F.D. 1983. Coronetted bust r.
           R. Royal arms with supporters. ONE POUND below.
           Edge: Grained. DECUS ET TUTAMEN.

No.	TYPE	DATE	R	VARIETIES, Remarks, etc.
3701	Ni-Br..........................	**1983**	C^3	
3702	—	—	C	Specimen in presentation folder
3703	—	—	N	Proof from the set
3704	.925 Æ........................	—	N	Proof in case
3705	—	—	S	Proof Piedfort in case

Type **B** *O*. As type A excepting the date.
           R. Sprig of Thistle (Scotland) within coronet. ONE POUND below.
           Edge: Grained. NEMO ME IMPUNE LACESSIT

No.	TYPE	DATE	R	VARIETIES, Remarks, etc.
3706	Ni-Br..........................	**1984**	C^3	
3707	—	—	N	Specimen in presentation folder
3708	—	—	N	Proof from the set
3709	.925 Æ........................	—	N	Proof in case
3710	—	—	S	Proof Piedfort in case

TYPE C   TYPE D

Type **C** *O.* ELIZABETH II. D. G. REG. F. D. (date). New mature bust r. R. Leek
(Wales) within coronet, ONE POUND below.
Edge: Grained. PLEIDOL WYF I'M GWLAD

No.	TYPE	DATE	R	VARIETIES, Remarks, etc.
3711	Ni-Br............................	**1985**	*C³*	
3712	—................................	—	*C*	Specimen in presentation folder
3713	—................................	—	*N*	Proof from the set
3714	.925 Æ.........................	—	*N*	Proof in case
3715	—................................	—	*S*	Proof Piedfort in case
3716	Ni-Br............................	**1990**	*C³*	
3717	—................................	—	*N*	Proof from the set
3718	.925 Æ.........................	—	*C*	Proof in case

Type **D** *O.* As type C.
R. A flax plant (Northern Ireland) within coronet, ONE POUND below.
Edge: As type A.

3719	Ni-Br............................	**1986**	*C*	
3720	—................................	—	*C*	Specimen in presentation folder
3721	—................................	—	*N*	Proof from the set
3722	.925 Æ.........................	—	*N*	Proof in case
3723	—................................	—	*S*	Proof Piedfort in case
3724	Ni-Br............................	**1991**	*C*	
3725	—................................	—	*N*	Proof from the set
3726	.925 Æ.........................	—	*N*	Proof in case

TYPE E   TYPE F

Type **E**   *O*. As type C. R. Oak tree (England) within coronet, ONE POUND
below. Edge: As type A.

No.	TYPE	DATE	R	VARIETIES, Remarks, etc.
3727	Ni-Br............................	**1987**	C^2	
3728	—	—	C	Specimen in presentation folder
3729	—	—	N	Proof from the set
3730	.925 Æ	—	N	Proof in case
3731	—	—	S	Proof Piedfort in case
3732	Ni-Br............................	**1992**	C	
3733	—	—	N	Proof from the set
3734	.925 Æ	—	N	Proof in case

Type **F**   *O*. As type C. R. Royal arms in plain, square-topped shield, ONE
POUND in larger letters below. Edge: As type A.

3735	Ni-Br............................	**1988**	C	
3736	—	—	N	Specimen in presentation folder
3737	—	—	N	Proof from the set
3738	.925 Æ	—	N	Proof in case
3739	—	—	S	Proof Piedfort in case

Type **G**   *O*. As type C. R. As type B (Scotland). Edge: As type B.

3740	Ni-Br............................	**1989**	C^3	
3741	—	—	C	Specimen in presentation folder
3742	—	—	N	Proof from the set
3743	.925 Æ	—	N	Proof in case
3744	—	—	S	Proof Piedfort in case

Type **H**   *O.* As type C. R. As type A (Royal Arms). Edge: As type A.

No.	Type	Date	R	Varieties, Remarks, etc.
3745	Ni-Br............................	**1993**	*C*	
3746	—	—	*N*	Proof from the set
3747	.925 Æ	—	*N*	Proof in case
3748	—	—	*S*	Proof Piedfort in case

APPENDIX I

Silver and Cupro-Nickel Coinage Tables from 1816

COLLECTORS have frequently commented that a list of the numbers of coins issued each year by the Mint would provide a useful addition to this work. Detailed records of seventeenth and eighteenth century mintings are incomplete but the tables below give the issues from 1816 to 1966 inclusive. However, we have some reservations in mind regarding these figures, as they are frequently misinterpreted. The amounts given are the numbers of coins *issued* by the Mint in a particular year, *not* the number of coins that bear a particular date. In many instances dies of one year continued to be used the following year, and it is only since 1950 that totals of particular dates can be computed with accuracy. Also in some years coins have been struck with the following year's date, but have been included in the total of coins issued in the year they were made. The figures given below have been compiled from Mint records but some amounts may require amendment following current research.

TABLE I — REGULAR DENOMINATIONS

Year	Crowns	Halfcrowns	Florins	Shillings	Sixpences	Groats	Threepences
1816[1]	—	—	—	—	—	—	—
1817	—	8,092,656	—	23,031,360	10,921,680	—	—
1818	155,232	2,905,056	—	1,342,440	4,284,720	—	—
1819	683,496	4,790,016	—	7,595,280	4,712,400	—	—
1820	448,272	2,396,592	—	7,975,440	1,488,960	—	—
1821	437,976	1,435,104	—	2,463,120	863,280	—	—
1822	124,929	—	—	—	—	—	—
1823	—	2,003,760	—	693,000	—	—	—
1824	—	465,696	—	4,158,000	633,600	—	—
1825	—	2,258,784	—	2,459,160	483,120	—	—
1826	—	2,189,088	—	6,351,840	689,040	—	—
1827	—	—	—	574,200	166,320	—	—
1828	—	49,890	—	—	15,840	—	—
1829	—	508,464	—	879,120	403,920	—	—
1830	—	—	—	—	—	—	—
1831	—	—	—	—	1,340,195	—	—
1832	—	—	—	—	—	—	—
1833	—	—	—	—	—	—	—
1834	—	993,168	—	3,223,440	5,892,480	—	—
1835	—	281,952	—	1,449,360	1,552,320	—	—
1836	—	1,588,752	—	3,567,960	1,987,920	4,253,040	—
1837	—	150,526	—	479,160	506,880	962,280	—
1838	—	—	—	1,956,240	1,607,760	2,150,280	—
1839	—	—	—	5,666,760	3,310,560	1,461,240	—
1840	—	386,496	—	1,639,440	2,098,800	1,496,880	—
1841	—	42,768	—	873,160	1,386,000	344,520	—
1842	—	486,288	—	2,094,840	601,920	724,680	—
1843	—	454,608	—	1,465,200	3,160,080	1,817,640	—
1844	94,248	1,999,008	—	4,466,880	3,975,840	855,360	—
1845	159,192	2,231,856	—	4,082,760	3,714,480	914,760	1,314,720
1846	140,976	1,539,648	—	4,031,280	4,268,880	1,366,200	47,520
1847	75,706[2]	367,488	—	847,440	586,080	225,720	—
1848	—	91,872	—	194,040	—	712,800	—

[1] The coins dated 1816 were not issued until 1817, so they are included in the figures for 1817.
[2] This includes 8,000 'Gothic' crowns.

Year	Crowns	Halfcrowns	Florins	Shillings	Sixpences	Groats	Threepences
1849	—	261,360	413,820	645,480	205,920	380,160	126,720
1850	—	484,613	—	685,080	498,960	594,000	950,400
1851	—	—	1,540	470,071	2,288,107	31,300	479,065
1852	—	—	1,014,552	1,306,574	904,586	—	—
1853	—	—	3,919,950	4,256,188	3,837,930	11,880	31,680
1854	—	—	550,413	552,414	840,116	1,096,613	1,467,246
1855	—	—	831,017	1,368,499	1,129,084	646,041	383,350
1856	—	—	2,201,706	3,168,000	2,779,920	95,040[3]	1,013,760
1857	—	—	1,671,120	2,562,120	2,233,440	—	1,758,240
1858	—	—	2,239,380	3,108,600	1,932,480	—	1,441,440
1859	—	—	2,568,060	4,561,920	4,688,640	—	3,579,840
1860	—	—	635,580	1,671,120	1,100,880	—	3,405,600
1861	—	—	839,520	1,382,040	601,920	—	3,294,720
1862	—	—	594,000	954,360	990,000	—	1,156,320
1863	—	—	938,520	859,320	491,040	—	950,400
1864	—	—	1,861,200	4,518,360	4,253,040	—	1,330,560
1865	—	—	1,580,040	5,619,240	1,631,520	—	1,742,400
1866	—	—	914,760	4,989,600	5,140,080	—	1,900,800
1867	—	—	423,720	2,166,120	1,362,240	—	712,800
1868	—	—	896,940	3,330,360	1,069,200	—	1,457,280
1869	—	—	297,000	736,560	388,080	—	—
1870	—	—	1,080,648	1,467,471	479,613	—	1,283,218
1871	—	—	3,425,605	4,910,010	3,662,684	—	999,633
1872	—	—	7,199,690	8,897,781	3,382,048	—	1,293,271
1873	—	—	5,921,839	6,489,598	4,594,733	—	4,055,550
1874	—	2,188,599	1,642,630	5,503,747	4,225,726	—	4,427,031
1875	—	1,113,483	1,117,030	4,353,983	3,256,545	—	3,306,500
1876	—	633,221	580,034	1,057,487	841,435	—	1,834,389
1877	—	447,059	682,292	2,980,703	4,066,486	—	2,622,393
1878	—	1,466,323	1,786,680	3,127,131	2,624,525	—	2,419,975
1879	—	901,356	1,512,247	3,611,507	3,326,313	—	3,140,265
1880	—	1,346,350	2,167,170	4,842,786	3,892,501	—	1,610,069
1881	—	2,301,495	2,570,337	5,255,332	6,239,447	—	3,248,265
1882	—	808,227		1,611,786	759,809	—	472,965
1883	—	2,982,779	3,555,667	7,281,450	4,986,558	—	4,369,971
1884	—	1,569,175	1,447,379	3,923,993	3,422,565	—	3,322,424
1885	—	1,628,438	1,758,210	3,336,527	4,652,771	—	5,183,653
1886	—	891,767	591,773	2,086,819	2,728,249	—	6,152,669
*1887	273,581	1,438,046	1,776,903	4,034,133	3,675,607	—	2,780,761
*1888	131,899	1,428,787	1,547,540	4,526,856	4,197,698	—	518,199
*1889	1,807,223	4,811,954	2,973,561	7,039,628	8,738,928	—	4,587,010
*1890	997,862	3,228,111	1,684,737	8,794,042	9,386,955	—	4,465,834
1891	566,394	2,284,632	836,438	5,665,348	7,022,734	—	6,323,027
1892	451,334	1,710,946	283,401	4,591,622	6,245,746	—	2,578,226
1893	497,845	1,792,600	1,666,103	7,039,074	7,350,619	—	3,067,293
1894	144,906	1,524,960	1,952,842	5,953,152	3,467,704	—	1,608,603
1895	252,862	1,772,662	2,182,968	8,880,651	7,024,631	—	4,788,609
1896	317,599	2,148,505	2,944,416	9,264,551	6,651,699	—	4,598,442
1897	262,118	1,678,643	1,699,921	6,270,364	5,031,498	—	4,541,294
1898	161,450	1,870,055	3,061,343	9,768,703	5,914,100	—	4,597,177
1899	166,300	2,863,872	3,996,953	10,965,382	7,996,804	—	6,246,281
1900	353,356	4,479,128	5,528,630	10,937,590	8,984,354	—	10,644,480
1901	—	1,516,570	2,648,870	3,426,294	5,108,757	—	6,098,400
1902	256,020	1,316,008	2,189,575	7,809,481	6,367,378	—	8,268,480
1903	—	274,840	1,995,298	2,061,823	5,410,096	—	5,227,200
1904	—	709,652	2,769,932	2,040,161	4,487,098	—	3,627,360
1905	—	166,008	1,187,596	488,390	4,235,556	—	3,548,160
1906	—	2,886,206	6,910,128	10,791,025	7,641,146	—	3,152,160
1907	—	3,693,930	5,947,895	14,083,418	8,733,673	—	4,831,200
1908	—	1,758,889	3,280,010	3,806,969	6,739,491	—	8,157,600
1909	—	3,051,592	3,482,829	5,664,982	6,584,017	—	4,055,040
1910	—	2,557,685	5,650,713	26,547,236	12,490,724	—	4,563,380
1911	—	2,914,573	5,951,284	20,065,901	9,155,310	—	5,841,084
1912	—	4,700,789	8,571,731	15,594,009	10,984,129	—	8,932,825
1913	—	4,090,169	4,545,278	9,011,509	7,499,833	—	7,143,242

* Double-florins issued only in: 1887, 483,347; 1888, 243,340; 1889, 1,185,111; 1890, 782,145.
[3] No groats known of this date, so they were probably dated 1855.

Year	Crowns	Halfcrowns	Florins	Shillings	Sixpences	Groats	Threepences
1914	—	18,333,003	21,252,701	23,415,843	22,714,602	—	6,733,584
1915	—	32,433,066	12,367,939	39,279,024	15,694,597	—	5,450,617
1916	—	29,530,020	21,064,337	35,862,015	22,207,178	—	18,555,201
1917	—	11,172,052	11,181,617	22,202,608	7,725,475	—	21,662,490
1918	—	29,079,592	29,211,792	34,915,934	27,558,743	—	20,630,909
1919	—	10,266,737	9,469,292	10,823,824	13,375,447	—	16,845,687
1920	—	17,982,077	15,387,833	22,825,142	14,136,287	—	16,703,597
1921	—	23,677,889	34,863,895	22,648,763	30,339,741	—	8,749,301
1922	—	16,396,724	23,861,044	27,215,738	16,878,890	—	7,979,998
1923	—	26,308,526	21,546,533	14,575,243	6,382,793	—	—
1924	—	5,866,294	4,582,372	9,250,095	17,444,218	—	—
1925	—	1,413,461	1,404,136	5,418,764	12,720,558	—	3,731,859
1926	—	4,473,516	5,125,410	22,516,453	21,809,621	—	4,107,910
1927	15,030[4]	6,825,872	116,497	9,262,344	68,939,873	—	15,022[4]
1928	9,034	18,762,727	11,087,186	18,136,778	23,123,384	—	1,302,106
1929	4,994	17,632,636	16,397,279	19,343,006	28,319,326	—	—
1930	4,847	809,051	5,753,568	3,137,092	16,990,289	—	1,319,412
1931	4,056	11,264,468	6,556,331	6,993,926	16,873,268	—	6,251,936
1932	2,395	4,793,643	717,041	12,168,101	9,406,117	—	5,887,325
1933	7,132	10,311,494	8,685,303	11,511,624	22,185,083	—	5,578,541
1934	932	2,422,399	—	6,138,463	9,304,009	—	7,405,954
1935	714,769[5]	7,022,216	7,540,546	9,183,462	13,995,621	—	7,027,654
1936	2,473	7,039,423	9,897,448	11,910,613	24,380,171	—	3,238,670
1937	418,699	9,106,440	13,006,781	15,107,997	22,302,524	—	8,148,156
1938	—	6,426,478	7,909,388	9,631,288	13,402,701	—	6,402,473
1939	—	15,478,635	20,850,607	21,316,569	28,670,304	—	1,355,860
1940	—	17,948,439	18,700,338	21,012,215	20,875,196	—	7,914,401
1941	—	15,773,984	24,451,079	19,477,913	23,086,616	—	7,979,411
1942	—	31,220,090	39,895,243	31,130,402	44,942,785	—	4,144,051
1943	—	15,462,875	26,711,987	21,228,427	46,927,111	—	1,379,220
1944	—	15,255,165	27,560,005	22,576,918	37,952,600	—	2,005,553
1945	—	19,849,242	25,858,049	30,249,674	39,939,259	—	
1946	—	22,724,873	22,300,254	33,861,645	43,466,407	—	—
1947	—	21,911,484	22,910,085	25,449,132	29,993,263	—	—
1948	—	71,164,703	67,553,636	90,928,860	88,323,540	—	—
1949	—	28,272,512	28,614,939	40,571,479	41,355,515	—	—
1950	—	28,335,500	24,357,490	33,543,473	32,741,955	—	—
1951	2,003,540[4]	9,003,520	27,411,747	20,918,104	40,399,491	—	—
1952	—	—	—	—	1,013,477	—	—
1953	5,962,621	3,883,214	11,958,710	61,606,422	70,323,876	—	—
1954	—	11,614,953	13,085,422	57,033,767	105,241,150	—	—
1955	—	23,628,726	25,887,253	73,210,814	109,929,554	—	—
1956	—	33,934,909	47,824,500	87,760,647	109,841,555	—	—
1957	—	34,200,563	33,071,282	60,734,205	105,654,290	—	—
1958	—	15,745,668	9,564,580	55,214,862	123,518,527	—	—
1959	—	9,028,844	14,080,319	20,455,766	93,089,441	—	—
1960	1,024,038	19,929,191	13,831,782	41,404,846	103,288,346	—	-
1961	—	25,887,897	37,735,315	42,579,465	111,284,384	—	—
1962	—	23,998,112	35,129,903	54,165,689	158,355.270[6]	—	—
1963[7]	—	17,572,800	25,580,000	78,520,000	124,860,000	—	—
1964[8]	—	4,576,800	16,313,000	18,864,000	137,352,000	—	—
1965[9]	12,080,000	8,124,800	48,723,000	11,236,000	149,948,000	—	—
1966[10]	7,560,000	14,811,200	84,574,000	31,364,000	171,636,000	—	—
1967	—	33,058,400	39,718,000	—	240,788,000	—	—
1968	Decimal Coinage Struck						

[4] Proof Coins.

[5] Includes 2,500 raised edge proofs.

[6] Includes 3,767,633 sixpences dated 1961.

[7] Figures include the following number dated 1962: 2/6, 15,200; 2/-, 18,000; 1/-, 1,506,000; 6d, 11,896,000.

[8] Figures include the following number dated 1963: 2/6, 77,600; 2/-, 909,000; 1/-, 5,038,000; 6d, 7,092,000.

[9] Figures include the following number dated 1964: 2/6, 1,474,400; 2/-, 1,135,000; 1/-, 4,000; 6d, 22,076,000.

[10] Figures include the following number dated 1965: 5/-, 7,560,000; 2/6, 3,228,000; 2/-, 575,000; 1/-, 758,000.

	50 Pence	25 Pence	20 Pence	10 Pence	5 Pence
1968	—	—	—	336,143,250	98,868,250
1969	188,400,000	—	—	314,008,000	119,270,000
1970	19,450,000	—	—	133,571,000	225,742,525
1971	—	—	—	4,708,000	60,633,475
1972	—	7,542,100	—	—	—
1973	89,775,000	—	—	152,174,000	—
1974	—	—	—	92,741,000	—
1975	—	—	—	181,559,000	141,539,000
1976	43,746,500	—	—	228,220,000	—
1977	49,536,000	37,061,160	—	59,323,000	24,308,000
1978	72,005,500	—	—	—	61,094,000
1979	58,680,000	—	—	115,457,000	155,456,000
1980	89,086,000	9,306,000	—	88,650,000	220,566,000
1981	74,002,000	26,773,600	—	3,487,000	—
1982	51,312,000	—	740,815,000	—	—
1983	62,824,904	—	158,463,000	—	—
1984	—	—	65,350,965	—	—
1985	681,103	—	74,273,699	—	—
1986	—	—	—	—	—
1987	—	—	137,450,000	—	48,220,000
1988	—	—	38,038,344	—	120,744,610
1989	—	—	132,013,890	—	101,406,000
1990	—	—	75,001,250	—	1,634,840,005(i)
1991	—	—	12,500(ii)	—	591,615,000
1992	—	—	—	—	—
1993	—	—	—	—	—

(i)   reduced size introduced
(ii) not necessarily the final figure

TABLE II — ENGLISH & SCOTTISH SHILLINGS

Year	English	Scottish	Total
1937	8,359,122	6,748,875	15,107,997
1938	4,833,436	4,797,852	9,631,288
1939	11,052,677	10,263,892	21,316,569
1940	11,099,126	9,913,089	21,012,215
1941	11,391,883	8,086,030	19,477,913
1942	17,453,643	13,676,759	31,130,402
1943	11,404,213	9,824,214	21,228,427
1944	11,586,751	10,990,167	22,576,918
1945	15,143,404	15,106,270	30,249,674
1946	18,663,797	16,381,501	35,045,298
1947	12,120,611	12,283,223	24,403,834
1948	45,576,923	45,351,937	90,928,860
1949	19,328,405	21,243,074	40,571,479
1950	19,243,872	14,299,601	33,543,473
1951	9,956,930	10,961,174	20,918,104
1952	—	—	—
1953	41,942,894	20,663,528	62,606,422
1954	30,262,032	26,771,735	57,033,767
1955	45,259,908	27,950,906	73,210,814
1956	44,907,008	42,853,639	87,760,647
1957	42,774,217	17,959,988	60,734,205
1958	14,392,305	40,822,557	55,214,862
1959	19,442,778	1,012,988	20,455,766
1960	27,027,914	14,376,932	41,404,846
1961	39,816,907	2,762,558	42,579,465
1962	36,395,179	17,470,510	54,165,689
1963[1]	44,723,200	33,796,800	78,520,000
1964[2]	13,617,440	5,246,560	18,864,000
1965[3]	9,218,900	2,017,100	11,236,000
1966[4]	15,002,000	16,362,000	31,364,000

[1] Figures include the following coins dated 1962: English 1/-, 9,200; Scottish 1/-, 1,496,800.
[2] Figures include the following coins dated 1963: English 1/-, 5,029,440; Scottish 1/-, 8,560.
[3] Figures include the following coins dated 1964: English 1/-, 2,900; Scottish 1/-, 1,100.
[4] Figures include the following coins dated 1965: English 1/-, NIL; Scottish 1/-, 758,000.

TABLE III — MAUNDY MONEY

Year	Fourpence	Threepence	Twopence	Penny
1816	1,584	1,584	2,376	4,752
1817	1,386	1,584	2,376	10,296
1818	1,188	1,584	2,376	9,504
1819	792	1,320	1,980	6,336
1820	990	1,320	1,584	7,920
1821	990	1,320	1,980	3,960
1822	2,970	3,960	5,940	11,880
1823	1,980	2,640	3,960	12,672
1824	1,584	2,112	3,168	9,504
1825	2,376	3,432	3,960	8,712
1826	2,376	3,432	3,960	8,712
1827	2,772	3,168	3,960	7,920
1828	2,772	3,168	3,960	7,920
1829	2,772	3,168	3,960	7,920
1830	2,772	3,168	3,960	7,920
1831	3,564	3,960	4,752	10,296
1832	2,574	2,904	3,564	8,712
1833	2,574	2,904	3,564	8,712
1834	2,574	2,904	3,564	8,712
1835	2,574	2,904	3,564	8,712
1836	2,544	2,904	3,564	8,712
1837	2,574	2,904	3,564	8,712
1838	4,158	4,312	4,488	8,976
1839	4,125	4,356	4,488	8,976
1840	4,125	4,356	4,488	8,976
1841	2,574	2,904	3,960	7,920
1842	4,125	4,356	4,488	8,976
1843	4,158	4,488	4,752	7,920
1844	4,158	4,488	4,752	7,920
1845	4,158	4,488	4,752	7,920
1846	4,158	4,488	4,752	7,920
1847	4,158	4,488	4,752	7,920
1848	4,158	4,488	4,752	7,920
1849	4,158	4,488	4,752	7,920
1850	4,158	4,488	4,752	7,920
1851	4,158	4,488	4,752	7,920
1852	4,158	4,488	4,752	7,920
1853	4,158	4,488	4,752	7,920
1854	4,158	4,488	4,752	7,920
1855	4,158	4,488	4,752	7,920
1856	4,158	4,488	4,752	7,920
1857	4,158	4,488	4,752	7,920
1858	4,158	4,488	4,752	7,920
1859	4,158	4,488	4,752	7,920
1860	4,158	4,488	4,752	7,920
1861	4,158	4,488	4,752	7,920
1862	4,158	4,488	4,752	7,920
1863	4,158	4,488	4,752	7,920
1864	4,158	4,488	4,752	7,920
1865	4,158	4,488	4,752	7,920
1866	4,158	4,488	4,752	7,920
1867	4,158	4,488	4,752	7,920
1868	4,158	4,488	4,752	7,920
1869	4,158	4,488	4,752	7,920
1870	4,569	4,488	5,347	9,002
1871	4,627	4,488	4,753	9,286
1872	4,328	4,488	4,719	8,956
1873	4,162	4,488	4,756	7,932
1874	5,937	4,488	5,578	8,741
1875	4,154	4,488	5,745	8,459
1876	4,862	4,488	6,655	10,426
1877	4,850	4,488	7,189	8,936
1878	5,735	4,488	6,709	9,903
1879	5,202	4,488	6,925	10,626
1880	5,199	4,488	6,247	11,088
1881	6,203	4,488	6,001	9,017
1882	4,146	4,488	7,264	10,607
1883	5,096	4,488	7,232	11,673

Year	Fourpence	Threepence	Twopence	Penny
1884	5,353	4,488	6,042	14,109
1885	5,791	4,488	5,958	12,302
1886	6,785	4,488	9,167	15,952
1887	5,292	4,488	8,296	17,506
1888	9,583	4,488	9,528	14,480
1889	6,088	4,488	6,727	14,028
1890	9,087	4,488	8,613	13,115
1891	11,303	4,488	10,000	21,743
1892	8,524	4,488	11,583	15,525
1893	10,832	8,976	14,182	21,593
1894	9,385	8,976	12,099	18,391
1895	8,877	8,976	10,766	17,408
1896	8,476	8,976	10,795	17,380
1897	9,388	8,976	11,000	16,477
1898	9,147	8,976	11,945	16,634
1899	13,561	8,976	14,514	17,402
1900	9,571	8,976	10,987	17,299
1901	11,928	8,976	13,539	17,644
1902	10,117	8,976	14,079	21,278
1903	9,729	8,976	13,386	17,209
1904	11,568	8,876	13,827	18,524
1905	10,998	8,976	11,139	17,504
1906	11,065	8,800	11,325	17,850
1907	11,132	8,760	13,238	18,388
1908	9,929	8,760	14,815	18,150
1909	2,428	1,983	2,695	2,948
1910	2,755	1,440	2,998	3,392
1911	1,768	1,991	1,635	1,913
1912	1,700	1,246	1,678	1,616
1913	1,798	1,228	1,880	1,590
1914	1,651	982	1,659	1,818
1915	1,441	1,293	1,465	2,072
1916	1,499	1,128	1,509	1,647
1917	1,478	1,237	1,506	1,820
1918	1,479	1,375	1,547	1,911
1919	1,524	1,258	1,567	1,699
1920	1,460	1,399	1,630	1,715
1921	1,542	1,386	1,794	1,847
1922	1,609	1,373	3,074	1,758
1923	1,635	1,430	1,527	1,840
1924	1,665	1,515	1,602	1,619
1925	1,786	1,438	1,670	1,890
1926	1,762	1,504	1,902	2,180
1927	1,681	1,690	1,766	1,647
1928	1,642	1,835	1,706	1,846
1929	1,969	1,761	1,862	1,837
1930	1,744	1,948	1,901	1,724
1931	1,915	1,818	1,897	1,759
1932	1,937	2,042	1,960	1,835
1933	1,931	1,920	2,066	1,872
1934	1,893	1,887	1,927	1,919
1935	1,995	2,007	1,928	1,975
1936	1,323	1,307	1,365	1,329
1937	1,325	1,351	1,472	1,329
1938	1,424	1,350	1,374	1,275
1939	1,332	1,234	1,436	1,253
1940	1,367	1,290	1,277	1,375
1941	1,345	1,253	1,345	1,255
1942	1,325	1,325	1,231	1,243
1943	1,335	1,335	1,239	1,347
1944	1,345	1,345	1,345	1,259
1945	1,355	1,355	1,355	1,367
1946	1,365	1,365	1,365	1,479
1947	1,375	1,375	1,479	1,387
1948	1,385	1,491	1,385	1,397
1949	1,503	1,395	1,395	1,407
1950	1,515	1,405	1,405	1,527
1951	1,580	1,468	1,580	1,480
1952	1,064	1,012	1,064	1,024
1953	1,078	1,078	1,025	1,050
1954	1,076	1,076	1,020	1,088

Year	Fourpence	Threepence	Twopence	Penny
1955	1,082	1,082	1,082	1,036
1956	1,088	1,088	1,088	1,100
1957	1,094	1,094	1,094	1,168
1958	1,100	1,100	1,164	1,112
1959	1,106	1,172	1,106	1,118
1960	1,180	1,112	1,112	1,124
1961	1,118	1,118	1,118	1,200
1962	1,197	1,125	1,197	1,127
1963	1,205	1,205	1,131	1,133
1964	1,213	1,213	1,137	1,215
1965	1,221	1,221	1,221	1,143
1966	1,206	1,206	1,206	1,206
1967	986	986	986	1,068
1968	964	964	1,048	964
1969	1,002	1,088	1,002	1,002
1970	1,068	980	980	980
1971	1,108	1,018	1,018	1,108
1972	1,118	1,026	1,118	1,026
1973	1,098	1,098	1,004	1,004
1974	1,138	1,138	1,042	1,138
1975	1,148	1,148	1,148	1,050
1976	1,158	1,158	1,158	1,158
1977	1,138	1,138	1,138	1,240
1978	1,178	1,178	1,282	1,178
1979	1,188	1,294	1,188	1,188
1980	1,306	1,198	1,198	1,198
1981	1,288	1,178	1,178	1,288
1982	1,330	1,218	1,330	1,218
1983	1,342	1,342	1,228	1,228
1984	1,354	1,354	1,238	1,354
1985	1,366	1,366	1,366	1,248
1986	1,378	1,378	1,378	1,378
1987	1,390	1,390	1,390	1,512
1988	1,402	1,528	1,526	1,402
1989	1,353	1,353	1,353	1,353
1990	1,523	1,523	1,523	1,523
1991	1,514	1,384	1,384	1,514
1992	—	—	—	—
1993	—	—	—	—

TABLE IV — PROOF SETS

These figures are included in the preceding tables and the number given includes both the silver coins issued with and without gold.

Year	Silver sets with gold	Silver sets without gold
1826	c. 400	—
1831	over 120	—
1839	c. 300	—
1853	Very few	—
1887	797	287
1893	6	556
1902	Long set 8,066	—
1902	Short set 7,057	
1911	Long set 2,812	2,243
1911	Short set 952	
1927	—	15,000
1937	—	20,901

	Cupro-nickel without gold
1950	17,513
1951	20,000
1953	40,000

Year	
1970	750,000
1971	350,000
1972	150,000
1973	100,000
1974	100,000
1975	100,000
1976	100,000
1977	193,800
1978	88,100
1979	81,000
1980	143,400
1981	100,300
1982	106,800
1983	107,800
1984	106,520
1985	102,015
1986	125,000
1987	88,659
1988	79,314
1989	85,074
1990	79,052
1991	—

TABLE V — UNCIRCULATED SETS

These figures are not included in Tables I and VI.

Year		Year	
1982	205,000	1988	134,067
1983	637,100	1989	77,569
1984	158,820	1990	102,606
1985	178,375	1991	—
1986	167,224	1992	—
1987	172,425		

TABLE VI — HIGH VALUE COINS

	One Pound	Two Pound	Five Pound
1983	443,053,510		
1984	146,256,501		
1985	228,430,749		
1986	10,409,501	8,212,184[1]	
1987	39,298,502		
1988	7,118,825		
1989	70,532,501	4,777,582[2]	
1990	97,122,802		
1991	8,895,990		
1992			
1993			

[1] Also 520,191 supplied in pack and 125,000 struck in .500 silver
[2] 'Bill of Rights' 4,431,754 ; 'Claim of Right' 345,828

TABLE VII — DECIMAL SILVER PROOF COINS

TWENTY FIVE PENCE

1972	Silver Wedding	100,000
1977	Silver Jubilee	377,000
1980	Queen Mother	83,672
1981	Royal Wedding	218,142

FIVE POUNDS

1990	Queen Mother	56,102

TWO POUNDS

		piedfort	proof
1986	Commonwealth Games	—	125,000
1989	Bill of Rights	10,000[1]	25,000[2]
1989	Claim of Right	10,000[1]	24,852[2]

[1] All supplied in cased pairs
[2] Most supplied in cased pairs

ONE POUND

1983	Royal Arms	10,000	50,000
1984	Scotland	15,000	44,855
1985	Wales	15,000	50,000
1986	Northern Ireland	15,000	50,000
1987	England	15,000	50,000
1988	Shield	15,000	50,000
1989	Scotland	10,000	22,275
1990	Wales	—	23,277
1991	Northern Ireland	—	—
1992	England	—	—
1993	Royal Arms	—	—

APPENDIX II

A SELECT BIBLIOGRAPHY

ANSELL, George F. The Royal Mint, with suggestions for its better management. *London*, 1870

COPE, Geoffrey M. and Rayner, P. Alan. The Standard Catalogue of English Milled Coinage in Silver, Copper and Bronze, 1662–1972. *London*, 1978.

CRAIG, Sir John. The Mint. A history of the London Mint from A.D. 287 to 1948. *Cambridge*, 1953.

CROWTHER, G. F. A Guide to English Pattern Coins. *London*, 1887.

DYER, G. P. The proposed coinage of King Edward VIII. *H.M.S.O.* 1973.

FEAVERYEAR, Sir A. The Pound Sterling. 2nd ed. *Oxford*, 1963.

GRUEBER, H. A. Handbook of the Coins of Great Britain and Ireland in the British Museum. *London*, 1989.

HAWKINS, E. The Silver Coins of England. 3rd ed. *London*, 1887.

HOCKING, W. J. Catalogue of the Coins, Tokens, Medals, Dies and Seals in the Museum of the Royal Mint, 2 vols. *London*, 1906.

HSUN, L. Ming. The Great Recoinage of 1696–1699. *London*, 1966.

LINECAR, H.W.A. The Crown Pieces of Great Britain and the British Commonwealth. *London*, 1962.

LIVERPOOL, Charles, Earl of. A Treatise on the Coins of the Realm in a letter to the King. *Oxford*, 1805.

OMAN, Sir Charles. The Coinage of England. *Oxford*, 1931.

PHILLIPS, M. The Token Money of the Bank of England. *London*, 1900.

RAYNER, P. Alan The Designers and Engravers of the English Milled Coinage. *London*, 1954.

RUDING, The Rev. Rogers. Annals of the Coinage of Great Britain and its Dependencies. 3rd ed. (3 vols.). *London*, 1840.

ROYAL MINT. Annual Report of the Deputy Master and Comptroller. *London*, 1870–1977.

SEABY, Peter. The Story of the English Coinage. *London*, Revised ed., 1990.

SEABY. Standard Catalogue of British Coins. Issued annually.

SPINK & SON. Catalogue of a collection of Milled English Coins, including Patterns and Proofs, formed by H. Montagu. *London*, 1891.

STRIDE, H. G. The Royal Mint: its evolution and development. In Seaby's *Coin and Medal Bulletin*, 1954–1960.

various papers in

THE NUMISMATIC CHRONICLE (the journal of the Royal Numismatic Society).

THE BRITISH NUMISMATIC JOURNAL (the journal of the British Numismatic Society).

SPINK'S NUMISMATIC CIRCULAR.